THE UNITED NATIONS
AND
THE RULE OF LAW

Charter Development Through The
Handling of International Disputes and Situations

John W. Halderman

1966

Oceana Publications, Inc.

Dobbs Ferry, New York

Acknowledgments

The Rule of Law Research Center and the author wish to express their gratitude to Ralph Price of Greensboro, North Carolina, for his support of the Center's United Nations Studies Program, of which this volume is a product.

The author wishes to express his gratitude and appreciation for permission to quote from the works listed below.

Books

D. W. Bowett, *Self-Defense in International Law* (Manchester: Manchester University Press, 1958).

D. W. Bowett, *United Nations Forces: A Legal Study* (New York: Frederick A. Praeger, 1964. Written under the auspices of the David Davies Memorial Institute of International Studies).

P. E. Corbett, *Law in Diplomacy* (Princeton, N. J.: Princeton University Press, 1959).

Richard N. Gardner, *In Pursuit of World Order* (New York: Frederick A. Praeger, 1964).

Hasluck, *Workshop of Security* (Melbourne: F. W. Cheshire, 1948).

Carlton J. H. Hayes, *A Political and Cultural History of Europe* (New York: The MacMillan Company, 1936).

Rosalyn Higgins, *The Development of International Law Through the Political Organs of the United Nations* (London: Oxford University Press, 1963. Published under the auspices of the Royal Institute of International Affairs).

Catherine Hoskyns, *The Congo Since Independence: January 1960-December 1961* (London: Oxford University Press, 1965. Published under the auspices of the Royal Institute of International Affairs).

Morton A. Kaplan and Nicholas de B. Katzenbach, *The Political Foundations of International Law* (New York: John Wiley & Sons, 1961).

Hans Kelsen, *The Law of the United Nations, A Critical Analysis of Its Fundamental Problems* and *Recent Trends in the Law of the United Nations: A Supplement to 'The Law of the United Nations'* (New York: Frederick A. Praeger, 1950 and 1951, respectively. Published under the auspices of The London Institute of World Affairs).

iii

Hans Morgenthau, *Politics Among Nations: The Struggle for Power and Peace* (New York: Alfred A. Knopf, 3d ed., 1961).

Ann Van Wynen Thomas & A. J. Thomas, Jr., *The Organization of American States* (Dallas: Southern Methodist University Press, 1963).

Periodicals

Academie de droit international, *Recueil des Cours,* (Leyden: A. W. Sijthoff).

American Society of International Law, *American Journal of International Law* (Washington).

Academy of Political Science, *Political Science Quarterly* (New York). The quotations on pages 59-60 are reprinted with permission from the *Political Science Quarterly,* December 1963, Vol. 78, No. 4.

Contents

Contents

Chapter I

Scope of the "Rule of Law"

Need for a System

Two characteristics of international relations since the rise of the independent state "system" at the close of the Middle Ages have been (a) the lack of anything that could genuinely be called a system in the conduct of these relations, and, (b) a situation of constant rivalry and insecurity among major power groupings. That the two characteristics are linked and form, in fact, two aspects of a single basic situation, seems beyond question. The need for a system in order to establish a secure peace has been stated by Secretary-General U Thant of the United Nations:

> The first task of leaders of men all over the world is to find the first steps toward a world system of preventing war . . .
>
> . . . No sane person can believe that either the United States or the Soviet Union will wage a nuclear war deliberately, but there are good reasons to think that the risk of an unintended war is very great.
>
> * * *
>
> . . . This means that some system must be found to limit and control the nuclear arms race before it gets out of hand.[1]

It also seems relevant to suggest that the United States and the Soviet Union may not always represent the main threats of nuclear war. Since the Secretary-General made the above statement, the Chinese People's Republic has demonstrated an incipient nuclear capability. The possible emergence of this and other countries as new great military powers, and the possibilities of new alignments and of new and unpredictable policies and points of view on matters pertaining to world peace, make it all the more important to develop a system capable of maintaining peace.

Although the United Nations was intended to serve from the outset as the framework of such a system, its potential in this respect is today virtually written off. Two essential factors which

---

[1] U Thant, "A Call for Temporary Standstill Agreements" (address), 9 United Nations Rev. 5 (May 1962).

1

have apparently never been widely grasped are, first, that the Charter, as originally written and adopted, was never anything more than the framework of a potential system, and second, that it nevertheless did, and still does, constitute such a potential framework.

The hope, entertained at the time the Charter was drafted in 1945, that the conditions for an effective system were already present, was concentrated upon the provision of machinery for the prevention or suppression of aggression. Lack of such machinery was believed to have been responsible for the failure of the League of Nations. Statesmen said, and it was widely believed, that the Charter provisions for the use of force would enable the United Nations to succeed where the earlier organization had failed. The effectiveness of these provisions depended upon the ability of the great powers to collaborate for peace, which capability was assumed. Had the hopes of great power collaboration been fulfilled, it would have meant, in effect, that conditions were present for an effective world order system and that the United Nations could have functioned successfully not only with respect to its "security" functions, but also with respect to "peaceful settlement" and all other essential aspects of such a system.

The failure of this hope soon became manifest when differences arose between the Western allies and the Soviet Union, and international situations arose in places like Germany and Korea which the United Nations could not solve. This division grew into the "cold war," which is widely blamed for the failure of the United Nations to fulfill its role in the manner originally planned.

For purposes of present discussion, the cause of the failure might better be stated as having been the unreadiness of the world's peoples and governments to provide the necessary support and backing for a system designed to safeguard international peace and security. Manifestations of this failure would then be represented by the cold war itself, by the breakdown of the projected United Nations system, and in other ways.

The nature of a successful "system" is thus indicated. There is only one way in which the people of a state may form an orderly society composed of free and equal members, namely through the development of a constitutional system. It is suggested, as a basis of discussion, that an orderly society composed of free and equal states must also be formed in this way, with the system finding its roots in the minds of the people concerned,[2] as well as in their governments. Without attempting further comparisons between a potential international system and domestic constitutions, it is ventured to suggest that either must be grounded in a basic frame of mind in which the peoples concerned desire to do justice as among themselves, have a common notion of what they mean by justice, and general agreement as to how to go about securing it.[3]

United Nations as Potential Framework

The basic aspiration of the "peoples of the world" for a secure peace, based on justice, was expressed in the preamble of the United Nations Charter, and in the basic principles and purposes set forth in Article 1. The United Nations still seems to be the most logical and potentially fruitful basis upon which to base the effort to realize this aspiration. It continues to be the main repository of the hopes of the world's peoples for peace and security. It contains the main outline of a potential system which seems capable of being adapted to achieve its own stated purposes, including definitions of basic powers which the governments and peoples of the world desired to see exercised by the Organization, and organs for their exercise. It is true that the method by which the United Nations was expected to fulfill its major purposes so far as concerned the handling of international disputes and situa-

---

[2] The corresponding need, as it applied to the League of Nations, has been thus stated:

"Peace machinery existed, but its successful operation required an effective will not only of idealistic statesmen and intellectuals but of the masses in the several countries. In other words, it required a public opinion within every nation favorable to the subordination of national interests and policy to international adjustment. This, however, was significantly lacking . . ." Hayes, *A Political and Cultural History of Modern Europe*, Vol. II, p. 1047 (1937).

[3] Such a notion as that of "public opinion" obviously consists of highly diverse factors in different countries and types of society. As pointed out by Professor McDougal, "effective control over decisions may be located in governmental institutions, but it may also be located in political parties or pressure groups or private associations." McDougal, "Law and Power," 46 Am. J. Int'l Law 102, 110 (1952). However, the broad notion of "public opinion" serves the purpose of the present discussion, since we are here concerned with types of United Nations activity which seem generally calculated either to advance or to discourage those elements which, on an overall world-wide basis, potentially constitute an "effective" public opinion upholding the "rule of law" in international relations.

tions—e.g., through the Security Council with the five permanent members acting in concert—proved unworkable in practice. However, steps were taken as early as 1950 to remedy this defect by recognizing a residual power in the General Assembly.[4] It must be recognized, at the same time, that the shift of power toward the Assembly represents a basic development in the search for world peace and security. The original anticipation of great power collaboration necessarily assumed that the basis for an effective system was already in existence. The failure of this collaboration proved that this was not the case. The shift toward an increased role for the Assembly is therefore believed to find a major part of its significance in the fact that, because of its much larger membership, the Assembly has far more potential than the Security Council as an instrument for developing the necessary basis for an effective system in the minds of the governing authorities and peoples of the world.

How such a system is to be achieved with world-wide force and effect cannot be foreseen by the present writer. It would seem that, for some time to come, progress should most logically be expected as among that important segment of states which share, as their foremost policy aspiration, the achievement of peace and security in a world of free and equal states. Since the United Nations itself is based on this principle, it would seem to serve as a logical meeting place and basis of collaboration as among states desiring to work toward this goal. To the extent that progress toward an effective "rule of law" could be made as among these states, their relative over-all strength in the world, as compared with countries whose regimes did not subscribe to the principles of freedom and equality, would necessarily increase and the prospects of these principles ultimately prevailing on a world-wide basis would be improved. Moreover, once some progress were made, and the effort enabled to move onto a higher plateau (or, in another analogy, to "get off the ground"), new possibilities for progress should come into view. It also seems possible that a conscientious endeavor to secure justice on the basis of Charter principles might evoke favorable responses among peoples whose governments did not subscribe to the principles of freedom and equality, and produce a gradual modification of the policies of those governments. Dedicated efforts might conceivably, in this or in other respects, bring results in ways not logically anticipated.

---

[4] *Cf.* p. 152 *infra.*

The present study is largely concerned with the possibility of advancing the rule of law in international relations through the application of law and principle in the handling of disputes and situations by the United Nations. In the view of this writer, the major beneficial result of improving the application of law and principle in these matters would relate to the development of world public opinion. If public education is important as a means of bringing about the requisite moral backing for the Organization, the example set by states in the handling of concrete cases would seem to be one of the most important educational methods. Thousands of words uttered in support of the United Nations and its principles can readily be nullified by actions which contradict the words or (as happens more frequently) which create confusion as to the true nature and powers of the Organization. It should, perhaps, be explained that the object here in mind is not so much the dualistic one which would regard "public support" and the United Nations as two different things, as it is to bring United Nations principles to life in the mind of the peoples of the world. This is where the "real" constitution must find its existence; the organization is only the potential instrument for giving it effect.

The subject-matter of the present discussion—e.g., the United Nations capability of handling disputes and situations—may be one of particular importance since, if other recourses fail, it might well constitute the last chance of preventing a given situation from deteriorating into a major world conflagration. While efforts in various fields are undoubtedly necessary to bring about a secure basis for peace, an effective system for the handling of disputes might seem well calculated to prove the catalytic agent causing the whole to fall into the desired pattern.

Role of Debate

The principles laid down in the Charter for the handling of disputes and situations are, generally, of so broad a character as to permit the most diverse interpretations, so that the structure of an effective system must be built by a process of Charter, or "constitutional," development. As one mode of entry into the problem, this approach may be said to be followed when governments, or the Secretary-General, endeavor to cause the United Nations to act on the basis of what they conceive to be sound principles. Efforts along this line should at least precipitate debate on relevant issues, and such discussions should, in turn, gradually serve to evolve a set of sound principles in the public mind and, no doubt more slowly, cause these principles to become operative in the conduct of foreign relations.

The desirability of full public debate of relevant issues can also be predicated, abstractly, on the proposition that the "peoples of the world" brought the Charter into existence and, among other things, charged the Organization with the task of resolving serious disputes and situations "in conformity with the principles of justice and international law."[5] The manner in which this task is fulfilled in individual cases is a public issue and one which, accordingly, deserves full and genuine public debate. Nevertheless, in many cases, relevant principles are ignored in United Nations discussions, or presented in distorted form. Not only may public opinion thus be left in ignorance of what the applicable principles are, but the principles themselves, as a result of being ignored or distorted, may be damaged without the public being made aware of what is being done.

Thus, the debate and elucidation of issues is one elementary aspect of the "constitutional approach." It has not been made effective to any significant extent for the reason, in part, that the scope and outline of debate tends to be established by the states directly concerned in particular disputes and situations, and because these states are usually absorbed in more immediate or apparent policy considerations. Notwithstanding that in many cases some states have taken stands in support of United Nations principles, such efforts have not, as a general rule, sufficed to prevent these principles being submerged under the tide of political controversy. Significant advancement toward an effective rule of law would seem to necessitate the devising of some method of assuring the elucidation of the correct issues as seen from a constitutional point of view. A suggestion along this line will be considered in the concluding chapter.

Stability and Change

Another aspect of the "constitutional approach," which may serve as a starting point for discussion in terms of concrete principles and procedures, involves the distinction between disputes concerning the interpretation and application of existing rules of law,

---

[5] U.N. Charter, Art. 1.

on one hand, and those which, on the other, involve demands for change in existing legal rules or situations. The distinction seems to be basic in international relations, as it is in domestic societies, being concerned with the formulation and application of law as law, and with enabling law to play its proper role as a stabilizing factor in society.

A concrete case involving this distinction arose in 1947 when Egypt brought before the Security Council its demand for the withdrawal of British troops from the Suez Canal Zone. The presence of the troops had been agreed to in a treaty in force between Egypt and the United Kingdom. The Egyptian Representative claimed that the case should not be decided on the basis of the treaty, stating among other arguments that:

> I have refrained from relying on juridical considerations. I have done so because I believe the Security Council is not limited to settlement of the legal aspect of a dispute brought before it. The Council is not called upon to adjudicate on the legal rights of the parties. Its mission —I shall say its higher mission—is to preserve peace and security, to see to it that conditions prevail in which peaceful and friendly relations may obtain among nations . . .[6]

The United Kingdom, for its part, denied that the Council could properly consider the desirability of changing the treaty:

> It is one of the fundamental purposes of the Charter, set forth in Article 1, paragraph 1, to bring about, by peaceful means, and in conformity with the principles of justice and international law, the settlement of international disputes. The principle *pacta sunt servanda* is perhaps the most fundamental principle of international law . . . If the treaty of 1936 is valid, the Security Council cannot, consistently with the purposes of the United Nations, take any other course than that of recognizing this fact and of removing this matter from the agenda.[7]

It was, of course, only normal for the United Kingdom to stand on its treaty rights when it saw these as being to its advantage. It was for Egypt, as the complaining state, to define the boundaries of the discussion. That country's position seems to have had as one purpose the avoidance of a decision based on existing law, and the tenor of the argument seems to have been to reject, in its entirety, the relevance of law to the case. Thus, the Egyptian spokesman said:

---

[6] U.N. Security Council Off. Rec. 2d year, 179th meeting 1861 (1947).
[7] *Id.* 176th meeting 1772.

> The Security Council cannot evade its "primary responsibility for the maintenance of international peace and security" because of the "legal" position of the parties of the dispute.
>
> In coming before the Security Council, the Egyptian Government has insisted upon bald political facts . . .[8]

The Egyptian Representative was here evidently giving expression to a distinction which is commonplace, but is nevertheless believed to involve a misapprehension, as between "legal" and "political" issues. In this view "law" corresponds with international law which, in the traditional sense here used, consists of the body of legal relationships existing between and among states, growing largely out of custom and treaty. The distinction under discussion regards "legal" issues as those which are governed by law in this sense, and "political" issues as those which are not. This distinction seems to represent a carry-over from domestic law concepts in which, however, it appears in somewhat different form. In the domestic context, "legal" issues are those suitable for adjudication; "political" issues those which are not.

In domestic law, a "political" issue, while not "justiciable," still falls within the general constitutional framework. It must be resolved peaceably and in accordance with law. In international relations, however, there is no such constitutional framework. Here, a "political" issue is commonly regarded as being unregulated except by political forces; stated otherwise, it appears to lie in the realm of anarchy. The goal of establishing the "rule of law" at the basis of international relations therefore has, as an essential aspect, the necessity of bringing matters generally regarded as "political" within a "legal" or "constitutional" framework.[9]

Several factors have contributed to the persistence of the view that law in international relations consists solely of the existing body of rules. Two such factors might be (a) that the International Court of Justice is clearly concerned with law, and (b) that it is the only permanent international organ having a clear re-

---

[8] *Id.,* 179th meeting 1873.

[9] So it was said by the Secretary-General that the principle of the rule of law "permeates the approach of the Charter to international problems far beyond the sphere of competence of the Court." *Introduction to the Annual Report of the Secretary-General on the Work of the Organization 16 June 1960-15 June 1961,* U.N. Gen. Ass. Off. Rec. 16th Sess., Supp. No. 1A, at 2 (A/4800/Add. 1) (1961). *Cf.* Brierly, "The Rule of Law in International Society," 7 Nordisk Tidsskrift for International Ret., Acta scandinavica juris gentium 3, 14-15 (1936), partially quoted in Bishop, *International Law: Cases and Materials* 4 (2d ed. 1962).

semblance to an organ of domestic government. Since domestic courts are concerned with law, the impression carried over to the international realm on the part of some may be that the International Court of Justice is the only organ concerned with law in the field of international relations. Another factor may be historical. Early advocates of the permanent judiciary, at around the turn of the present century, placed their main hopes for peace in the development of the role of law in the sense of the body of rules suitable for application by judicial process. Several factors may, in turn, have contributed to this hope. At the time, the world "community" of independent states, which had been largely responsible for the development of international law as it then existed, consisted principally of countries of European and European descended populations. The preceding period of relative stability may have encouraged the idea that law—in the sense of the body of rules existing at a given time—was capable of resolving disputes among these states and thus of assuring world peace. The accompanying growth of the role of arbitration could have contributed to this hope. The proposal for a permanent international judiciary of high quality, empowered to decide disputes on the basis of law, was designed to promote this anticipated role for law, and to bring it to fruition. These hopes may have even been heightened by the outbreak of World War I, and the accompanying growing opinion that states in the future *must* find ways of settling their disputes peacefully. The proposed permanent judiciary probably appeared to some leaders of opinion as providing the logical answer to this need. What no one could have foreseen was that World War I was introducing the era of greatest change that the world had ever seen. Any idea of a society that could be regulated by a more or less fixed body of law was exploded by political developments such as led up to World War II, to say nothing of the profound transformation of the world scene that has taken place subsequently. One of the results of these developments may be that whereas, in the original view pertaining to the Court, too little attention was given to the necessity of "change" —commonly referred to as the "political" element of international relations—the recent attitude has been to concentrate attention upon the "political" approach to the virtual exclusion of the rightful role of the judicial process. The persistence into the present day of the attitude toward "law" which prevailed at the time of World War I has resulted in a present tendency to regard "law" in its entirety as being outmoded and inapplicable to present day conditions. A corollary tendency has, then, been to regard most important disputes and situations as being "political" and unrelated to law.

The tendencies just referred to are, naturally, most strong on the part of countries which, for the time being, are holding themselves in a position of opposition to the western European tradition. Communist countries and those of Asia and Africa thus tend to regard the body of rules embraced by international law as being alien to them, tainted with "colonialism," etc. This attitude seriously impedes efforts to make "international law," in this sense, the basis of the "rule of law" in international relations.

In the view of the present discussion, the most practical method of achieving the "rule of law" is by bringing the processes of "change" within a broad constitutional system. While the role of the judiciary is recognized as essential to an ultimate, effective system, it is believed that, for some time to come, the most important function must consist in non-judicial processes of "change." Practically speaking, the most available procedure relevant to this function is that of non-binding recommendations of the General Assembly and Security Council. It is to be expected that, in the future, as in the past, a sizeable proportion of such recommendations will be rejected by one or more of the parties to particular disputes and situations. The important consideration is, however, that any degree of increased effort to bring about solutions of disputes *in accordance with law and Charter principle* must, inevitably, bring about *some* degree of constitutional development, e.g., some change in the format in which international relations are conducted.[10]

Such evolution, to the extent carried out through the United Nations, would have the participation of all the members. The substantive law so evolved through gradual process would necessarily tend to become gradually more acceptable to all concerned. In so far, then, as the United Nations could be employed in the manner under discussion, the resulting trends, psychologically as well as legally, would be in the direction of increased acceptance of, and confidence in, the role of the Organization and of international law.

---

[10] Pollux, "The Interpretation of the Charter," 23 Brit. Yb. Int'l Law 54 (1946); Robinson, "Metamorphosis of the United Nations," 94 Academie de droit international, Recueil des Cours 493, 558-59 (1958-II).

In the effort to achieve the "rule of law," then, the matter of utmost importance is not the substantive content of the body of law, nor the consistency with which the rules are applied. The essence of the matter is still not quite reached by regarding law as an evolutionary process. These factors all enter into the result, but the really decisive factor is believed to lie in the nature of the effort made, and seen to be made, on the part of the competent authorities to achieve justice through the equal and dispassionate application of law and principle.

If, by means of a requisite effort, an evolutionary trend of the kind under discussion is gotten underway and caused to continue and develop, the stage would inevitably be reached at which states would begin to demonstrate their confidence in the system in the most practical manner, that is, through the submission to binding adjudication of important cases involving the interpretation and application of their existing legal positions and relationships.

The development just referred to would not, however, be the only one to result from a growth of public confidence in the "system." The growth of such confidence would seem bound to bring about a heightened effectiveness of all aspects of law. It should be expected to result, for example, in significant advance toward the effective control of armaments, since this problem is generally agreed to be inextricably linked with that of creating an environment of general international security. It thus becomes possible to catch a glimpse of a potential "rule of law" of the future which, resting upon the base of popular consensus, would consist in a coherent constitutional system embracing, as its central visible characteristic, the capability of maintaining peace and security among the members of the system. Such, indeed, would seem to be the necessary character of effective law in all communities in which (as contrasted to systems in which law is handed down by superior authorities) the law has to be devised by the members on the basis of their mutual juridical equality.

Efforts to develop an effective "rule of law" in international relations would therefore have as their proper goal the development of the requisite degree of public confidence in the "system" being sought after. There are doubtless many ways in which this goal can be pursued. The present discussion considers that one possibly effective approach lies in the endeavor to apply United Nations principles in the handling of international disputes and situations. This approach seems important, in part, because the proper use of these principles tends to build up the United Nations, which is conceived as the best available basis upon which to build a future rule of law for the conduct of international relations.

The attempt is made, in the present discussion, to give the "constitutional" approach as practical a context as possible by discussing some aspects of it in terms of past cases. The purpose in referring to these cases is therefore to use them as models having a basis in reality, and not to criticize what was done.

The Suez "troops" case is, then, one in which the complaining state demanded a change in the existing legal relationship, whereas the respondent insisted that the matter was governed by existing law.

The Council is given appropriate powers of recommendation applicable to both situations. Article 36 provides in part:

> 3. In making recommendations under this Article the Security Council should . . . take into consideration that legal disputes should as a general rule be referred by the parties to the International Court of Justice. . . .

If the matter is not regarded by the Council as being of this character, that organ has the power, under the same Article, to "recommend appropriate procedures or methods of adjustment," or, under Article 37, "to recommend such terms of settlement as it may consider appropriate." It is thus perceived that the system contemplated by the Charter makes provision for disputes involving demands for change, and that its basic power in such matters is the power of recommendation.

While various problems pertaining to this power will be considered in ensuing chapters, it is necessary to keep in mind, from the outset, such considerations as that (a) if a dispute cannot, for any reason, be submitted to adjudication, the only remaining recourse, from the standpoint of a "constitutional" approach, is the working out of a new agreement, between the parties, to govern the situation; (b) the devising of new agreements, involving the possibility of new rules of law, or modifications of existing rules, is not left unregulated in the system contemplated by the Charter; (c) the authority to "recommend" represents the practical limit of power which the peoples and governments of the world were willing to have the Organization exercise, in this respect, as against themselves; and (d) the power in question represents an important opportunity by which the Organization can make appropriate recommendations on the basis of principle, reason, etc., and thus cause the processes of "peaceful settlement" and "change" to contribute to the development of a system based on law.

While the remainder of the present chapter will be largely concerned with issues involved in deciding whether a given case should be referred for adjudication on the basis of existing law, or handled as a demand for change in existing relationships, it may be noted, at this point, that, in the Suez "troops" case under discussion, the Egyptian Government rejected not only the recourse to adjudication, but also that of Security Council recommendation. It may have been felt that this latter recourse was too mild to meet the needs of the situation, and it may have been for this reason that the Egyptian authorities requested, in the letter initiating the complaint, that the Security Council "direct the total and immediate evacuation of British troops from Egypt . . ."[11]

The general Egyptian approach in this case, in appearing to reject "law," in professedly following a "political" approach, and in seeking to cause the Council to "direct" one of its permanent members to relinquish a position based on treaty, provides an illustration of a kind of problem which appears to impede the development of law and the Charter as the foundation of international relations, and which will be considered in various aspects in ensuing chapters.

It is, of course, normal for states to pursue courses of action designed to promote their apparent interests in the immediate situation, rather than policies designed to further the longer range interests represented by the United Nations, and it is a matter of concern to this discussion whether the "practical" disadvantage of such long-range policies is necessarily as great as is evidently, in some cases, assumed.

In the case under discussion, the Security Council adopted no resolution, and it is difficult to estimate whether the course followed by Egypt in the Council furthered, hindered, or made no difference to the peaceful settlement of the dispute which eventuated seven years later. It seems at least possible that the course followed may have tended to harden the British position, and that a more moderate approach, attuned to the role of persuasion assigned to the United Nations in such matters by the Charter, might have tended, more than the course actually followed, to expedite the solution of the problem.

---

[11] U.N. Security Council Off. Rec. 2d year, 159th meeting 1344 (S/410) (1947).

Claims Based on Both Law and Equity

The issue as between adjudication and "change" arises in different form when states consider that their demands for change are justified in law as well as in justice and equity. A state, considering that an existing rule is being wrongfully interpreted or applied by another state, might suggest that the issue be referred to the World Court for decision. In the event that the adjudication resulted in an adverse decision from its point of view, the same state might then initiate a new demand that the rule of law thus validated be changed on the ground that it is unjust and inequitable. Although this course of action is perfectly justified, and even logical, it is seldom followed, so that examples to illustrate the discussion of the matter are hard to come by.

A factual situation of this kind emerged in the Suez "troops" case in which, as just mentioned, the basic Egyptian demand was for a change in an existing treaty relationship. Mixed into the Egyptian argument was language indicating that the treaty in question had become inoperative by operation of law. Thus, in the Egyptian letter initiating the complaint in the Security Council, it was said that the treaty "cannot bind Egypt any longer, having outlived its purposes, besides being inconsistent with the Charter."[12] Two grounds thus appear to be stated, both of which are legal in character. The first invokes the doctrine *rebus sic stantibus,* under which a treaty ceases to be binding in the event of a change in the state of facts which existed at the time it was entered into. Even though the doctrine itself may be of disputed validity, there is no question but that to invoke it involves the assertion that the treaty has become inoperative by operation of law. The second ground advanced by Egypt is purely legal, being based, as was made clear during the Council debate, on the stipulation contained in Article 103 of the Charter that, in the event of a conflict, the Charter would prevail over any other international agreement.

Since the United Kingdom based its position upon the treaty, a legal issue could be said to have been joined concerning the continuing force and effect of this instrument. However, when it was suggested that the case be referred to the World Court, the Egyptian Representative strongly opposed the proposal, stating:

> What point can there be in mentioning in the resolution a possible dispute concerning the validity of the Treaty of 1936? On any hypothesis, that Treaty has been so disintegrated by events that it

---
[12] *Ibid.*

can no longer serve as a foundation for the continuance of friendly relations.[13]

It is, perhaps, unusual to find a party to a dispute thus denying the validity of a treaty upon which the other party is basing its case and, in the same breath, denying the only method by which a definitive determination of the question of validity is possible. However, the political approach thus exemplified is not unusual. The particular juxtaposition of ideas here advanced can only have served to confuse the world public as to the role of the United Nations in such matters, and to have set back any prospect that the Organization might, eventually, be able to fulfill its purposes in this respect.

From a "practical" point of view, moreover, it might apparently have been to Egypt's advantage if its case had been argued more along constitutional lines in this respect than was actually done. Its Representative might thus have said that while he regarded the treaty as invalid in law, he was willing to forego this issue in order to concentrate upon his main plea which sought the removal of the troops on grounds of equity and justice. Even if the treaty remained in force, he might have argued, it had become unjust and inequitable in today's conditions, and therefore ought to be terminated. The tendency of this approach would have been to focus attention upon the equity of the demand for change, and to have made it somewhat more difficult for the British Representative to rest his case upon the claim that the treaty governed the situation. As it was, by mixing into his argument language which, intentionally or not, had the effect of asserting that the treaty was legally invalid, the Egyptian Representative may have assisted the British Representative by giving him increased justification for stressing the continued validity of that instrument, and the argument that the case was governed by the treaty and by the rule that treaties must be observed.

In such "mixed" cases as this, a complaining state may, as just mentioned, forego its contention based on the existing law in order to concentrate attention upon its demand for change, or it may press for a determination of the legal question while reserving its right to bring up its demand for change at a later date if this seems necessary and desirable.

---

[13] *Id.* 193d meeting 2166. In addition to this general denial that its claim was based on law, the Egyptian Representative specifically denied that he had invoked the doctrine of *rebus sic stantibus. Id.* 179th meeting 1861.

Cases illustrative of the second course of action are difficult to find. Even though states desirous of seeing an existing situation changed may contest the validity of the law underlying the situation, they appear usually to be insufficiently sure of their legal positions to be willing to entrust them to the judicial process and the risk of binding adverse decisions. Also entering into the attitude of such states is the prevailing notion, to be discussed below, that a judicial decision is determinative of the whole dispute. "Mixed" cases of the kind under discussion arise, of course, in a variety of circumstances, so that the attitudes referred to are justified more in some cases than in others.

A case illustrating certain aspects of the problem concerns the refusal of Egypt to permit use of the Suez Canal by Israeli-connected ships and cargoes. This practice gave rise to an Israeli complaint before the Security Council in 1951. Egypt defended its position in part by asserting that it was at war with Israel and consequently had the right of "visit and search" which, under traditional international law, permits belligerent states to detain enemy ships and enemy cargoes, even though the latter may be on neutral vessels. It also claimed to be acting under the right of self-defense.

Israel and some members of the Council argued in rebuttal that the Egyptian-Israeli Armistice of 1949 was intended to bring about a permanent cessation of hostilities, that hostilities had actually ceased at the time of the armistice, and that Egypt could not, in consequence, justifiably assert belligerent rights as an excuse for interfering with Suez Canal shipping. The Israeli complaint, in so far as pertinent to the present discussion, was that the Egyptian actions were unlawful. Thus the Israeli spokesman said, during the Security Council debate:

> The right of ships to traverse the high seas and international highways of the world is a cornerstone of the laws of nations . . .

> When a ship of a maritime Power pursues its innocent course with cargoes for Israel, and Egypt intervenes to obstruct passage and remove the cargo, then the result is not a lawful assertion of Egyptian sovereignty, but an unjustifiable arrogation of rights and an unlawful encroachment on the sovereignty of the maritime power concerned and of Israel as the State to which the cargo is consigned. Any State has a right to send any ship with any cargo to Israel and Egypt has no right to block the free intercourse between the sender and the recipient of such goods.[14]

---

[14] *Id.* 6th year, 549th meeting 12-13 (S/PV. 549) (1951).

A legal issue was thus joined as to which either Egypt or Israel might have suggested adjudication by the World Court. However, neither side did so, presumably because neither was sufficiently sure of its position to wish to take the risk of a judicial proceeding. Had Israel suggested this recourse, an Egyptian refusal might have been somewhat difficult since, presumably, its representative could only have said that, while he was relying on the existing rule of law, he was unwilling to see the matter submitted to the only procedure capable of rendering a decision validating this rule. He did not here have open to him the alternative course of action, followed by his predecessor in the Suez "troops" case, of demanding a change in the existing law. However, in the "ships" case the position in this respect never became noticeable to the world public since no one suggested that the issue be adjudicated.

The United Kingdom Representative, speaking in support of Israel in the "ships" case, expressed the view that the dispute should be settled not on the basis of what Egypt's rights might be, but rather on the basis of what was just and equitable in the circumstances. Referring to the draft resolution before the Council (co-sponsored by the British, United States and French Representatives) he said:

> [T]he draft resolution does not attempt to say whether or not Egypt can technically claim to be entitled to belligerent rights. What the draft resolution does say is that, in the light of the Armistice Agreement and of what has taken place since it was signed, the maintenance of the present restrictions is unjustified and unreasonable and must be held to constitute an abuse of any rights which Egypt may claim to possess . . .[15]

Egypt and the United Kingdom thus took up, *vis-à-vis* each other, roughly opposite positions to those they had taken in the earlier "troops" case. In the "ships" case it was Egypt that was standing on its asserted legal rights and the United Kingdom which desired to bypass the legal issue and pursue the question on the basis of what seemed just and equitable. However, several differences may be noted. First, in the earlier "troops" case, the United Kingdom acquiesced in a Belgian suggestion that the case might be referred to the Court. In the later "ships" case Egypt made no such suggestion, nor did any other state involved in the Council debate. Secondly, in the earlier case, the pertinent rule of law

---

[15] *Id.* 552d meeting 3 (S/PV. 552). The resolution is quoted in part at p. 85 *infra*.

affected only Great Britain and Egypt;[16] consequently, these countries could have proceeded directly to the negotiation of a new rule without seriously affecting the interests of other states. In the "ships" case, however, Egypt was asserting a general rule of law which, by its nature, affected the interests of other states. While this fact did not make it mandatory that the dispute be referred to adjudication, it made a stronger argument for doing so than existed in the earlier case.

Some of the issues that might have been (or still might be) adjudicated in the "ships" case are: Under the Charter can war still take place in the legal sense? If it can, do belligerents continue to have the right of "visit and search" notwithstanding the cessation of hostilities pursuant to an armistice that is intended to remain in force until the conclusion of permanent peace?

The practical question is again whether the states party to the dispute would consider such clarification advantageous to their respective positions in the immediate dispute. Obviously they did not in the Suez "ships" case, since no one proposed this course of action. The case may, however, be taken as illustrating factors such as might enter into possible future situations in which complaining states might feel impelled to pursue their arguments on the basis of existing law, while reserving their right to pursue demands for change at a later stage. It may be observed in this connection that the Israeli argument emphasized the alleged illegality of the Egyptian actions whereas the British Representative considered it best for the Council to leave aside the legal question and to "call upon" Egypt to acquiesce in a legal regime which would permit free transit of the canal for the ships and cargoes in question. It is not difficult to imagine this case in slightly changed circumstances in which a complaining state, being an important maritime power, would consider itself obliged, first of all, to attempt to vindicate its view of the existing law. In terms of the case under discussion, this would have entailed the effort to establish that the right of free transit existed and continued to exist in the indicated circumstances. The only way in which this rule could be established would be by a decision of a judicial tribunal. If, then, hypothetically, this recourse were attempted and failed—the court upholding what is, in effect, the Egyptian position in the actual Suez case—the com-

---

[16] For purposes of this discussion regard is had only to the issue concerning troops in the Canal Zone; that part of the case concerning Sudan is disregarded.

plaining state might then wish to pursue the matter further through initiating a demand that the existing law be changed. It would be perfectly in order in doing this. In domestic societies such a course of action is routine. Many illustrations have occurred in the United States, among which a well-known example involved a Supreme Court decision declaring unconstitutional certain Illinois legislation on the ground that the state could not regulate railway rates on traffic destined to go beyond the state borders.[17] Advocates of the proposed regulation, being defeated on the basis of the existing law, went to Congress and obtained, through the Interstate Commerce Act, the desired power of regulation on a nation-wide basis.[18] In the international sphere the principle involved would be similar, though the mode of vindicating it would, of course, be different. In some cases, in which the terms of settlement would affect many states, the solution might be sought through conclusion of a broad multilateral treaty. This procedure would represent a *de facto* application of the process of codification of international law, which is made a function of the United Nations by Article 13 of the Charter.

A major obstacle preventing states from pursuing the course of action under discussion, insofar as it involves recourse to the judiciary, lies in the prevailing view that substantive decisions of the World Court are, in general, final determinations of the entire disputes to which they apply. This view is doubtless linked with the opinion which maintains, as stated by Kaplan and Katzenbach, that the Court can play only a limited role because "disputes about treaty interpretation or the application of rules of customary law are often a means of asserting what is really a desire for legislative reform; that is, for changing the content of the rules."[19] In the present submission it is considered that these elements of a case can be readily separated out if it is desired to do so, and that while perhaps the majority of disputes will have to be treated solely in the context of demands for "change," there are bound to be some as to which it would be highly desirable, in the first instance, to obtain a determination of the existing legal situation.

The view which regards a decision of the Court as equivalent to a decision of the whole dispute may have emerged out of an essen-

---

[17] Wabash, St. L. and P. Ry. Co. v. Illinois, 118 U.S. 557 (1886).

[18] 24 Stat. 379.

[19] Kaplan and Katzenbach, *The Political Foundations of International Law* 277 (1961).

tially "dispute-centered" view of international relations in which people, as is natural, tend to focus attention upon international disputes and upon modes of settling such disputes. One aspect of the matter may be that the permanent international judiciary evolved, in a sense, out of the arbitration concept.[20] For example, one of its principal founders, Elihu Root, believed that a permanent judiciary would represent an improvement and strengthening of the latter procedure.[21] The arbitration and judicial processes are quite similar in a number of respects but arbitration is broader, since the parties to disputes may, if they wish, charge arbitral tribunals with deciding on bases other than law. Such tribunals, being properly authorized, may therefore, by basing decisions on such considerations as they deem just and equitable in the circumstances, in effect bring about a change in the existing legal situation as between the parties. A judicial decision, on the other hand, must, by definition, be limited to the interpretation and application of existing law. Thus the arbitration process is, by its nature, better adapted than the judicial process to settling disputes in their entirety. It is also true that in Mr. Root's day, as now, the more important and politically sensitive disputes were not submitted to third-party determination. Disputes referred to arbitration were generally of a kind that could be given final settlement in this way, and consequently the state of mind evolved in which this process is regarded as having the purpose of settling disputes in their entirety. This attitude, on the part of officials and public alike, has largely carried over to the World Court. The Charter itself may tend to perpetuate the prevailing view of the matter since, in Article 33, it lumps the judicial process with other methods which might be employed for the settlement of disputes:

> The parties to any dispute . . . shall, first of all, seek a solution by negotiation, enquiry, mediation, conciliation, arbitration, judicial settlement . . .

This provision obviously has to be read as meaning not that the judicial process can settle "any dispute" in its entirety, but that it can be employed to determine those cases, or parts of cases, that properly come within the jurisdiction of a court.

---

[20] See Jenks, *The Prospects of International Adjudication* 102-103 (1964).

[21] Instructions to the American Delegates to the Hague Conference, 1907, *Foreign Relations of the United States,* 1907, Part II, 1128, 1135; 2 Jessup, *Elihu Root* 75-76 (1938).

The prevailing view of the matter was exemplified by both the United Kingdom and Egypt in the Suez "troops" case discussed above. The United Kingdom wanted consideration confined to the legal question of the validity of the treaty, considering that if it won the verdict on this point it would have won the case, notwithstanding Egypt's demand for change. Egypt was evidently in agreement with this view of the matter and therefore wanted to avoid any reference of the case to the Court, or any discussion of the validity of the treaty in the Council. In the "ships" case Egypt had to stand on its view of the law, but evidently desired to avoid an adjudication of the question for fear that the decision would go against it. Opposing states, though they might have considered Egypt wrong on the law, were apparently unwilling to risk a decision of the Court for fear that if Egypt won in this forum it would have won its case in the eyes of public opinion, and that it would have been practically impossible thereafter to have pursued a demand that the law be changed.

It might be agreed by all concerned that it would be desirable, in the interests of the development of the role of law, for the elements of "mixed" cases to be separated out and taken up in proper order.[22] The problem is again encountered, in this connection, that what might seem desirable from a long-range view of constitutional development might not appear to be in the practical and immediate interests of states involved in disputes. On the other hand, however, it would appear that, at least in some cases, this difficulty might be made to yield to the beneficial effects of full discussion and elucidation of the elements involved. For example in the Suez "troops" case, Egypt could have said, in effect: We believe the treaty in question has become invalid because of changed conditions, and we want this question decided first. If, however, the

---

[22] The Secretary-General suggested in 1958 that for states to refer legal cases to the Court in mixed cases of the kind under discussion "would clear the ground for processes of peaceful negotiations in the political organs of the United Nations." *Introduction to the Annual Report on the Work of the Organization 16 June 1958-15 June 1959*, U.N. Gen. Ass. Off. Rec. 14th Sess., Supp. No. IA at 4 (A/4132/Add.1) (1959). In the Egyptian "troops" case the United States Representative urged that Egypt accept the suggestion that the dispute should be referred to the Court, stating that if the treaty should be held technically valid, there would be nothing to preclude Egypt from later pursuing the case along other lines. U.N. Security Council Off. Rec. 2d year, 198th meeting 2296 (1947). See also statement by Soviet Representative to the Security Council, *id.* 17th year, 998th meeting 1 (S/PV. 998) (1962).

treaty should be upheld and determined still to be in force, we would then want to bring our plea for a change in the treaty on grounds of equity and justice. In the "ships" case, the argument contesting the Egyptian actions could have been along somewhat similar lines, as follows: We believe that the ships in question have the legal right to transit the Suez Canal, and we insist upon having this question adjudicated. However, even if Egypt's claim of right should be upheld by the Court, we are clear that this rule would be unjust and inequitable in the circumstances, considering that hostilities ended two years previously and that such cessation of hostilities was contemplated by all concerned as being permanent. Therefore, if the Court should uphold Egypt's position on the basis of existing law, we would reserve our right to press our demand that that applicable rule should be changed, so as to be brought into accord with this new kind of armistice, and the conditions of life under the Charter.

It is, of course, possible that states desiring change in particular situations may feel that their prospects of success are difficult enough without being further prejudiced by adverse court decisions. However these are matters for determination in the light of particular cases, and states always have the choice whether they wish to seek a definitive determination of the existing law, or whether to concentrate their efforts on their demands for a change.

Turning to consider the longer-range objective of developing law as the basis of international relations, the distinction under discussion appears of such fundamental importance that its better elucidation and application in terms of concrete cases would appear as an indispensable prerequisite to this goal. If an international system is to be developed which gives appropriate weight to both the elements of "stability" and "change," then it would seem to be essential that efforts be made to vindicate both elements, where appropriate, in concrete cases, including "mixed" cases, whenever possible. It is particularly in "mixed" cases that the proper juxtaposition of these elements comes directly in issue. The distinction under discussion is, in other words, indispensable to a successfully functioning international system for the same reason that it is in domestic societies. By the same token, there would not seem to be any great difficulty in its being readily comprehensible by all concerned, including the world public.

Chapter II

Disputes and Situations Involving Charter Law

Charter Evolution Both Possible and Necessary

When we turn from the consideration of cases arising under general international law and treaty law, such as those discussed in the preceding chapter, to disputes involving particular points of Charter law, we find that some special problems are presented. In particular, when governments find that their policy aspirations are hindered or obstructed by specific provisions of the Charter—or the absence of desired provisions—they are not so free as they are in other cases to seek changes in the existing law. True, the Charter contains provision for its own amendment. It is also true that, as in the case of most written constitutions, this amendment procedure is restrictive and difficult to use. The first amendments to have passed the Assembly and Security Council—to enlarge the Security Council and Economic and Social Council—are awaiting ratification at the time of writing.

Since, however, change may also be carried out through practice acquiesced in by the general membership, the Charter has the capability, prerequisite to any effective constitution, of evolving to meet changing conditions. In this connection the opinion may be recalled, ventured above in Chapter 1, that the principles of the Charter must find their real and effective existence in the minds of the world public, or its effective leaders. Here, also, must take place the evolution of the Charter necessary to enable it to serve as an effective constitutional instrument.

The best-known instance of Charter modification through practice and acquiescence concerns the Security Council voting rule set forth in Article 27 (3), stipulating that decisions on nonprocedural matters shall require "an affirmative vote of seven members including the concurring votes of the permanent members." Through practice generally acquiesced in, it has become well estab-

23

lished that the abstention of a permanent member will not defeat a decision of this kind.[1] This Charter modification can be said to have been fully explained and elucidated in the course of its being carried out. Permanent members of the Council, which were the states mainly concerned, made it clear, on occasion, that they did not wish to vote in favor of a particular resolution but, at the same time, did not desire to prevent its adoption. The practice was sometimes challenged on constitutional grounds, and in ensuing discussions it was not disputed that the Charter language required the votes of all five permanent members; however the challenges were overridden on the practical ground that the modified rule was more desirable than the original. As a British Representative said on one occasion:

> Irrespective of the strictly legal position, it was unwise to abandon a practice whereby the permanent members of the Council were attempting to avoid hampering decisions by exercising their veto.[2]

It may be doubted that the desired practice could be adopted "irrespective of the strictly legal position" since the question was whether resolutions of the Council adopted in this way were legally adopted. Since the Council clearly regarded resolutions as adopted, notwithstanding abstentions by permanent members, the conclusion appears unavoidable that the voting rule as laid down in the Charter was, in this respect, modified by practice and the acquiescence of states.

The possibility of modifying the Charter has been brought up

[1] Professor Gross traced this development up to early 1951 at which time he could say that the modified rule had not become effective with respect to the Security Council's use of force. Gross, "Voting in the Security Council: Abstention from Voting and Absence from Meetings," 60 Yale L.J. 209, 227-28 (1951). Subsequently, however, the Council adopted its resolution of February 21, 1961 urging the U.N. Force in the Congo to use force "if necessary" and "in the last resort" to prevent civil war in the Congo, and this was universally regarded as a valid decision notwithstanding the abstention of the Soviet and French Representatives. Professor Gross now recognizes the modified rule as being effective as to all types of cases:

"In the absence of effective procedure for authoritative interpretation, differences are bound to arise and remain unresolved unless a general consensus emerges as it did, for instance, in connection with the abstention of permanent members of the Security Council contrary to the letter of Article 27, paragraph 2." Gross, "Expenses of the United Nations for Peace-Keeping Operations: The Advisory Opinion of the International Court of Justice," 17 Int'l Org. 1, 10 (1963).

[2] U.N. Gen. Ass. Off. Rec. 3d Sess., Pt. 2, *Ad Hoc* Pol. Comm. 201 (1949).

of the Charter itself. The purpose of the present discussion is also to demonstrate that this practice, inevitably detrimental from the standpoint of Charter development, is, at least in some cases, unnecessary even from the "practical" point of view of states resorting to it.

The remainder of the present chapter is taken up with consideration of two groups of cases in which states found their policies to be impeded by provisions or omissions of the Charter. In the first group, desired action appears to have called for Charter modification by adding a power not originally included; some steps in the direction of such modification appear to have been taken. In the second group, moves have been taken in the direction of deleting an important provision from the Charter.

Charter Modification: Addition of New Power

The first group of cases just referred to concerns the power of the United Nations to exercise governmental or administrative authority over territory. The earliest case in this group concerned the Permanent Statute of the Free Territory of Trieste, which was annexed to the Italian Peace Treaty concluded in 1947,[8] and which provided in Article 2:

> The integrity and independence of the Free Territory shall be assured by the Security Council of the United Nations Organization. This responsibility implies that the Council shall:
> (a) ensure the observance of the present Statute and in particular the protection of the basic human rights of the inhabitants.
> (b) ensure the maintenance of public order and security in the Free Territory.

Other clauses provided that the Governor would be appointed by the Council and subject to suspension by that body,[9] and that he would have the status of the Council's representative.[10] In the legislative realm, the Governor was given a power of veto over acts of the popular Assembly; however if the popular Assembly thereafter insisted upon passing legislation and the Governor refused to agree, the final decision would rest with the Security Council.[11]

---

[8] Annex VI, Treaty of Peace with Italy, Feb. 10, 1947, 61 Stat. 1245, 1429; T.I.A.S. No. 1648; 49 U.N.T.S. 127, 186; 42 Am. J. Int'l L. Supp. 47, 97 (1948).

[9] *Id.* Art. 11.

[10] *Id.* Art. 17.

[11] *Id.* Art. 19.

When the Council took up the request that it assume these powers, several members queried its authority under the Charter to do so. It was generally recognized, in the ensuing debate,[12] that there was no specific provision in the Charter enabling the Council to assume such responsibilities. However, a consensus emerged holding that the necessary authority could be found in Article 24, the relevant parts of which provide:

1. In order to ensure prompt and effective action by the United Nations, its Members confer on the Security Council primary responsibility for the maintenance of international peace and security. . . .

2. In discharging these duties the Security Council shall act in accordance with the Purposes and Principles of the United Nations. The specific powers granted to the Security Council for the discharge of these duties are laid down in Chapters VI, VII, VIII, and XII.

In reaching its decision on this basis, the Council recognized that authority for the desired action was not to be found in any of the chapters of the Charter enumerated in paragraph 2 of this article. There was, in this connection, some disposition to accept the theory of a memorandum, presented by the Secretariat,[13] stating that it was understood, at the San Francisco Conference, that when the maintenance of peace and security is in issue, the Council should not be regarded as limited by specific Charter provisions other than the fundamental principles and purposes found in Chapter I. The British Representative, for example, said that the Council should hesitate before creating a precedent which would debar it, in the future, from accepting any responsibilities not specifically laid upon it in the Charter.[14] The Colombian Representative said that the Council should be able to act on the basis of the spirit of the Charter, rather than being limited to definite provisions.[15] There were other statements indicative of this approach to the problem.

Before taking up more specific aspects of the Trieste and other similar cases, it is desirable to consider the theory set forth in the Secretariat memorandum just referred to, namely that the Security Council's powers with respect to the maintenance of peace and security are limited only by the broad purposes and principles of

---

[12] U.N. Security Council Off. Rec. 2d year, 89th and 91st meetings (1947).
[13] *Id.* 91st meeting 44-45.
[14] U.N. Security Council Off. Rec. 2d year, 89th meeting 9-10 (1947).
[15] *Id.* 18.

the United Nations. This theory has not been applied with any consistency; on the other hand it has not been effectively denied. Its existence as at least one alternate theory of interpretation[16] as to the extent of Charter powers has no doubt contributed to the prevailing tendency in which the United Nations is caused by member states to take decisions and actions which appear to be practically unlimited by Charter considerations—except as to voting requirements—but as to which, at the same time, various Charter justifications are advanced, not necessarily valid or mutually consistent. Ensuing chapters of the present study are devoted in large part to consideration of these practices.

The theory of the Secretariat memorandum under discussion is herein considered not to reflect any consensus of the San Francisco Conference[17] and to be, on its merits, untenable. By the same token it is believed impossible, from the standpoint of a "constitutional approach," to sustain the proposition that decisions such as that in the Trieste case can properly be attributed to Article 24 of the Charter. This provision, it will be recalled, confers primary responsibility upon the Security Council for the maintenance of peace and security. The maintenance of peace and security is, in turn, the first-stated major "Purpose" of the United Nations found

---

[16] Schachter, "The Development of International Law Through the Legal Opinions of the United Nations Secretariat," 25 Brit. Yb. Int'l L. 91, 97-101 (1948); Goodrich and Hambro, *Charter of the United Nations: Commentary and Documents* 205-207 (2d ed. rev. 1949). A more general theory that the legal powers of the United Nations and other international organizations are not confined to such acts and rights as are specified in their constitutions is set forth in Seyersted, "United Nations Forces: Some Legal Problems," 37 Brit. Yb. Int'l L. 351, 447-71 (1961).

[17] The reference in the memorandum, in this connection, was to the 14th meeting of Committee III/1 of the Conference. Kelsen, with whom the present writer agrees, maintains that the discussion in this meeting does not lead to the conclusion indicated in the memorandum:

"This discussion at the San Francisco Conference shows that some delegates were of the opinion that the Security Council was not restricted to the specific powers set forth in Chapters VI, VII and VIII (Chapter XII was not yet inserted into the text of the Charter). But it does not show a generally accepted opinion that the powers conferred upon the Council by Article 24 are limited only by being 'subject to the purposes and principles of the United Nations,' as the Secretary-General maintained in his statement." Kelsen, *The Law of the United Nations* 284 n. 6 (1950).

Further evidence in support of this view is believed to be found in the record of the 25th meeting of the Coordination Committee of the Conference. Doc. No. WD 422, CO/186, 17 U.N. Conf. Int'l Org. Docs. 169, 171-72 (1945).

in Article 1 of the Charter. The thesis of the present discussion is that the development of a system capable of maintaining peace and security means the development of a set of "constitutional" principles and procedures. Valuable as such concepts as "peace" and "justice" are as starting points for constitutional development they are, in themselves, too broad to serve as the effective principles of such a system. States can and do invoke them as justifications for the most diverse and mutually inconsistent policies.

When it is herein suggested that it is necessary to develop a more precise set of principles, it is realized that the principles comprising an effective system may not prove to be very precise, especially when applied to particular factual situations. The decision-maker may have a close choice as to which of several principles ought to be applied in a given case and the preferable decision even may represent a merger of parts of several principles. Such methods of decision are, however, characteristic of legal processes.[17a] As has been observed in Chapter 1, the essential factor is considered to be neither the rules themselves nor the consistency with which they are applied, but rather the nature of the effort that is made by the proper authorities to achieve justice on the basis of principle.

The nature of the problem under discussion comes more clearly into focus if we assume the converse approach, in which the powers of the United Nations are said to be unlimited, except by broad principles such as "peace" and "justice." For reasons which have been indicated, this view is believed equivalent to saying that there are no limits except the requirements pertaining to voting majorities. To the extent that this view of the United Nations prevails, questions of principle naturally tend to become subordinated to the desirability of gaining votes and voting victories, and of avoiding defeats. This attitude, which appears to prevail in the United Nations today (and which will be discussed further in Chapter 8, below), is believed practically to rule out prospects of effective Charter development.

It is, then, necessary to reconsider, in light of these considerations, the general consensus of the Council, in the Trieste case, that authority for the desired United Nations action could be found in Article 24 of the Charter. From the point of view which regards the United Nations as an Organization of delegated pow-

---

17a As it was put by Justice Holmes, "general principles do not decide concrete cases." Lochner v. New York, 198 U.S. 45, 76 (1904).

ers, the Council has, for the fulfillment of its broad responsibility under Article 24, certain more specific powers, notably those pertaining to "collective measures," "provisional measures," and the "peaceful settlement" function. The function assumed in the Trieste case appears to have been essentially different from a collective or a provisional measure, and while it may be said to have been part of a broader effort to achieve the peaceful settlement of a dispute between Italy and Yugoslavia, it was also essentially different from the "peaceful settlement" function of the Council, as this is defined in Chapter VI of the Charter. The basic United Nations "peaceful settlement" function *vis-à-vis* the parties to a dispute is the power of recommendation. Undoubtedly the United Nations may also take ancillary actions, such as carrying out investigations to inform itself, or the parties, of the facts of the case; or the appointment of conciliation or mediation commissions to assist the parties in reaching agreement. Such actions seem naturally related to the "peaceful settlement" function. However, the assumption of responsibility for territory, as in the Trieste case, appears to have a different focal point, and an essentially different constitutional character.

The motivation for assuming such a function may also, by the same token, be essentially different from that of maintaining peace and security.[18] This possibility is suggested by the case of Jerusalem, to be mentioned further below, in connection with the Palestine case of 1947. While the United Nations decision to assume governmental responsibility for Jerusalem as an international city was motivated in part, no doubt, by considerations relating to the maintenance of peace and security, it had also, certainly, in part, the purpose of assuring protection of, and free access to, holy places of three religions.

Since the administration or government of territory thus appears as a type of function distinct from other United Nations functions, and since no reasonably specific authority for it is found in the Charter, it is believed that the Council's action in the Trieste case is preferably to be regarded as a first step in a potential process of Charter modification. We are not, of course, here referring to formal Charter amendment, but rather to modification of that instrument through practice and acquiescence of states. From this point of view, the basic elements of the Council's action may be

[18] See statement of the Australian Representative, U.N. Security Council Off. Rec. 2d year, 91st meeting 56-57 (1947).

said to have consisted in a demonstrated awareness of the need for
this authority by the United Nations, and the disposition to take
steps to establish the necessary Charter basis, notwithstanding the
lack of a specific authorization in the Charter as written.

In view of what appears to be a basically satisfactory handling
of the Trieste case, it is all the more surprising that, in subsequent
cases, raising substantially similar questions concerning the powers
of the Assembly, no similarly candid recognition of the existence
of a problem of Charter law, or of a disposition to solve it, has
been manifested.

The question was precipitated in several forms by the Assembly's
Plan of Partition with Economic Union of Palestine,[19] which was
recommended later in the same year as the Trieste debate (1947).
The Plan was formulated in response to the announcement by the
British Government that it was relinquishing the role of Mandatory Power earlier assigned to that country by the League of Nations, and in response to the accompanying suggestion that the
United Nations make provision for the future government of
Palestine. The Plan, which was in the form of a recommendation
by the Assembly, called for the division of Palestine between an
Arab and a Jewish state, with Jerusalem becoming an international city under United Nations supervision. It was rejected by
the Arabs of Palestine and by the surrounding Arab states, and
never came into force.

To effect the transition from the Mandate to the proposed new
regime, the Plan provided for the establishment of a United Nations Palestine Commission. This Commission was to take over the
administration of Palestine as the Mandate came to an end, establish provisional councils of government for the new Arab and
Jewish states, and exercise supervision over these councils until,
in due course, full governmental responsibility would be turned
over to them.[20] In answer to a challenge by Arab states as to the
Charter authority of the United Nations to exercise the powers
thus assigned to the Palestine Commission, it was said by the
Polish Delegate, Pruszynski, chairman of the Committee which
drafted the Plan, that

> The Commission . . . was not to act as the government of Pales-
> tine but solely as the body through whose agency the administration

[19] Res. 181 (II), *Resolutions* 131, 132, U.N. Gen. Ass. Off. Rec. 2d Sess.
(1947).
[20] Part I, B, paragraphs 1-9 of the Plan.

of the country would be transferred to the provisional councils of government. . . .[21]

The United States Delegation argued along similar lines in the plenary session:

> In view of the nature of these administrative functions, I do not believe that we can seriously question this temporary and transitory assistance which would be extended to the non-self-governing peoples of territories which will become two States, in their efforts to establish themselves as free and independent members of the family of nations.[22]

The Plan also envisioned the assumption of administrative and/or governmental powers by the United Nations with respect to Jerusalem and the Joint Economic Board.

Jerusalem was to be established as a *corpus separatum* under a special international regime to be administered by the United Nations. The Trusteeship Council was designated to discharge the responsibilities of the United Nations in this connection.

The Joint Economic Board was to have been established under the Plan with the function of carrying out the measures required to realize the objectives of the economic union, and it was to have the necessary powers to enable it to fulfill this function. The United Nations, through the Economic and Social Council, was to appoint three neutral members of the Board. Of the other six members, three were to be appointed by each of the new states; consequently, the United Nations appointees would hold the balance as to any matters on which the states were in disagreement. It was objected, at the time, that "the net effect of this proposal is . . . to authorize the United Nations to take a direct part in the administration of the economic life of the country."[23]

The proposals pertaining to Jerusalem and the Joint Economic Board were approved by the Assembly as part of the Plan of Partition with Economic Union, without any effort to answer challenges by Arab delegations[24] to the authority of the United Nations to assume the powers in question.

The final case in the group under discussion is that of West

[21] U.N. Gen. Ass. Off. Rec. 2d Sess., *Ad Hoc* Committee on The Palestinian Question 160 (1947).

[22] *Id.* Plenary 1326-27.

[23] *Id. Ad Hoc* Committee on the Palestinian Question, Annex 25 at 279 (A/AC. 14/32 and Add. 1).

[24] See also remarks of Sir Mohammed Zafrullah Khan, *Id.*, Plenary 1370-73.

Irian. The United Nations undertook the administration of this territory for a period in 1962-1963 as a means of effectuating the transfer of the territory from the Netherlands to Indonesia, pursuant to an agreement between the two countries. The Secretary-General assisted in arriving at the settlement, and the resulting agreement required approval of the Assembly, which was duly given. Article V of the agreement provides:

> The United Nations Administrator, as chief executive officer of the UNTEA [United Nations Temporary Executive Authority], will have full authority under the direction of the Secretary-General to administer the territory for the period of the UNTEA administration in accordance with the terms of the present agreement.[25]

The Secretary-General said that the United Nations would have "temporary executive authority" over the territory in question[26] but went on to say:

> This novel settlement may well be a step in the gradual evolution of the United Nations as an increasingly effective instrument for carrying out policies agreed upon between Member Governments for the peaceful resolution of their differences, in line with the Charter.[27]

There is thus recalled, first of all, a certain paradoxical element of the Palestine case in which official spokesmen for the majority avoided any statement to the effect that the United Nations would be undertaking the government of territory while, at the same time, the majority was causing the United Nations to undertake precisely that kind of activity. Here, in the West Irian case, the Secretary-General indeed states that the United Nations is undertaking the exercise of "executive authority" over the territory, but proceeds to indicate that the peaceful settlement function of the Organization may form the Charter basis of the action. His above-quoted statement on this point is self-evidently true if it is interpreted as meaning that the United Nations may take any action to assist the parties in reaching a peaceful settlement of a dispute so long as the action is "in line with the Charter." If this last clause is made the focal point of the statement, the interpretation might then be that, since the action in question is "in line with the Charter," the Charter must provide for the assumption of govern-

---

[25] 437 U.N.T.S. 273; U.N. Gen. Ass. Off. Rec. 17th Sess., Annexes, Agenda Item No. 89, at 2 (A/5170 and Add. 1) (1962).

[26] *Id.* Plenary 53 (A/PV. 1127) (1962).

[27] *Ibid.*

mental authority by the United Nations. Pursuant to this interpretation the Secretary-General's statement could be said to follow the precedent of the Trieste case in tending to build up authority of the United Nations to exercise this kind of power. While this would seem to be the most logical interpretation to give the Secretary-General's statement, the formulation of the statement itself appears as too vague and uncertain to serve a useful purpose from the standpoint of Charter evolution, which must include the necessary development of public opinion.

In attempting to understand the difficulty evidently encountered by the competent authorities in assigning a Charter basis for the decisions under discussion with respect to the Palestine and West Irian cases, it may be pertinent to recall that the Palestine case was debated only a few months after the Trieste debate in the Security Council. If the Palestine case had come up in the Security Council, it is only logical to assume that the precedent of the Trieste case would have been followed with respect to the question of Charter authority here under discussion. The possibility thus suggests itself that the source of difficulty was doubt that the Assembly had the authority to take such decisions. It will be recalled, in this connection, that the Security Council found authority for the Trieste decision in Article 24 of the Charter—a provision that refers only to the Security Council. Also entering into the problem may have been the opinion that the Assembly is constitutionally without power to do more than recommend. This view was prevalent not only at the time of the Palestine case, but continues to be prevalent today so far as theory—as opposed to actions—is concerned. It may, therefore, conceivably have entered into the Secretary-General's pronouncement concerning the nature of the West Irian operation under the Charter.[28]

---

[28] An explanation of the policy followed based on the "practical" interests of states in the immediate situations, as opposed to the long-range interests represented by the Charter, hardly seems credible in respect to these cases. In the first place, only in the Palestine case, among the group under discussion, was there a dispute involving the authority of the United Nations to assume administrative or governmental powers. It seems to be true that, in this case, there was a general disposition among the majority to subordinate constitutional questions in their efforts to secure a solution of the dispute as to the future of Palestine. A constitutional question concerning the power of the United Nations to enforce the Plan of Partition with Economic Union, to be discussed in the ensuing chapter, would seem, more than the issue presently under discussion, to involve possible divergencies as between the immediate interests of states and the long-range interests represented by the United Na-

The precedent of the Trieste case would not seem to be an insurmountable obstacle to the making of corresponding decisions by the General Assembly, even if it is considered (contrary to the view of the present discussion) that the proper basis of the power in question may be found in the Charter purpose pertaining to the maintenance of peace and security. In the first place, while Article 24 charges the Security Council with responsibility for the maintenance of peace and security, there is underlying this provision the delineation of the same concept in Article 1 (1) where it appears, however, not as a particular function of the Security Council, but as a major "Purpose" of the United Nations as a whole. Secondly, the entrusting of this responsibility to the Security Council in Article 24 is, by its terms, not exclusive. Rather, it is there stated that the responsibility of the Council is "primary," thus implying the existence of secondary authority elsewhere. The Assembly acted upon this theory of interpretation in adopting the Uniting for Peace resolution in 1950, wherein that organ asserted the power to initiate necessary measures when the Council was prevented by the veto, in particular cases, from doing so.[29]

It is not, however, herein considered that the Charter authority for the administration or government of territory properly rests upon the broad United Nations purpose of maintaining peace and security. Rather, for reasons indicated above in connection with the Trieste case, it is believed that the assumption of responsibility for territory by the United Nations really involves the modification of the Charter through recognition of a power not spelled out in that instrument and not contemplated by its framers. If this is the case, and if this power should be (or, perhaps, if it has been) brought into existence by evolutionary process, it would belong to the United Nations as a whole, and not to any particular organ. That the Assembly, along with the Security Council, should be recognized as an appropriate organ for its exercise would seem to be indicated by the fact that four out of the five decisions made

tions. As to the issue presently under discussion—concerning the power of the United Nations to administer territory—it seems rather unlikely that the majority would have thought that its suppression or distortion would have advanced the prospects of a peaceful solution. It must, on the contrary, have appeared as evident that concessions on such points would have been well worthwhile if they contributed to agreement, in principle, on the basic issue pertaining to the partition of Palestine.

[29] *Cf.* p. 153 *infra.*

in the past, looking toward the assumption of responsibilities of the kind under discussion, have been taken by the Assembly.

Suppression of Unwanted Charter Provisions

The final group of cases for consideration in this chapter concerns the encounter of certain states with a United Nations Charter provision which they deemed obstructive of their interests, and a resulting course of action tending toward the elimination of this clause from the Charter. The provision in question is the "authorization clause" found in the second sentence of Article 53:

> 1. The Security Council shall, where appropriate, utilize such regional arrangements or agencies for enforcement action under its authority. But no enforcement action shall be taken under regional arrangements or by regional agencies without the authorization of the Security Council . . . .

The regional agency involved in these cases is the Organization of American States (OAS).

In the earliest of the cases under discussion the OAS, in 1960, found that the Dominican Republic had committeed wrongful acts against Venezuela and decided that, for this reason, its members should withdraw their diplomatic representation from the Dominican Republic and impose a partial interruption of economic relations with that country, beginning with an arms embargo.[30]

In the second case the OAS, at its meeting at Punta del Este in early 1962, suspended all trade in arms between its members and Cuba on account of subversive activities of the latter country found to be in serious violation of the fundamental principles of the inter-American system.[31]

Measures such as arms embargoes and the withdrawal of diplomatic representation appear to fall within the concept of "enforcement action" as used in Article 53 of the United Nations Charter. This function—defined as "collective measures" in Article 1 of the Charter[32]—embraces the authority of the Organization to

---

[30] See 43 Dep't State Bull. 358 (1960).

[31] See 46 id. 282 (1962).

[32] So far as terminology is concerned, although the Charter provisions actually defining the concept (quoted in principal text infra) speak of "collective measures" (Art. 1) and "measures" (Art. 39) and not to "enforcement" measures, etc., terms such as "enforcement arrangements," "enforcement measures," etc., were most generally used at San Francisco to describe the generic

employ tangible pressures in the handling of disputes and situations, and authorizes such measures including both force and measures short of force when deemed necessary to deal with aggression, other breaches of peace or threats to peace. A generally similar power is possessed by the OAS as to American regional matters.[33] The concept is thus defined in the United Nations Charter:

Article 1

The Purposes of the United Nations are:

1. To maintain international peace and security, and to that end: to take effective collective measures for the prevention and removal of threats to the peace, and for the suppression of acts of aggression or other breaches of the peace . . . .

Article 39

The Security Council shall determine the existence of any threat to the peace, breach of the peace, or act of aggression and shall make recommendations, or decide what measures shall be taken in accordance with Articles 41 and 42, to maintain or restore international peace and security.

Article 41

The Security Council may decide what measures not involving the use of armed force are to be employed to give effect to its decisions, and it may call upon the Members of the United Nations to apply such measures. These may include complete or partial interruption of economic relations and of rail, sea, air, postal, telegraphic, radio, and other means of communication, and the severance of diplomatic relations.

Article 42

Should the Security Council consider that measures provided for in Article 41 would be inadequate or have proved to be inadequate, it may take such action by air, sea, or land forces as may be necessary to maintain or restore international peace and security. Such action may include demonstrations, blockade, and other operations by air, sea, or land forces of Members of the United Nations.

---

concept in question. Thus the function of Committee III/3, which drafted the relevant provisions found in Chapter VII, was generically described by the Steering Committee of the Conference as "enforcement arrangements." *United Nations Conference on International Organization: Selected Documents* 23 (1946).

[33] See Inter-American Treaty of Reciprocal Assistance (The "Rio Pact") OAS Treaty Series 8; 21 U.N.T.S. 77; 62 Stat. 1681 (1948); T.I.A.S. No. 1838.

In the first of the cases under discussion the Soviet Representative, while approving the action taken by the OAS, thought that it required Security Council approval pursuant to Article 53, and introduced a resolution in that organ which would have had the effect of giving such approval. The American states and some others, apparently fearing that if this precedent were established the Soviet Union could use it in future cases to obstruct OAS action, introduced a resolution of their own, which was adopted, and in which the Council merely took note of the action taken by the OAS.[34]

In the second case the Cuban Representative in the Security Council asserted, in that body, that the OAS measure directed against his country was an enforcement measure requiring authorization under Article 53, and proposed that, if this position were not agreed to, the question be referred to the World Court for decision. This position was rejected by a majority of the Council and no resolution on the case was passed by that body.[35]

Several arguments were advanced on behalf of the majority position. They were somewhat interrelated, and had a clear tendency to declare the "authorization" clause inapplicable, at least as concerns regional measures short of force. What was, perhaps, the principal line of argument in this connection was stated as follows by the British Representative in the 1960 debate:

> In the opinion of the United Kingdom Government, it is common sense to interpret the use of this term in Article 53 as covering only such actions as would not normally be legitimate except on the basis of a Security Council resolution. There is nothing in international law, in principle, to prevent any State, if it so decides, from breaking off diplomatic relations or instituting a partial interruption of economic relations with any other State. These steps, which are the measures decided upon by the Organization of American States with regard to the Dominican Republic, are acts of policy perfectly within the competence of any sovereign state. It follows, obviously, that they are within the competence of the members of the Organization of American States acting collectively.[36]

[34] For the Council debate see U.N. Security Council Off. Rec. 15th year, 893d and 894th meetings (S/PV. 893, 894) (1960). For resolution adopted see *id.* Supp. July-Sept. 1960, at 145 (S/4491, Sept. 9, 1960).

[35] For the Council debate see *id.* 17th year, 992d-998th meetings (S/PV. 992-998) (1962). For a good analysis of the debates in the Dominican and Cuban cases see Claude, "The OAS, the UN, and the United States," *International Conciliation* No. 547, at 47-63 (March 1964).

[36] *Id.,* 15th year, 893d meeting 16 (S/PV. 893) (1960).

This argument was employed by several representatives in both the 1960 and 1962 cases. A variant, also brought forward in both cases, was that the phrase "enforcement action," as used in Article 53, refers only to measures involving the use of physical force.

The argument, in both its aspects, is believed to be, at the least, debatable. Referring to the last sentence of the above-quoted statement of the British Representative, it seems far from obvious that the powers of the OAS correspond to those of the member states, acting individually, under international law. The OAS is an international organization, the powers of which are determined by relevant treaties, including the Charter of the United Nations. The argument that the "authorization" requirement does not apply to measures short of force seems to be at variance with the language of Article 53 which makes it applicable to all "enforcement actions." As indicated above, "enforcement action" appears to be embraced within the Charter concept of "collective measures" including tangible pressures short of force as well as measures of force.

Another line of argument, in the debates in question, can be interpreted as looking to the deletion of the "authorization" clause in its entirety. In the 1960 debate, for example, the Argentine, United States and Ecuadoran Representatives co-sponsored the resolution adopted by the Council which merely took note of, instead of authorized, the OAS action against the Dominican Republic. In support of this resolution the Argentine Representative said that it would amount to a "complete demonstration of the coordination which should exist between the regional agency and the international Organization"[37] and went on to say:

> It is therefore our conviction that, however Article 53 may be interpreted in the future,[38] legally organized regional groups . . . must have sufficient authority to solve problems confined within the limits of the region involved.[39]

The Ecuadoran Representative, another sponsor of the resolution, said:

---

[37] *Id.* at 6.

[38] It does not, however, seem possible, pursuant to a constitutional approach, to take a position which leaves a legal issue out of account. If, for example, in this case, a representative's position purports to be without reference to Article 53, one unavoidable effect is to weaken the force and effect of that provision.

[39] U.N. Security Council 15th year, 893d meeting 7 (S/PV. 893) (1960).

[Article 53] cannot and should not be used to make a regional agency's action rigidly dependent upon authorization by the Security Council. On the contrary, the relations between the Council and the regional agencies should be so flexible as to permit these agencies to take effective action for the maintenance of international peace and security in the light of regional conditions and without necessarily bringing regional problems before a world forum.[40]

The United States Representative, the third co-sponsor, said that "the Security Council can best affirm its faith in the inter-American system by the adoption of the draft resolution submitted by the members of the Organization of American States in the Council."[41]

The basic issue thus posed is not, by this writer, considered to be whether Charter language should be rigidly adhered to, but rather what is best to be done taking into account both the interests of states in particular situations, and the desirability of developing the Charter as the basis of a system capable of maintaining peace and security.

Certainly one tendency of the arguments against the use of the "authorization" clause in these cases was to favor a rule that the clause should not be applied to regional measures not involving the use of force. Proposals to modify the Charter to this extent have a reasonable appearance, including the corollary that measures involving force should have United Nations authorization. If, however, in the heat of an actual situation states are unwilling to accept the risks involved in seeking authorization in the lesser categories of cases, would they be more inclined to do so in those more serious cases which are deemed to require the application of military force? What would seem to be the logical expectation of a negative answer seems to be confirmed by the refusal of the OAS to seek authorization for its application of force in the Dominican case of April, 1965. This expectation is also upheld by certain arguments advanced by United States officials in connection with the Cuban "quarantine" crisis of 1962.[42] These matters will be discussed below in the present chapter.

[40] *Id.* at 12.

[41] *Id.* at 9.

[42] In the Security Council debate on the missile crisis, the Ghanaian Representative claimed that the United States had estopped itself, by these earlier arguments, from denying that the "quarantine" was an enforcement measure requiring United Nations authorization. *Id.* 17th year, 1024th meeting 19 (S/PV. 1024) (1962).

Taking up, first, the measures short of force in the Dominican and Cuban cases above referred to, it is to be observed that the Council debates in neither of these cases effectively brought out the facts that the whole issue pertaining to the "authorization" requirement had already been the subject of a major controversy at San Francisco, and that the clause in question had been included in the Charter, after full debate, because of its significance to the major United Nations purpose of maintaining peace and security.

Although regional organizations are juridically separate from the United Nations, provisions designed to assure coordination, and to prevent conflict as between them and the world Organization, are incorporated in the Charter of the United Nations. The only one of these provisions going so far as to require United Nations authorization of a regional activity is the one under consideration, pertaining to regional enforcement actions. Proponents of the clause at San Francisco were apprehensive that to allow regional organizations to proceed on their own initiative to the application of tangible pressures, including the possible use of force, in international situations, could well prove disruptive of the over-all world role of the United Nations. Some states, on the other hand, when they saw the "authorization" clause as proposed in the Dumbarton Oaks Proposals, feared that it might lead to the frustration of needed regional action by the United Nations, through the veto or otherwise. Sentiments in favor of regional organizations were especially strong among the American states which had just agreed, at the Chapultepec Conference, to incorporate a regional security system into the long-existing inter-American system. The resulting dilemma at San Francisco led to one of the major controversies of the Conference, which was only resolved by a compromise[43] and after a considerable effort.[44] As one part of the solution, the "authorization" requirement was incorporated in the Charter. The other main part consisted of the writing of a new Charter provision (Art. 51) recognizing the right of collective self-defense in case of armed attack:

> Nothing in the present Charter shall impair the inherent right of individual or collective self-defense if an armed attack occurs against a Member of the United Nations, until the Security Council has

---

[43] See summary reports of second and fourth meetings of Committee III/4 of the San Francisco Conference, Doc. 196, III/4/4 and Doc. 576, III/4/9, 12 U.N. Conf. Int'l Org. Docs. 668, 679, 680-84 (1945).

[44] *The Private Papers of Senator Vandenberg* 186-93 (A.H. Vandenberg, Jr. ed. 1952).

taken the measures necessary to maintain international peace and security. Measures taken by Members in the exercise of this right of self-defense shall be immediately reported to the Security Council and shall not in any way affect the authority and responsibility of the Security Council under the present Charter to take at any time such action as it deems necessary in order to maintain or restore international peace and security.

In the ensuing years, when it became apparent that certain major international problems could not be solved through the United Nations, there was a considerable resort to regional security organizations, which tended to emphasize the aspect of regional self-defense. While such organizations were entirely consistent with the letter of the Charter, they necessarily incorporated tendencies with potentialities of danger to the United Nations. Apprehensions of this character were thus expressed by Secretary-General Hammarskjold:

> [D]evelopments outside the organizational framework of the United Nations, but inside its sphere of interest, do give rise to certain problems which require serious consideration. In the short view, other approaches than those provided by the United Nations machinery may seem more expedient and convenient, but in the long view they may yet be inadvisable. To fail to use the United Nations machinery on those matters for which Governments have given to the Organization a special or primary responsibility under the Charter, or to improvise other arrangements without overriding practical and political reasons—to act thus may tend to weaken the position of the Organization and to reduce its influence and effectiveness, even when the ultimate purpose which it is intended to serve is a United Nations purpose.
>
> The balance to be struck here must be struck with care.[45]

---

[45] *Annual Report of the Secretary-General on the Work of the Organization 1 July 1953-30 June 1954.* U.N. Gen. Ass. Off. Rec. 9th Sess., Supp. No. 1, at xi (A/2663) (1954). To similar effect see remarks by U Thant on May 27, 1965, N.Y. Times, May 28, 1965, p. 1., col. 2. Professor Corbett thus refers to a comparable development in the period of the League of Nations:
"Sharp misgivings were voiced by representatives of some humbler States as the 'Locarno Powers' took over the making of decisions vested by the Covenant in the League Council or Assembly. . . . But the dominant note was one of confidence that the way had at last been cleared for effective implementation of the universal law of the Covenant. Any suggestion that Locarno was to prove the beginning of a general retreat from universalism to regional and particular security arrangements, with their inevitable diversion of attention and influence from the League, was drowned in hosannas to the newly discovered 'spirit of Geneva.' " Corbett, *Law in Diplomacy* 207 (1959).

The use or non-use made of the "authorization" requirement of Article 53 has an obvious relevance to the problem as to which the Secretary-General thus indicated concern. It may, at the same time, be acknowledged that if the "authorization" requirement were to be abandoned, the United Nations would not thereby lose all control over enforcement measures of regional organizations. The world organization would, of course, retain its basic purpose and responsibility with respect to the maintenance of peace and security. Regional organizations and their members would still be bound by the basic Charter principle that member states must refrain from the use of force in any way inconsistent with the "Purposes" of the United Nations (Article 2 (4)). If a regional organization were to embark on a measure which the United Nations considered to be a wrongful breach of peace, or threat to peace, the latter organization would have the right to take such measures as it deemed appropriate to deal with the situation.

Nevertheless, the authority conferred upon the United Nations by the "authorization" provision, giving it a control over such regional measures from the outset, is a fundamentally important power abandonment of which would tend to be divisive. Such was the view of the San Francisco Conference when, after a full discussion, it decided to retain the clause with the exception, above noted, pertaining to emergency situations justifying collective self-defense.

The 1960 and 1962 cases under discussion seem to have represented a re-emergence of the dilemma of San Francisco just referred to, but in concrete rather than abstract form. To contrary effect it may be argued with some logic that, since the United Nations Charter did not bring about a real change in the nature of international relations, it should not be allowed to diminish the role of such an organization as the OAS, a regional security organization which *had* been evolved to meet the needs of the real situation. By the same token, however, the question still remains whether it is not still just as essential as it was at the time of San Francisco to establish a world system capable of maintaining peace and security. The question also still persists as to whether the "peoples of the world" do not still desire to see the United Nations fulfill the basic function of maintaining peace and security with which it was entrusted, in principle, in 1945. This same question was posed in 1950 when, in connection with the Korean case, it became clear to all that the security system originally envisioned in the Charter could be frustrated and prevented from functioning because of the inability of the Security Council to fulfill the responsibility entrusted to it. At that time, by means of the Uniting for Peace resolution, the Assembly asserted its power to initiate measures deemed necessary for the maintenance of peace and security when the Council was prevented, by the veto, from fulfilling its primary responsibility.[46] In a more fundamental sense, the "peoples of the world" can be said to have decided that the United Nations should not be prevented from fulfilling its major purpose pertaining to the maintenance of peace and security by reason of the breakdown of the original theory under which this function had been entrusted to the Council. If this is what the "peoples of the world" still want, questions would seem to present themselves as to the desirability of a course of action such as that under discussion. The "authorization" clause, although perhaps, as just indicated, not absolutely vital to the ultimate success of the United Nations, was deliberately placed in the Charter as an important means of preserving the world role of the Organization as against the tendency of dissolution into regional blocs. A move to nullify the clause, while keeping the world public in the dark as to what is being done, would seem to be a course of action which leaves aside basic questions of constitutional development.

There were, of course, practical reasons for the policies followed in these cases by the American states. As to the Dominican case of 1960, it will be recalled that the Soviet Union did not object to the anti-Trujillo measures of the OAS. If the American states had sought Security Council authorization for the OAS measures in that case, such authorization could apparently have been obtained without difficulty. In insisting that authorization was required, the Soviet Union was no doubt mainly concerned with preserving the opportunity afforded by the "authorization" clause for discussing American affairs, or possibly obstructing American actions, in future cases. It was probably out of apprehension of such future communist activity that the American states and others denied the applicability of the provision in question.

The foresight of both sides was vindicated in the case of the 1962 arms embargo applied by the OAS against Cuba. Any re-

---

[46] Res. 377 (V), Nov. 3, 1950, U.N. Gen. Ass. Off. Rec. 5th Sess., Supp. No. 20 at 10 (A/1775) (1950). The resolution is discussed further at pp. 152-54 *infra*.

quest for Security Council authorization of the OAS action in that case would undoubtedly have met with a Soviet veto. No doubt for this reason, the American states, and others, rejected the Cuban assertion that authorization was required, as well as the demand that the question be submitted for adjudication. These rejections would have been difficult to make if, in the earlier Dominican case, these states had acquiesced in the Soviet position that authorization was required.

If, in the 1962 case, a request for authorization had been made in the Security Council, and there vetoed, the request might then have been taken into the Assembly pursuant to the principle underlying the Uniting for Peace resolution which has just been mentioned, and which would seem clearly applicable to the granting of United Nations authorization for measures deemed necessary by regional organizations. It seems likely, however, that if this recourse had been pursued in the Cuban case of 1962, the result would have been a defeat for the American states. The main emphasis of the Punta del Este Conference had been less on specific acts of subversion by Cuba than on the general proposition that the introduction of communism constitutes a threat to the hemisphere. It seems possible that a number of non-American states in the General Assembly would have entertained doubts that this was a sufficient threat to justify the application of measures of tangible pressures. If American governments had thus tried and failed to obtain United Nations authorization, and had thereby been forced to abandon the proposed embargo, they would undoubtedly have been subjected to considerable criticism from within their own countries. The only explanation they could have offered would have been that they were seeking to uphold a basic Charter principle, important to the achievement of the long-range objectives of the United Nations. It is hardly to be supposed that this justification would have proved acceptable, or would, indeed, have been widely understood. If it is true, as herein argued, that one of the best ways of developing a constitutional basis for the conduct of international relations is the use of the Charter in accordance with its principles, this case illustrates the proposition that there must be a development of public opinion in this respect before the Charter can be so used. A vicious circle thus exists which must be broken if substantial progress is to be made.

A new phase of the Cuban case unfolded in 1963 and 1964. An investigating committee of the OAS reported, in February,

1964, that "Venezuela has been the target of a series of actions sponsored and directed by the Government of Cuba, openly intended to subvert Venezuelan institutions and to overthrow the democratic government of Venezuela through terrorism, sabotage, assault and guerilla warfare," and that Cuban agents had clandestinely shipped arms into Venezuela.[47] On the basis of this report, the OAS decided, by resolution of July 26, 1964, that "the acts verified by the Investigating Committee constitute an aggression and an intervention on the part of the Government of Cuba in the internal affairs of Venezuela."[48] In consequence of this finding, the OAS proceeded to apply far-reaching diplomatic and economic measures against Cuba.[49]

Again, the American states did not seek the authorization of the United Nations for these measures. Neither, in this case, did Cuba or the Soviet Union raise the issue. Considering the earlier efforts of the American states, and some others, to deny the applicability of the "authorization" clause in similar cases, and the absence of a request from either side that it be employed in the 1964 Cuban case, it appeared at the time that the provision in question was almost deleted from the Charter by common consent, at least so far as concerns measures short of force.[50] Yet it is not difficult to discern an advantage that might have been derived by the American states in bringing this latest phase of the Cuban case into the world forum of the United Nations. The purpose of bringing this case into the OAS, as well as of the

---

[47] N.Y. Times, Feb. 25, 1964, p. 10, col. 3-4.

[48] 51 Dep't. State Bull. 181 (1954).

[49] *Ibid.*

[50] The following statement of the United States Government, stating that the 1964 OAS action again Cuba was governed solely by the Inter-American Treaty of Reciprocal Assistance, and refraining from any explicit reference to the United Nations Charter, seems deliberately calculated to write off the role of the United Nations in these matters:

"We consider that the Rio Treaty was correctly applied by the foreign ministers. . . . The juridicial issues were fully discussed . . . and were resolved in the way which the treaty itself specifically provides for, namely, by a two thirds majority vote, which by the terms of the treaty is binding on all members. We therefore see no need for review of the foreign ministers' decisions by any other international organization. The United States has faith in the efficacy of the inter-American system and is confident that in the future, as in the past, whatever differences may exist will be resolved in a manner consistent with the traditions of inter-American co-operation and solidarity." 51 Dep't State Bull. 271 (1964).

diplomatic and economic measures themselves, was probably in large part to impress upon the world public the breaches of international standards by the Castro regime. If this procedure had been considered valuable for the purpose indicated, how much more effective it would have been for the Venezuelan spokesmen to have come into the United Nations and, in that world forum, to have presented their proofs of the outrages of the Castro agents in their country. It would seem that such a course of action would have served both the immediate interests of the American states in the dispute at hand, and the long-range interests represented by the Charter.

Another possible course of action might have been to bring the Cuban case into the United Nations directly, and there have sought appropriate action against Cuba by the United Nations itself.

The reasons underlying the decisions not to pursue either of these courses of action are speculative so far as the present writer is concerned. A possible reason might have been fear of defeat. A veto of any proposed action against Cuba in the Security Council would, of course, have been inevitable. A question might then have existed as to the fate of the proposal if it had been taken into the General Assembly. If defeat were envisioned as a reasonable possibility in that organ also, a question might still have existed as to whether the interests of states opposing the Cuban actions would not still have been served, on balance, by the considerable psychological gain that would have accrued from the process of debating and voting upon the issue in the General Assembly. This question is considered further, in somewhat broader context, in the concluding chapter below.

Also entering into the decision may have been the consideration that, by denying the applicability of the "authorization" clause in the two earlier cases, the American states had estopped themselves from using it in the later Cuban case. This factor would, however, seem most likely to have been subsidiary to larger policy considerations to the effect that it is safer and preferable, as a general rule, to restrict the international handling of American disputes and situations to the American regional organization. The pursuit of such a policy naturally has the tendency to downgrade the clause in question. It also has the inevitable consequence, which was foreseen at the time of San Francisco, of damaging the role of the United Nations. It may, for instance, be taken as a certainty that if other regional groups were to embark on forcible action on their own initiative, and were challenged on the basis of the "authorization" clause of the Charter, they would cite the American precedent as justification for their actions. At the same time, their actions might be wholly out of accord with the Charter by common consent of the rest of the world, and might, indeed, constitute a menace to world peace.

The general proposition that the application of force or lesser pressures by regional organizations, without reference to the United Nations, does not tend to promote the development of law and is, in fact, a manifestation of the traditional "political" approach to international relations, seems to be demonstrated by the Dominican case of 1965. In that case, it will be recalled, the United States intervened with force in an armed revolt in the Dominican Republic, after which the United States force was quickly transformed into an OAS operation by being placed under the jurisdiction of that Organization and by the addition of troop contingents from several American countries. Deployed originally for the purpose, in part, of saving lives of United States citizens and other foreigners endangered by the hostilities, the armed intervention continued for what was generally understood to be the purpose of preventing a communist take-over of the Dominican Republic.[51]

In answer to Soviet and Cuban claims in the Security Council that the Dominican operation was a case of wrongful intervention in the affairs of a state, the United States Representative (who was the principal spokesman in support of the OAS position) cited the decision of the OAS, at the Punta del Este Conference of 1962, that the principles of communism were incompatible with the principles of the inter-American system.[52] He refrained, however, from asserting that the measure was a justifiable use of force by the OAS in order to deal with a threat to peace. To have done so would have raised the question whether the operation was a collective measure, and thus subject to the "authorization" clause of the Charter. The United States Representative also upheld the measure on the basis of Article 52 of the Charter, which authorizes independent efforts on the part of regional organizations to bring about peaceful solutions of regional disputes and situa-

[51] 52 *id.* 739-48, 854-85, 977-80 (1965). For the OAS resolution establishing the Force see *id.* 862.
[52] 2 U.N. Monthly Chronicle No. 6, at 4 (June 1965).

tions. The ensuing Article, however, in its reference to "enforcement actions" seems to refer to the only relevant category in which force or other tangible pressures may be employed, and specifies that these require the authorization of the United Nations. It seems probable that it was with this provision in mind that the United States Representative denied that the Dominican operation was an enforcement action.[53] As will be discussed more fully in ensuing chapters, such apparent attempts to avoid the limitation of the "collective measures" concept by assimilating uses of force and other pressures with the "peaceful settlement" function involves a blurring of major Charter concepts, which appears to be inimical to prospects of Charter development.

Although an effort thus seems to have been made, on the part of the supporters of the OAS action in the Dominican case, to downgrade legal aspects of the case, the impingement upon it of a certain element of law was nevertheless unavoidable. It is manifested by Article 2(4), which many consider to be the key provision of the United Nations Charter:

> All Members shall refrain in their international relations from the threat or use of force against the territorial integrity or political independence of any state, or in any other manner inconsistent with the Purposes of the United Nations.

This provision is a restatement of a part of the rule of non-intervention, which is older than the Charter, and which has a real existence in the minds of large elements of world public opinion including government authorities. No group of states has done more to give it force and effect than the American states.

The strength of the rule of "non-intervention" is such that, unless there is an affirmative body of law justifying a given intervention, the presumption that the intervention is wrongful is likely to become prevalent in large parts of the world. When the United States is charged with wrongful intervention in one of the less-developed areas, some of the elements making the accusation do their best to brand it as "imperialism." To the extent that such efforts are persuasive, an operation like that of the Dominican case, designed to prevent the spread of communism, may tend to produce effects contrary to those intended.

The task of building up a body of affirmative law capable of counteracting the presumption of wrongful intervention in such

---

[53] *Id.* No. 7, at 5 (July 1965).

cases—a body of law which, like the rule of non-intervention itself, would have to find its real existence in the minds of people —is obviously a formidable one.

So far as concerns the possible substantive content of such a body of law, the possibility which first suggests itself, in light of the Dominican case, would be the development of a rule of law empowering the competent international organization to enforce democratic regimes upon member states. Proposals along this line have, in fact, long been considered by the American states. During World War II a resolution was adopted by the Emergency Advisory Committee for the Political Defense of the Continent recommending that American states should not recognize regimes constituted by force except after consultation.[54] However, subsequent efforts along this line have indicated that American states are far from agreement on any such policy.[55]

Speaking of the constituent treaties of the inter-American system, a recent treatise states:

> [T]here exists in these treaties no right of collective intervention for democracy per se; but should a nation have an internal government which creates an international problem threatening the independence, the sovereignty, or the inviolability or the integrity of the territory of any American state, methods have been established by treaties to take care of this. A paramount and primary purpose of the OAS is the maintenance of hemispheric peace, and the realization of political democracy within each nation is apparently left up to the people of that nation.[56]

Such may be supposed to be the attitude of states and peoples generally throughout the world. In the broader area, indeed, the prospects would seem to be less than in the Americas for the development of the kind of rule under discussion, since less effort has been made along this line. It is, of course, on the broader world scene no less than in the Western Hemisphere, that it is important to overcome the presumption of wrongful intervention in cases such as the Dominican case. What is believed to be

---

[54] For English Text of resolution see Emergency Advisory Committee for Political Defense, *Second Annual Report . . . July 15, 1943-October 15, 1944,* at 79 (English ed. Montevideo 1944). For its history and application see *id.* 13-20; Spaeth and Sanders, "The Emergency Advisory Committee for Political Defense," 38 Am. J. Int'l L. 218, 227 (1944).

[55] Thomas and Thomas, *The Organization of American States,* 214-222 (1963). See also N.Y. Times, July 3, 1964, p. 5, col. 1.

[56] Thomas and Thomas, *op. cit. supra* note 55, at 221-22.

the general unwillingness of states and peoples to permit the United Nations to impose, against themselves, decisions as to their internal regimes is discussed in various contexts in ensuing chapters.

However, there seems to be general agreement, in principle, that the United Nations may take necessary measures to deal with breaches of peace or threats to peace. It is in respect of this power —"collective measures"—that the best basis appears to exist for the building of an affirmative rule of law capable of overcoming the presumption of wrongful intervention in cases such as that under discussion.

For the development of such a rule adequate to the purpose just indicated, it might be necessary to establish the proposition that communist expansionist activities are, *per se,* threats to international peace. While this would seem to be a formidable task, it has just been observed that certain opportunities for progress along this line appear to have existed in the Cuban "Punta del Este" case of 1962, taken in conjunction with the Cuban-Venezuelan dispute of 1963-1964.

If it should be desired to build such a rule of law as that under discussion it is, of course, important that such direct opportunities as those just mentioned should be exploited to the full. It must be emphasized, however, that the problem under discussion is broader than the Dominican case. The basic problem, in somewhat different form, exists in the Vietnamese case, and in respect to the general effort to stem the spread of communism. It goes, indeed, to the essence of the major East-West struggle. While the fuller exploitation of the Cuban cases above referred to would, no doubt, have contributed to the development of law capable of dealing with the problem, a development adequate to the real dimensions of the problem could only be achieved as the result of a broadly-based and persistent effort directed to the achievement of a general system based on law, capable of maintaining peace and security on a world-wide basis.

The present discussion stems from the limited question whether it is desirable to attempt to delete the "authorization" clause of Article 53 of the United Nations Charter, with the consequent tendency to confine the handling of regional cases to regional authorities. This question appears, however, to be part of the larger question whether or not the effort just referred to should be made.

In the Cuban missile crisis of October 1962, the policy of American states again became involved with the "authorization" clause of Article 53. In this case, the Organization of American States found that Soviet missiles with offensive capabilities were being introduced into Cuba, and that the peace of the western hemisphere was thereby endangered within the meaning of Article 6 of the Inter-American Treaty of Reciprocal Assistance. As a consequence of this finding, the OAS recommended that:

> the member states in accordance with Articles 6 and 8 of the Inter-American Treaty of Reciprocal Assistance, take all measures, individually and collectively, including the use of armed force, which they may deem necessary to ensure that the Government of Cuba cannot continue to receive from the Sino-Soviet powers military material and related supplies which may threaten the peace and security of the Continent and to prevent the missiles in Cuba with offensive capacity from ever becoming an active threat to the peace and security of the Continent.[57]

The resulting measure, carried out mainly by the United States, was a naval "quarantine" of Cuba having the purpose of stopping and searching Soviet vessels with a view to preventing the introduction of further such weapons into Cuba.

The "quarantine" measure thus seems to have been an application of force by the OAS with the purpose of dealing with a situation deemed to constitute a threat to peace. It therefore seems to conform to the objective criteria of "collective measures" under the United Nations Charter which, in turn, as has been observed, appears to embrace the phrase "enforcement action" found in Article 53. The operation would, then, seem to require United Nations authorization under the last-mentioned provision unless it properly fell within the category of "collective self-defense" which forms an exception to the "authorization" requirement.

Discussion of the nature of the "quarantine" measure under the Charter has naturally centered upon these two basic Charter concepts. Perhaps the most important pronouncements on the subject, however, which emanate from the United States Department of State, appear, in the end, to deny that the measure was in either of these categories, and to refrain from indicating what its affirmative nature was supposed to be.

The Legal Adviser of the Department of State in his first public comment upon the legal nature of the "quarantine,"[58] invoked

---

[57] Res. of Oct. 23, 1962, 47 Dep't State Bull. 722-23 (1962).

[58] Chayes, "The Legal Case for U.S. Action on Cuba." *Id.* 763.

the theory of the Uniting for Peace resolution which holds the responsibility of the Security Council for the maintenance of peace and security to be "primary" and not "exclusive." He pointed out that the Council had proved incapable of fulfilling the security function originally planned for it, and that other bodies had consequently come to be relied on, including the Assembly, the Secretary-General and regional organizations. He went on to say that the OAS was subordinate to the United Nations, but indicated that this relationship was satisfied, in the missile crisis, by the fact that the situation was discussed in the Security Council with a view to finding a peaceful solution.[59] Since the Legal Adviser did not mention Article 53 in this connection, his statement can be interpreted as a step in the direction of eliminating the "authorization" requirement from the Charter. This theory was somewhat modified by the same authority in a subsequent statement[60] in which, in discussing the relationship between the United Nations and regional organizations in these matters, he brought in Article 53. However, he proceeded to discuss this provision in terms tending to deprive it of force and effect. He achieved this result by asserting that the requirement could be complied with by United Nations action merely taking note of the OAS action (as in the Dominican case of 1960), or even by non-action on the part of the United Nations (as in the Cuban case involving the OAS arms embargo of early 1962).[61]

These pronouncements indicating that the "authorization" requirement had been complied with, seem, by inference, to affirm the nature of the "quarantine" as an "enforcement action."

Subsequently, however, a change in the position of the Department of State may have taken place, as seems to be indicated in a statement of the Deputy Legal Adviser.[62] According to this statement, no measure of the United Nations or regional organization is to be regarded as an "enforcement action" if it is initiated by recommendation of the organization to its members—if, in other words, participation in the measure is optional on the part of the member states.[63] The "quarantine" measure was initiated

[59] Id., 765.

[60] Chayes, "Law and the Quarantine of Cuba," 41 Foreign Affairs 550 (1963).

[61] Id. at 556.

[62] Meeker, "Defensive Quarantine and the Law," 57 Am. J. Int'l L. 515 (1963).

[63] Excerpt quoted at pp. 202-03 infra.

by an OAS resolution which was, in its terms, a recommendation
to the member states that they carry out the measure in question.
Moreover, under the Inter-American Treaty of Reciprocal Assistance, no state is obliged to take part in OAS measures involving
the use of force; all such OAS measures are, therefore, in effect,
recommendatory. The theory propounded by the Deputy Legal
Adviser would then have the result that no OAS measure involving the use of force could be an "enforcement action" and that
United Nations authorization for such measures under Article 53
would accordingly never be required.

The enunciation of this theory takes its place in a line of development involving the use of the notion of "recommendation"
as a means of initiating measures of the United Nations and
regional organizations, and is discussed further in this context
below, in Chapter 7. For purposes of present discussion it need
only be suggested that the distinction here propounded seems
to be one of form rather than substance. Whether the measure
in question was initiated by recommendation or by binding order
on the member states, it still constituted an application of tangible
pressure designed to deal with a threat to peace, and would thus
seem to conform to the objective criteria of the Charter concept
of "collective measures."

Both of the above interpretations emanating from the Department of State have the tendency of removing the force and effect
of the "authorization" clause, and thus of eliminating an important principle deliberately incorporated in the Charter to
assist the United Nations in fulfilling its world role and in preventing the dissolution of the incipient world system into regional
blocs. The opinion has already been ventured in this Chapter
that this course of action is detrimental from the point of view
of Charter development.

The other main Charter category under consideration as the
possible basis of authority for the "quarantine" measure is that
of "collective self-defense" within the meaning of Article 51 of
the Charter.[64] Recourse to this provision has a certain basic logic
since it was placed in the Charter to provide an exception enabling
regional groups to act in emergency situations without the necessity
of obtaining United Nations authorization.

However, the emergency situations as to which this recourse

---

[64] Quoted at pp. 42-43 *supra*.

is authorized are limited by the terms of Article 51 to cases of actual armed attack. No such attack occurred in the missile crisis.

The case might then be taken as posing the question of the relative desirability and appropriateness of pursuing, respectively, the following possible modifications of the Charter: (a) the elimination of the "authorization" requirement, as to which important steps have already been taken, and (b) the deletion of the limitation which restricts the "collective self-defense" concept to cases of actual armed attack.

Turning to the second of these possibilities, reference may first be had to the traditional right of self-defense which has always been claimed and exercised by states, and which is not limited to cases of actual armed attack.[65] The right of collective self-defense under Article 51 is to be distinguished since, as has been observed, this provision was put in the Charter for the specific purpose of providing a loophole through which regional organizations might act without the necessity of obtaining United Nations authorization. The traditional right was taken up by the appropriate Committee of the San Francisco Conference, namely, Committee I/1, which drafted the fundamentally important Chapter I of the Charter on the "Purposes and Principles" of the United Nations, including Article 2(4), quoted above.[66] No provision was included on the general right of self-defense; however, this Committee made clear in its report that "the use of arms in legitimate self-defense remains admitted and unimpaired."[67] An important school of thought considers, on the basis of these developments, that Article 51 should not be regarded as limiting the right of self-defense to cases of actual armed attack.[68]

---

[65] "[T]he right has, under traditional international law, always been 'anticipatory,' that is to say its exercise was valid against imminent as well as actual attacks or dangers." Bowett, *Self-Defence in International Law* 188-89 (1958).

[66] *Cf* p. 50 *supra.*

[67] *United Nations Conference on International Organization: Selected Documents* 490, 498 (1946).

[68] Bowett, *op. cit. supra* note 65, at 187-90; Stone, *Aggression and World Order* 43-44 (1958); McDougal and Feliciano, *Law and Minimum World Public Order: The Legal Regulation of International Coercion* 232-38 (1961); Mallison, "Limited Naval Blockade or Quarantine-Interdiction: National and Collective Defense Claims Valid Under International Law" 31 Geo. Wash. L. Rev. 335, 360-64. Mallison, in the article just cited, considers that the "quarantine" was a proper exercise of the right of collective self-defense. Accord: Larson, letter to N.Y. Times, Nov. 12, 1962, p. 28, col. 7.

However, if, as some authorities maintain,[69] Article 51 does not permit of such an interpretation, the possibility of Charter modification still exists. The following argument, in support of this possibility, is thought to be consistent with a constitutional approach to the problem. The right of self-defense was limited to cases of armed attack, in Article 51, presumably because the framers of the Charter anticipated that the security system they were formulating would function and that the Security Council would, accordingly, be able to handle all situations except immediate emergencies created by actual, and unexpected, armed attacks. It will be observed that under Article 51 the right is recognized only until such time as the Security Council is able to act for the maintenance of peace and security. If this was the attitude of the framers with respect to the necessary scope of the right of self-defense accorded to regional organizations in Article 51, they must have entertained a similar view as to the traditional right of self-defense enjoyed by states. It was apparently mere accident that the presumed limitation as to the future necessary scope of the right should have become crystallized in Charter language in respect of the notion of "collective self-defense" and not as to the traditional right as enjoyed by states.

Since the security system has not been able to function in the manner envisioned at San Francisco, and since this fact has been recognized in various readjustments of a constitutional character such as, notably, the Uniting for Peace resolution, it is logical to suppose that a corresponding adjustment has taken place in the minds of governments and peoples concerning the basic right of self-defense. There can, in fact, be no doubt that states are, today, claiming and exercising this right in its traditional scope, which is not limited to cases of actual armed attack. It would seem reasonable to suppose that the right as enunciated in Article 51 has been similarly adjusted in the minds of the "peoples of the world" and thus in the true constitutional sense. It therefore appears as probable that the basis exists, in terms of public opinion, for considering that the right of collective self-defense is not limited to cases of actual armed attack, notwithstanding the language of Article 51. Such a modification of the Charter is admittedly retrogressive in that the world would be a more secure

---

[69] See, e.g., Kelsen, *Law of the United Nations* 797-98 (1950); Kunz, "Individual and Collective Self-Defense in Article 51 of the Charter of the United Nations," 41 Am. J. Int'l L. 872, 878 (1947).

place if states were never required to exercise the right of self-defense except in cases of actual armed attack. However, it is believed that the best way of developing the Charter so that it will provide greater security—especially in regard to such a subjective matter as this, which may, at any time, become involved in crises of international relations—may be the taking, as a starting point, of a Charter interpretation which corresponds to the actual thinking of the peoples of the world.

In regard to this subject-matter, attention has naturally tended to focus, to a considerable extent, upon its relationship to the threat of nuclear war which developed since the Charter was drafted. As early as 1946 the United States Delegation to the United Nations Atomic Energy Commission made the following observation in a memorandum to the Commission:

> Interpreting its provisions [Article 51] with respect to atomic energy matters, it is clear that if atomic weapons were employed as part of an "armed attack," the rights reserved by the nations to themselves under Article 51 would be applicable. It is equally clear that an "armed attack" is now something entirely different from what it was prior to the discovery of atomic weapons. It would therefore seem to be both important and appropriate under present conditions that the treaty define "armed attack" in a manner appropriate to atomic weapons and include in the definition not simply the actual dropping of an atomic bomb, but also certain steps in themselves preliminary to such action.[70]

Although the Soviet Delegation appeared to be protesting that this suggestion would lead to the amendment of the Charter by unauthorized means,[71] the Commission, in its first report to the Security Council, took up the suggestion to some extent, as follows:

> 4. In consideration of the problem of violation of the terms of the treaty or convention, it should also be borne in mind that a violation might be of so grave a character as to give rise to the inherent right of self-defense recognized in Article 51 of the Charter of the United Nations.[72]

President Kennedy, in his initial public statement on the missile crisis, pointed out that:

> We no longer live in a world where only the actual firing of weapons represents a sufficient challenge to a nation's security to constitute

---

[70] Report to the Security Council, U.N. Atomic Energy Comm'n Off. Rec., Spec. Supp. 109-10 (1946).

[71] Id. at 118.

[72] Id. at 19.

maximum peril. Nuclear weapons are so destructive and ballistic missiles are so swift that any substantially increased possibility of their use or any sudden change in their deployment may well be regarded as a definite threat to peace.[73]

Although the Legal Adviser of the United States Department of State later said that the President did not invoke "collective self-defense" as authorization for the "quarantine,"[74] the passage just quoted nevertheless carries connotations of that concept. Professor McDougal states:

> [U]nder the hard conditions of the contemporary technology of destruction, which makes possible the complete obliteration of states with still incredible speed from still incredible distances, the principle of effectiveness, requiring that agreements be interpreted in accordance with the major purposes and demands projected by the parties, could scarcely be served by requiring states confronted with necessity for defense to assume the posture of "sitting ducks." Any such interpretation could only make a mockery, both in its acceptability to states and in its potential application, of the Charter's major purpose of minimizing unauthorized coercion and violence across state lines.[75]

The threat of nuclear war has also served as the focus of arguments to the opposite effect, namely that the limitation of Article 51 should be upheld and maintained.[76] Professor Henkin holds that Article 2(4)—prohibiting any use of force contrary to the purposes of the Charter—is the heart of the Charter and maintains that if this rule is to serve its purpose, the right of self-defense should be limited to cases of actual attack as provided in Article 51. This criterion, he says, "is clear, unambiguous, subject to proof, and not easily open to misinterpretation or fabrication."[77] He goes on to say:

> Surely today's weapons render it even more important that nations should not be allowed to cry "vital interests" or "anticipatory self-defense" and unleash the fury. It is precisely in the age of the major

---

[73] "The Soviet Threat to the Americas," (address by President Kennedy), 47 Dep't State Bull. 715, 716 (1962).

[74] Chayes, *supra* note 58, at 764.

[75] McDougal, "The Soviet-Cuban Quarantine and Self-Defense," 57 Am. J. Int'l L. 597, 600-01 (1963). To similar effect see McDougal and Feliciano, *op. cit. supra* note 68 at 238-40.

[76] Wright, "The Cuban Quarantine," 57 Am. J. Int'l L. 546, 559-63 (1963); Henkin, "The United Nations and Its Supporters: A Self-Examination," 78 Pol. Sci. Q. 504, 527-35 (1963). See also Jessup, *A Modern Law of Nations* 167 (1949).

[77] Henkin, *supra* note 76, at 532.

deterrent that nations should not be encouraged to strike first under pretext of prevention or pre-emption.[78]

This authority points out, at the same time, that

> A nation planning all-out attack will not be deterred by the Charter, though it may well talk "anticipatory self-defense" to any left to listen. Nor does one prescribe rules for the nation threatened with such an attack. If a nation is satisfied that another is about to obliterate it, it will not wait.[79]

This latter statement is believed not only to be true, but to reflect the fundamental problem involved in a "constitutional" approach to the problem under discussion. If states will not be deterred or guided by the Charter in the determination of their policies in relevant practical situations, then, perhaps, the governing consideration with respect to Charter analysis should be the long-range development of that instrument and of the rule of law. Only through such development can the United Nations come to exercise practical influence upon states in their policy determinations in such matters; the sooner it is enabled to do this, the better.

Proceeding in this light, it is to be observed that, as stated by a leading authority: "The measures of self-defence taken must be reasonable, limited to the necessity of protection, and proportionate to the danger."[80] This rule conforms to the realities of international relations. The proposition may be illustrated by the "quarantine" measure itself, if that action is interpreted as an exercise of "collective self-defense." In that case the American states, having nothing but defense in mind, carefully formulated the measure so as to ward off the threatened danger, while reducing to a minimum the risk that the crisis might lead to war.[81] States are bound to follow this course if they do not want war and are concerned only with defending their security.

In this aspect of the matter, then, the "quarantine" measure conformed to the realities of international life—it was such a reality—and also would conform to the Charter concept of "collective self-defense" if that concept were to be considered as not strictly limited to cases of actual armed attack.

In another aspect, some may question whether there was actually such a threat in this case as to justify invoking the right

---

[78] *Ibid.*

[79] *Ibid.*

[80] Bowett, *op. cit. supra* note 65, at 269.

[81] See Mallison, *supra* note 68, at 358-59, 379-80, 393-94.

of self-defense. The initial decision, of course, had to be made by the American states, in accordance with the essential nature of the self-defense concept. If the United Nations had considered the action wrongful, it would then have had the responsibility of repudiating, or otherwise dealing with it. It has not done so, and the impression has been given of general acquiescence that the measure was justified.

It is, then, concluded that if the "quarantine" measure had been designated a measure of "collective self-defense," this categorization would have conformed to the concept as it exists in the minds of the governments and peoples of the world. This course of action would, of course, involve the interpretation of the Charter, or a step toward its modification, tending to remove the rigid restriction of this concept to cases of actual armed attack. The general effect of this course of action on the Charter itself would seem to be, at least, not to weaken it. By bringing an important Charter concept more into line with reality, it might be said to strengthen, to some extent, that instrument's potentiality of future development.

The categorization of the "quarantine" as a measure of "collective self-defense" seems, from the point of view of the present discussion, preferable to the two recourses mentioned above as being suggested by officials of the United States Department of State. The first of these, it will be recalled, seems to infer that the measure had the character of an "enforcement action," and interprets Article 53 to the effect that "authorization" (at least positive authorization) is not required. This interpretation, continuing the downgrading of the "authorization" clause already well under way as a result of the earlier Dominican and Cuban cases of 1960 and 1962 respectively, is believed detrimental to the long-range devlopment of the Charter for reasons which have been indicated above. The second of the positions mentioned, holding the "quarantine" not to have been an enforcement measure because instituted by recommendation to the member states (instead of by binding order), refrained from indicating what the affirmative nature of this measure was. For reasons suggested above (some of which will be developed further in Chapter 7, below) this position also seems detrimental to the development of the Charter and the rule of law.

It may then be concluded that, as between the major Charter concepts of "collective measures" and "collective self-defense," the "quarantine" measure should preferably be regarded as falling within the latter.

Before concluding the discussion of this measure, however, we may consider two other possible means of regarding it from a constitutional point of view.

The first of these would regard the "quarantine" as being contrary to the Charter and illegal. This position can be defended on the grounds (a) that the action had the characteristics of an "enforcement action," but violated the Charter requirement that such measures by regional organizations have the authorization of the United Nations, and (b) that it did not conform to the criteria of a measure of "collective self-defense"—the only Charter exception to the "authorization" requirement—since there was in this case no armed attack. As against this possible position, the point may be reiterated that the missile crisis proves that when states feel sufficiently threatened, they will take action deemed necessary for their security. To hold all such actions to be contrary to the Charter *per se,* if no actual armed attack is involved, would seem to place the Charter, in this respect, on a level of unreality. Such a course would seem retrogressive from the standpoint of the major goal presently under discussion, which is to build up the Charter as the basis of the rule of law in international relations.

The final possibility to be considered is that the "quarantine" be regarded as a move toward developing a new rule of Charter law. How such a move might develop would, of course, have to be assessed in light of particular proposals. In principle, however, it is to be considered that the "peoples of the world" know and generally accept the "collective measures" function which authorizes the application of tangible pressure (including both measures of force and measures less than force) by the United Nations when deemed necessary to deal with threats to peace, aggressions and other breaches of peace. This Charter concept seems to constitute a logical starting point upon the basis of which further development might prove possible. In its objective criteria it seems readily to embrace the "quarantine" measure.[82]

There is believed to be a danger in suggesting new Charter concepts involving the application of tangible pressures in interna-

---

[82] Susidiary to this main proposition are the requirements that collective measures undertaken by regional agencies must have the authorization of the United Nations, and the exception to this requirement provided by the Charter recognition of the right of collective self-defense in Art. 51.

tional relations since, unless they are developed in step with developing consent and acquiescence on the part of governments and leaders of public opinion, they may tend toward confusion and prove detrimental to the development of the Charter and the rule of law. One aspect of the problem is represented by the position of the Deputy Legal Adviser of the United States Department of State in holding the "quarantine" measure not to be a "collective measure," but in refraining, at the same time, from indicating what it is affirmatively considered to be. The problem thus suggested, which is herein believed to constitute one of the major issues affecting the development of the Charter, is discussed in ensuing chapters.

The following seems to represent an affirmative suggestion of the kind under discussion, made by Professor Henkin with reference to the "quarantine" measure:

> The President recognized, apparently, that to read Article 51 as permitting the unilateral use of force merely because another nation achieves some capacity to strike would jeopardize the Charter. He suggested a far more limited extension of the Charter. His action claimed only the right, in order to preserve international stability, to take moderate, non-destructive, revocable measures; and these (and even the limited, more active force which he threatened) he justified because they were taken following authorization by the Organization of American States.[83]

It seems to the present writer that this suggestion of a category of United Nations or regional action might go somewhat beyond Professor Henkin's description of it as contemplating a "small extension of the Charter." It seems to suggest recognizing the power of regional organizations to apply pressures of considerable potential, on their own responsibility and decision, "in order to preserve international stability." This motive for the use of force, or measures short of force, seems somewhat broader than the present Charter criteria applicable to "collective measures," and somewhat suggestive of the kind of danger to which efforts to expand the basic Charter concept of "collective measures" are believed likely to prove susceptible.

This proposal may be left, however, as a concrete suggestion of a possible course of action in cases such as the missile crisis, while we turn to consider in more detail the nature of the danger just referred to.

---

[83] Henkin, *supra* note 76 at 534.

Chapter III

Attribution to United Nations of Quasi-Legislative and Judicial Authority

A problem of a somewhat different order from those discussed in the preceding chapters arises when majorities of states in United Nations bodies undertake to cause the General Assembly or Security Council to appear to be making interpretations or decisions which are legally binding on certain states without their consent. Notwithstanding that it was well understood from the outset that the Organization possesses no such legislative or judicial power except with the acquiescence of the states concerned, member states have attempted rather persistently, from the time the Charter came into force, to make the United Nations appear as if it had such powers.

For a concrete illustration of the kind of problem under discussion, reference may be had to the resolution adopted by the General Assembly during the first year of the United Nations, concerning the Franco regime of Spain, in which:

The General Assembly . . .

> *Recommends* that if, within a reasonable time, there is not established a government which derives its authority from the consent of the governed, committed to respect freedom of speech, religion and assembly and to the prompt holding of an election . . . the Security Council consider the adequate measures to be taken in order to remedy the situation;

> *Recommends* that all Members of the United Nations immediately recall from Madrid their ambassadors and ministers plenipotentiary accredited there.[1]

This resolution seems clearly to assert a power on the part of the Organization to make and enforce a decision designed to alter the internal regime of Spain.

---

[1] Res. 39 (I), U.N. Gen. Ass. Off. Rec. 1st Sess., Pt. 2, Resolutions 63.

During the debate on this matter in Committee 1 of the Assembly, the United States Delegation opposed, as wrongful intervention, an earlier version of the resolution which, if adopted, would have recommended that member states carry out a complete break of diplomatic relations with Spain.[2] In more recent situations, however, the United States and some other countries have taken the position with respect to similar resolutions that if the United Nations does no more than "recommend" that states take coercive measures with a view to enforcing a decision, the resulting measure would not infringe Charter limitations with respect to enforcement or the use of coercive pressures, and would not constitute wrongful intervention. However, the view of the matter taken by the United States in the committee stage of the Spanish case seems correct. If the United Nations initiates pressure designed to enforce a decision, it must regard the decision as enforceable and therefore as binding.[3] Whether the pressure is initiated by recommendation or otherwise would seem to be irrelevant.

The initiation of enforcement measures is not the only means by which member states have attempted to cause the United Nations to give the impression that it has quasi-judicial or -legislative powers without regard to the consent of states concerned. As remarked above, efforts along this line have been rather persistent since the Organization was founded. The question therefore suggests itself as to whether a course of Charter modification may not have been in progress. This question was raised in 1962 by the delegation of the United Arab Republic in the General Assembly, in connection with the case concerning *apartheid* in the Union of South Africa:

> In 1945, the framers of the Charter had seen United Nations action mainly in terms of recommendations supported only by moral sanctions. However, the role of the United Nations had steadily developed and the time might have come for recommendations to give way to the imposition of the will of the United Nations.[4]

---

[2] *Id.* 1st Comm. 298-99 (A/C. 1/131) (1946). The United States Delegation did not comment on the modified version of this measure (calling only for withdrawal of ambassadors and ministers, and not for a full diplomatic break) as taken up and passed in the plenary session. *Id.*, Plenary 1217-18, 1221-22 (1946).

[3] Kelsen, "Sanctions in International Law under the Charter of the United Nations," 31 Iowa L. Rev. 499, 522 (1946).

[4] U.N. Gen. Ass. Off. Rec. 17th Sess., Spec. Pol. Comm. 12 (A/SPC/SR. 329) (1962).

Such a development does not appear to have taken place or to be foreseeable.[5] While it is possible to modify the Charter through practice and general acquiescence of the members, such acquiescence is not believed to be present in support of the kind of development suggested by the United Arab Republic. It seems out of the question that any of the major powers, or any substantial portion of the over-all membership of the United Nations, would acquiesce in such a grant of power to the Organization with the understanding that it would be equally applicable against themselves. The United Arab Republic has indicated its own lack of acquiescence in the case concerning the passage of Israeli-connected ships and cargoes through the Suez Canal. This is the case referred to above in Chapter 1 as the Suez "ships" case. In its resolution of September 1, 1951, in this case the Security Council

> *Calls upon* Egypt to terminate the restrictions on the passage of international commercial shipping and goods through the Suez Canal . . . and to cease all interference with such shipping . . .[6]

In subsequent debates certain states spoke of this decision as being legally binding. Egypt rejected this view when, in response to a New Zealand proposal that the Security Council call upon Egypt to carry out the resolution of September 1, 1951 "in accordance with its obligations under the Charter," the Egyptian Delegation demanded to know: "What are these obligations? What article of the Charter has Egypt contravened?"[7] The correct answer must be "none" since this was a matter in which Egypt claimed to be acting by legal right, and since the United Nations has no authority to make binding interpretations of the legal positions of states without their consent. So, it is believed, would most states reject assertions that they are bound by such decisions without their consent. Any suggestion that the United Nations might develop a rule under which majorities could apply such decisions to other states while the states composing the majority, at the same time, denied the right of the United Nations to apply such measures against themselves, would seem to run counter to basic legal propo-

---

[5] But see Falk, "The Legitimacy of Legislative Intervention by the United Nations," in *Essays on Intervention* (Stanger, ed. 1964); Falk, "Janus Tormented: The International Law of Internal War," in *International Aspects of Civil Strife* 185, 241-42 (Rosenau, ed. 1964).

[6] U.N. Security Council Off. Rec. 6th year, 558th meeting 2-3 (S/PV. 558) (1951). The resolution is set out more fully at p. 85 *infra*.

[7] *Id.* 9th year, 662d meeting 13 (S/PV. 662) (1954).

sitions such as that any rule of law must be reciprocal in character, capable of being applied equally and dispassionately to all concerned, and that law must have a general basis of acceptance on the part of the members of the community in which it is supposed to apply.

Having thus briefly outlined the nature and scope of the problem under discussion in the present chapter, it is desirable to consider in more detail how it developed.

In the first place it is to be observed that never, since the emergence of the modern state system, have sovereign states recognized that they were subject to a higher law-making or law-interpreting authority. States have frequently conceded that they recognize the higher authority of international law; however, since they do not generally submit to the jurisdiction of any authority capable of determining the applicable law in concrete situations, this recognition has something of a nebulous character. Strenuous efforts have been made to secure the general submission of member states of both the League of Nations and the United Nations to the jurisdiction of a higher law-interpreting authority, the World Court; these efforts, however, have not been successful.

A suggestion that the Security Council should have a limited power of a quasi-legislative character seems, in fact, to have been made at San Francisco. In the Dumbarton Oaks Proposals, which formed the basis of discussion at that conference, Chapter 8 B, corresponding to Chapter VII of the Charter, began with two provisions which were susceptible of interpretation as authorizing the Council to enforce terms of settlement on parties to disputes. However, as pointed out by Goodrich and Hambro,

> The smaller powers in particular, with the memory of the Munich settlement fresh in their minds, were opposed to giving to the Security Council any power to impose a particular settlement. . . .[8]

It was no doubt, at least in part, as a result of this sentiment that the paragraphs in question were modified to form the present Article 39 of the Charter, providing as follows:

> The Security Council shall determine the existence of any threat to the peace, breach of the peace, or act of aggression and shall make recommendations, or decide what measures shall be taken in

---

[8] Goodrich and Hambro, *Charter of the United Nations: Commentary and Documents* 264 (2d ed. rev. 1949).

accordance with Articles 41 and 42, to maintain or restore international peace and security.

This formulation was suggested by the delegation of China, one of the participants in the Dumbarton Oaks Conversations, which also proposed that the word "recommendation," in this context, should be given a different meaning than it had in Chapter 8 A of the Dumbarton Proposals (the forerunner of Chapter VI of the Charter), dealing with the Council's "peaceful settlement" function, on the ground that "In Section B the question was not one merely of a dispute but of a threat to the peace which had gone beyond the stage of a dispute."[9] Apparently it was intended to give the Council's power of "recommendation" in "Chapter VII" situations (e.g. situations constituting aggressions, breaches of peace or threats to peace), a somewhat stronger binding force than this word ordinarily connotes. However, while the Chinese formulation of the present Article 39 was accepted, the proposal as to the meaning of "recommendation" therein was not.[10] On the contrary, the committee which drafted the provision stated in its report that the power of "recommendation" was incorporated to make clear that, in dealing with the more serious "Chapter VII" type situation, the Council still had available to it the "peaceful settlement" procedures outlined in the preceding Chapter. The report went on to elucidate the point that the availability of this procedure to the Council in no way derogated from the duty of that organ to apply enforcement measures in appropriate situations.[11]

It is recorded in the Report of Committee III/2, which drafted Chapter VI of the Charter, that when, on the proposal of the four sponsoring powers, the provision was inserted authorizing the Security Council to "recommend such terms of settlement as it may consider appropriate" (in what became Article 37 of the Charter) "the Delegates of the United Kingdom and the United States gave assurance that such a recommendation of the Security Council possessed no obligatory effect for the parties."[12] The United Nations was not, then, being accorded the power to make

---

[9] Doc. No. 628, III/3/33, 12 U.N. Conf. Int'l Org. Docs. 380 (1945).
[10] *Id.* at 381.

[11] Report of Rapporteur of Committee III/3 to Commission III on Chapter VIII, Section B, *The United Nations Conference on International Organization: Selected Documents* 761, 765 (1946).

[12] Report of Rapporteur of Committee III/2 to Commission III, *id.* at 756, 759 (1946).

binding decisions with respect to the substantive issues of disputes and situations.[13]

Before leaving the provisions of the Charter on this matter it is desirable to take note of Article 40, which provides as follows:

> In order to prevent an aggravation of the situation, the Security Council may, before making the recommendations or deciding upon the measures provided for in Article 39, call upon the parties concerned to comply with such provisional measures as it deems necessary or desirable. Such provisional measures shall be without prejudice to the rights, claims, or position of the parties concerned. The Security Council shall duly take account of failure to comply with such provisional measures.

While "provisional measures" laid down by the Council pursuant to this Article may have binding force (a question not relevant to the present discussion), it is clear that these measures are provisional—"without prejudice to the rights, claims, or position of the parties"—and thus to be distinguished from the "peaceful settlement" function, properly speaking, which is concerned with finding permanent solutions of international disputes and situations.

Since the Charter itself is so clear that the basic power of the United Nations in the fulfillment of its "peaceful settlement" function is the power of recommendation and since, indeed, no suggestion of a higher law-making authority over states has ever been seriously entertained, it must appear as a surprising development that no sooner had the United Nations been founded than states began to use it in a manner to suggest that it was possessed of such powers.

This is not, of course, to suggest that states at the same time abandoned the basic rule, just referred to, that the United Nations is *not* empowered to make such binding decisions. We have already seen, in the present chapter, two instances in which such a power was denied. First, the United States Delegation, in the committee stage of the Spanish case, objected that the imposition of diplomatic sanctions would be wrongful intervention in the absence of a threat to international peace. Reference has also been made to the objection of Egypt to contentions that it was bound to accept the Council's decision of September 1, 1951, concerning

---

[13] Accord: Goodrich and Hambro, *op. cit. supra* note 8, at 208-09 (2d ed. rev. 1949); Wright, "Toward a Universal Law for Mankind," 63 Colum. L. Rev. 435, 453 (1963).

the passage of Israeli-connected shipping through the Suez Canal. As another example, the United States Delegation to the Tenth Session of the General Assembly, speaking in connection with the case concerning "Treatment of Indians in the Union of South Africa," was reported to have said in effect:

> While the United Nations could not impose a solution upon the parties to a dispute, it could properly express the consensus of opinion in the form of a resolution favouring direct negotiation and he hoped that the moral force of the United Nations judgment would persuade the parties to negotiate in good faith.[14]

Other cases are numerous in which delegations have considered it in their countries' interests to deny the existence of the power in question. However, in the present discussion we are concerned with the fact that the power has been asserted with, it is believed, the inevitable result of creating confusion among the world public as to what the real powers of the Organization in such matters are.

The first case of the kind was the Spanish case, which was briefly described at the outset of the present chapter to illustrate the nature of the problem presently under consideration. The Assembly's resolution in the case, designed to apply pressure in favor of the replacement of the Franco Government with a more liberal Spanish regime, failed of its purpose. The recommendation that states withdraw their ambassadors and ministers from Spain was only partially observed. Since this measure proved both ineffective and inconvenient to a number of the states concerned, the recommendation was repealed by the Assembly in its fifth session, in 1950.[15]

While political sentiments provided a considerable degree of public support for the Assembly's measure against Spain, it must, at the same time, have been somewhat confusing to the world public to find that the General Assembly could be employed as a means for overturning the government of a country. Certainly no powers of the kind were to be implied from anything said at San Francisco. Furthermore, the failure of the measure and its repeal must have had an adverse effect on the Organization's prestige in the eyes of world opinion. Had the United Nations in this case limited itself to the simple power of recommendation, even this action might have been objected to as a wrongful intervention in the affairs of Spain; however, since states are not bound to carry

---

[14] U.N. Gen. Ass. Off. Rec. 10th Sess., *Ad Hoc* Political Comm. 159 (A/AC. 80/SR. 34) (1955).

[15] Res. 386 (V), *id.*, 5th Sess., Supp. No. 20 at 16 (Doc. A/1775).

out recommendations, the failure of this move could not have had such serious adverse effects on the prestige of the Organization as probably resulted from the course of action followed.

An early case in which the Security Council gave the impression of exercising a judicial role was the Corfu Channel case, in which the British Government asserted that Albania was responsible for the loss of life and other damage caused when British naval units struck mines in an unnotified minefield adjacent to the Albanian coast. The following draft resolution, based on a United Kingdom proposal, would have been adopted by the Council except for a Soviet veto:

The Security Council
*   *   *

1. *Considers* that the laying of mines in peace-time without notification is unjustified and an offense against humanity;

2. *Finds* that an unnotified minefield was laid in the immediate vicinity of the Albanian coast, resulting in serious injury to two of His Majesty's ships with loss of life and injury to their crews; that this minefield could not have been laid without the knowledge of the Albanian authorities;

3. *Recommends* that the United Kingdom and Albanian Governments should settle the dispute on the basis of the Council's finding in paragraph 2 above. . . .[16]

The final paragraph, which would merely have recommended that the parties reach a negotiated settlement, might seem to have been in accord with the authorization conferred upon the Council by Article 36 of the Charter to "recommend appropriate procedures or methods of adjustment" or, if paragraph 2 of the draft resolution appears to pre-judge the decision, to be in accord with Article 37 which authorizes the Council to "recommend such terms of settlement as it may consider appropriate." A difficulty in this interpretation is, however, suggested by the fact that, following the veto of the proposed resolution, the case was referred to the World Court, which duly found Albania responsible for the incident in dispute and made an award of damages against that country in favor of the United Kingdom.[17] Even though the two procedures —resort to Council and Court—are essentially different, the course followed may have tended to give the impression to the world public that they are two alternate procedures available for essen-

---

[16] U.N. Security Council Off. Rec. 2d year, 122d meeting 608-09 (1947).
[17] *Corfu Channel Case* [1949] I.C.J. Rep. 4, 244.

tially the same purpose. The use of the word "finds" in paragraph 2 of the draft resolution could be expected to heighten the misapprehension on this point. Since this word has a legal connotation as a definitive determination, its use may well have conveyed the impression that the Council's determination as to these matters was conclusive. Also contributing to this impression may have been the fact that the Council *is* empowered, in some matters, to make definitive decisions, such as with respect to the existence of threats to peace, breaches of peace, and acts of aggression under Chapter VII; its conclusions of fact in such matters are necessarily conclusive and have the nature of "findings" in the legal sense of the word.

Although the distinction referred to may appear to some as rather finely drawn, it is believed to be of vital importance. The basic consideration in this connection is that the case was, by its nature, appropriate for judicial determination and not for submission to the Security Council. The real question to be determined was whether Albania had violated the legal rights of the United Kingdom and, if so, what reparation should be made. The Statute of the International Court of Justice specifically recognizes the Court's jurisdiction as embracing "legal disputes concerning . . . the existence of any fact which, if established, would constitute a breach of an international obligation," and "the nature or extent of the reparation to be made for the breach of an international obligation." If the British complaint, and that country's desired remedy, were properly matters for judicial determination, they were not, by the same token, properly for the Security Council, since these organs perform essentially different kinds of functions.[18]

The role of the Security Council in such a matter would necessarily have to fall within its "peaceful settlement" function. Its preferred course of action in this situation would seem to be indi-

---

[18] A somewhat similar case in 1960 involved the shooting down by Soviet action of a United States plane over the Barents Sea. A dispute of fact existed as to whether the incident occurred over the high seas or within Soviet territory. The Soviet Representative asked that the Council decide that the plane had wrongfully penetrated Soviet territory whereas the United States Representative, correctly, it is believed, proposed a Council resolution recommending that the parties resolve their differences either (a) through an investigating commission set up by agreement of the parties, or (b) by referring the case to the International Court of Justice. U.N. Security Council Off. Rec. 15th year, 881st meeting 7-8 (S/PV. 881) (1960).

cated in Article 36, which empowers it to "recommend appropriate procedures or methods of adjustment," and goes on to provide that:

> In making recommendations under this Article the Security Council should also take into consideration that legal disputes should as a general rule be referred by the parties to the International Court of Justice. . . .

It has to be recognized, of course, that in most disputes, one or more of the parties prove unwilling to resort to the Court. If, in the event of such refusal, the Council should then proceed in the exercise of its "peaceful settlement" function, its ultimate role *vis-à-vis* the parties would evidently be limited to the making of recommendations. Notwithstanding that the United Nations is entitled to take certain "actions," such as investigations of facts, or the setting up of mediation or conciliation commissions, etc., as part of the "peaceful settlement" process, such activities do not detract from the basically persuasive character of the "peaceful settlement" function. Any conclusions of law or fact incidental to such proceedings would, by the same token, be without legally binding effect.

While this aspect of the Corfu Channel case may not appear as having outstanding importance, it serves to illustrate how Council actions may have a tendency to confuse proper Council functions with the judicial function. It is believed to be in just such situations, with a natural tendency to confuse, that United Nations organs should be most meticulous in explaining exactly what is being done in terms of applicable Charter principles.

It seems quite possible that at least a part of the interested element of the world public might have been led by the circumstances of this case to question whether the Council was not purporting to act in a judicial capacity in undertaking to determine the essential question of the location of responsibility. Such further questions as the following might then have been asked: if the Council is empowered to take this sort of decision by majority vote, how does this competence differ from the "compulsory jurisdiction" which was denied to the Court? If this authority was actually vested in the Council at San Francisco, why did it not become a major issue of debate, as did the question of compulsory jurisdiction for the Court?

A factor in the handling of the Corfu Channel case may have been that at that time—the second year of the United Nations—

there existed a tendency on the part of some to accord to the United Nations in such matters (and especially to the Security Council) a larger degree of power than is indicated by the actual language of the Charter. Such a tendency may have been natural in view of the great emphasis placed upon the right of the Organization to decide upon the use of force when necessary to deal with aggression or other breaches of peace or threats to peace. The world, at the time, was mainly concerned with preventing or suppressing aggressions such as had precipitated World War II. There was no doubt a consensus that the Organization must act boldly and decisively in these matters and perhaps a concomitant—perhaps partly subconscious—feeling that it was perfectly entitled to order the solution of disputes—"cracking down" and "knocking heads together" as it was sometimes put—if necessary to accomplish this end. If the requisite degree of unified public backing had existed in support of the United Nations in these matters, a development along these lines might have taken place. Had the member states been able to agree on the resolution proposed by the United Kingdom in the Corfu Channel case, this might have become part of a development in which the "peoples of the world" manifested willingness to see the Security Council, in the handling of disputes and situations, exercise powers going beyond what was provided for or contemplated by the framers of the Charter.

The foregoing discussion of the Corfu Channel case necessarily touched upon some matters going beyond that case itself which, at the time it came before the United Nations, did not involve a threat to peace.

The Palestine case, however, which arose in the same year brought strongly into issue the need for applying both the "peaceful settlement" and "police" functions of the United Nations, and may be said to have demonstrated the lack of adequate public backing to enable it to fulfill its function in either of these respects.

As was briefly indicated in the preceding chapter, this dispute arose out of the determination of the Jewish population of Palestine to establish a separate Jewish state in that country, and the determination of the Arab population and the surrounding Arab states to prevent the establishment of such a state. When the dispute came before the United Nations, Palestine was continuing under the Mandate which had been established by the League of Nations and assigned to the United Kingdom as Mandatory Power. The Mandatory Power brought the case before the United Nations in early 1947 with the announcement that it would terminate the Mandate in the following year, and requested that the United Nations make provision for the future government of Palestine. As a result of this initiative the General Assembly took up the case and, in November, 1947, recommended the Plan of Partition with Economic Union calling for separate Arab and Jewish states in Palestine.

Among the pressures brought on the Arabs[19] to induce acceptance of the Plan were strong indications that it was enforceable and would be enforced if necessary. It may be pertinent to the present discussion to observe that these efforts were made in an early stage of the United Nations, before the "cold war" atmosphere had become prevalent, and in a case in which the five permanent members of the Council were in agreement in support of the recommended solution. The Organization was thus able to act in the spirit of the original concept of the Charter to a much greater degree than was later possible. While in retrospect it appears that the dispute was of such severity that a much more highly developed international system would have been required for its solution than actually existed at the time (or exists today), it is understandable that, at the time and in the circumstances, strong pressures should have been brought in an effort to induce a settlement, and that this was done without great regard for the legal distinctions appearing in the Charter. Had these efforts proved successful, the case would no doubt have become a landmark of Charter development in the direction of increased decision-making powers on the part of the Organization with respect to the substantive issues of international disputes. However the Plan failed and the dispute finally went to the arbitrament of force. The case in consequence stands for the proposition that a considerable development of the Charter was required to enable the United Nations to produce a peaceful solution of a problem of this magnitude.

The notion that the United Nations was legally empowered to enforce the Plan of Partition with Economic Union is believed to involve a breaking down of the distinction between the "peaceful settlement" and "collective measures" functions, both of which find their basic statement in Article 1, paragraph 1 of the Charter:

The Purposes of the United Nations are:
1. To maintain international peace and security, and to that end: to take effective collective measures for the prevention and removal

---

[19] E.g., the Arab population of Palestine and the surrounding Arab states.

of threats to the peace, and for the suppression of acts of aggression or other breaches of the peace, and to bring about by peaceful means, and in conformity with the principles of justice and international law, adjustment or settlement of international disputes or situations which might lead to a breach of the peace;

The two major functions here stand side by side, both forming component parts of the first-stated major "Purpose" of the United Nations, namely the maintenance of international peace and security. Since these functions are obviously interdependent for the fulfillment of the broader goal, it is proper that they should be thus juxtaposed; at the same time, however, it is to be reiterated that they are essentially different functions. Only the "peaceful settlement" function is concerned with the substantive issues of disputes. The "collective measures" function, which is, in effect, a "police" function, is to be employed only to deal with threats to peace, breaches of peace and acts of aggression.[20]

The "collective measures" function is normally identified with Chapter VII of the Charter, where it is spelled out in more detail than in Article 1 (1). This Chapter is entitled "Action with Respect to Threats to the Peace, Breaches of the Peace, and Acts of Aggression" and is introduced by Article 39. Articles 41 and 42 then go on to authorize, respectively, the use of measures short of force and the use of actual force, if deemed necessary to give effect to the "decisions" of the Council.[21] The "decisions" here referred to seem clearly those pertaining to the "collective measures" function, e.g., those deemed necessary to deal with threats to peace, breaches of peace and acts of aggression. That they do not mean "decisions" on the substantive issues of international disputes, or as to procedures for settling such issues, seems clear from the fact that the Council's powers in these latter respects are affirmatively stated in Articles 36 and 37 to be basically recommendatory in character.

With this brief explanation of the relative roles of the "peaceful settlement" and "police" functions, we may return to the Palestine case. In the face of Arab refusal to accept the Plan of Partition with Economic Union, the United Nations did not go so far as it had in the Spanish case, in which tangible pressures against Spain were

---

[20] The distinction emerges clearly in the remarks in Commission I of the San Francisco Conference of the Rapporteur of Committee I/1 (Zeineddine) and by Lord Halifax. *The United Nations Conference on International Organization: Selected Documents* 534-35, 536-37 (1946).

[21] For texts of these provisions see p. 38 *supra*.

actually initiated. Efforts along this line in the Palestine case did not go beyond intimating that the Plan would be enforced if necessary. Unlike the Spanish case, the Palestine case involved an actual threat to peace[22] and, since such a situation forms a clear-cut Charter basis for invoking the "police" function, it was natural that the possibility of enforcement action was placed partly on this ground. It was also, however, taken up, in part, in terms suggesting that the United Nations had the right to enforce the Plan as such. This was the first case in which these mixed motives for enforcement action were brought forward, with their inevitably confusing effect on public opinion.

The impression that the Plan of Partition with Economic Union would be enforced was, perhaps, most strongly conveyed in paragraphs (b) and (c) of the Assembly Resolution of November 29, 1947[23] (to which the Plan was annexed), in which the mixed motives just referred to may be discerned:

The General Assembly . . . Requests that
*   *   *

(b) The Security Council consider, if circumstances during the transitional period require such consideration, whether the situation in Palestine constitutes a threat to the peace. If it decides that such a threat exists, and in order to maintain international peace and security, the Security Council should supplement the authorization of the General Assembly by taking measures under Articles 39 and 41 of the Charter, to empower the United Nations commission, as provided in this resolution, to exercise in Palestine the functions which are assigned to it by this resolution.

(c) The Security Council determine as a threat to the peace, breach of the peace or act of aggression, in accordance with Article 39 of the Charter, any attempt to alter by force the settlement envisaged by this resolution.

Paragraph (c) appears especially likely to have conveyed the impression that the Plan, as such, would be enforced, since compliance with the clause in question would apparently have meant that the Council would have suppressed the resort to force by the Arab states in their effort to prevent the establishment of the Jewish state. This action, in turn, would have enabled the Jewish population to proceed to set up their state and would have amounted to enforcement of the Plan, or at least that vital part of it which contemplated the establishment of a Jewish state.

[22] This aspect of the Spanish case is discussed at pp. 174-75 *infra.*
[23] Res. 181 (II), *Resolutions* 131, U.N. Gen. Ass. Off. Rec. 2d. Sess. (1947).

The impression of enforceability as thus conveyed by paragraph (c) only reached its full force and effect as the result of certain accompanying statements which seemed to assume that measures of implementation and enforcement were part of the Plan. Thus the New Zealand Delegation questioned whether the Assembly should gamble on the peaceful implementation of the Plan, and urged that adequate provision on this point should be made.[24] The Danish Delegation said that these views of the New Zealand Delegation should receive most serious consideration,[25] and later introduced the above-quoted paragraphs (b) and (c) of the Assembly resolution.[26] The Canadian Delegation said with respect to these paragraphs:

> If . . . [the Security Council thought that the situation constituted a threat to peace], then the powers of the United Nations commission to act under the General Assembly resolution would be supplemented by authority from the Security Council. . . .
>
> With regard to sub-paragraph (c), Mr. Pearson felt that the wording proposed by Denmark would remove or lessen some of the doubts concerning the strength behind the provisions for implementation and enforcement.[27]

That paragraph (c) contemplated enforcement of the Plan was also the view of the Cuban Delegation which, however, considered the resolution illegal for this reason.[28]

At an earlier stage of the debate a United States spokesman made the following statement, which might be regarded as an explanation of the same principle as was later adopted in paragraph (c):

> We assumed that there would be Charter observance. The life of this Union depends upon obedience to the law. If any Member should violate its obligations to refrain in its international relations from the threat or use of force, the Security Council itself must act.[29]

---

[24] Id., Ad Hoc Comm. on the Palestinian Question 166 (1947).

[25] Id. at 170.

[26] Id., Annexes 20 and 20a, at 266-67 (A/AC. 14/43 and A/AC. 14/43 Rev. 1).

[27] Id. at 221.

[28] Id., Plenary 1383-84 (1947).

[29] This passage from the (unpublished) verbatim records of the 11th meeting of the Assembly's Ad Hoc Committee on the Palestinian Question (not appearing fully in the published Summary Record) was later read into the record of the Security Council by the United States Representative. U.N. Security Council Off. Rec. 3d year, 253d meeting 265 (1948).

Later, but still in the Committee stage, the United States Delegation emphasized that the determination as to when a threat to the peace existed, such as would justify enforcement measures, was a decision for the Security Council acting on its own discretion:

> Under the Charter the Security Council could determine when a threat to the peace existed, and the revised sub-paragraph (*b*) constituted a request to the Security Council to act if such a threat arose in Palestine. . . .[30]

This statement appears to have a somewhat different import from that of the passage quoted just previously which seems, like paragraph (c) of the resolution, to stress a duty on the part of the Security Council to put down any forcible Arab opposition and thus, in effect, enforce the part of the Plan pertaining to the creation of the Jewish state. The stress upon the Council's discretionary powers in the later statement of the United States Delegation may have been even stronger in the verbatim text than in the above-quoted summary.[31] It thus appears that formulas intermixing these concepts can be drawn upon, on occasion, for quite different if not flatly contradictory interpretations. So far as the Assembly proceedings are concerned, the fact of overriding importance is, no doubt, that, in the end, the United States supported both paragraphs (b) and (c) of the Danish proposals.

---

[30] U.N. Gen. Ass. Off. Rec. 2d Sess., *Ad Hoc* Comm. on the Palestinian Question 221 (1947).

[31] Later, the United States Representative read into the record of the Security Council the following verbatim text of the statement of a United States spokesman in the same meeting of the *Ad Hoc* Committee referred to in note 30, *supra*:

> "My delegation . . . would not have been able to support the original amendment put up by the Delegation of Denmark. We are prepared, however, to accept this revised version. The revised version does not ask the Security Council to act upon a hypothetical situation, but requests that it act in the event that a situation which constitutes a threat to international peace and security should arise. This, at best, can only be an admonition to the Security Council. The Security Council by its own constitution has the duty to exercise surveillance over such situations, and to determine when a threat to international peace and security exists."
> U.N. Security Council Off. Rec. 3d year, 260th meeting at 401.

The Security Council record indicates that this statement was made in regard to paragraph (c) of the resolution, and not paragraph (b). However, it has a resemblance to the passage in the Summary Record set forth in the principal text at the preceding footnote, including the reference to a revised Danish proposal. There was such a revision as to paragraph (b) of the proposal but not as to paragraph (c) so far as observed by the writer.

Since the Assembly's resolution in the case formally "recommended" acceptance of the Plan of Partition with Economic Union, there was a question logically antecedent to that concerning its enforceability: how did a recommendation take on the force of a binding decision? Probably the most important argument on this point during the debate resembled the line of paragraph (c) of the resolution, quoted above, in asserting that attempts to frustrate the resolution by force were illegal under the Charter.[32]

The case entered a new phase when, following adoption of the Plan by the Assembly, the Arabs persisted in their refusal to accept it. The Palestine Commission, established by the resolution and charged with implementation of the Plan, found the situation in the country deteriorating toward war, and sent an appeal for military assistance to the Security Council.[33] This appeal, which would seem inevitably to have made a considerable impact on public opinion, appears to have anticipated the use of force to enforce the Plan, rather than as an exercise of the "collective measures" function to deal with a breach of, or threat to, international peace. The Security Council then took up the requests, pertaining to the possible use of force, contained in paragraphs (b) and (c) quoted above, of the Assembly's resolution.

At this point the Secretariat submitted a memorandum to the effect that the Security Council was empowered under the Charter to employ force if necessary to enforce the Plan.[34] The action thus contemplated was sharply distinguished from the Charter power of "collective measures" which are authorized for dealing with aggressions, other threats to peace or breaches of peace:

> An international armed force set up on this basis would not be one in the sense of Chapter VII of the Charter. It would have the char-

---

[32] Cf. p. 168 infra. That recommendations have some degree of binding force was evidently attempted to be established by the United States Delegation in stating that "Recommendations of the General Assembly were made to all Members of the United Nations and, once adopted by a two-thirds majority, had virtually the force of law" (U.N. Gen. Ass. Off. Rec. 2d Sess., Ad Hoc Comm. on the Palestinian Question 221 (1947)), and by the earlier statement that:

> "In the view of the United States Delegation, no member of the United Nations would attempt to defy the decision of the United Nations. In that sense, the greatest test of its integrity was being offered to the United Nations." Id. at 169.

[33] U.N. Security Council Off. Rec. 3d year, Spec. Supp. No. 2, at 10 et. seq. and esp. 18-19 (S/676) (1948).

[34] Id., Supp. Jan.-March 1948, at 14 (A/AC. 21/13) (1948).

acter of an international police force for the maintenance of law and order in a territory for which the international society is still responsible.[35]

The maintenance of law and order in the Palestine case would have meant the putting down of Arab resistance to the setting up of a Jewish state and, in effect, the enforcement of the Plan. The position taken in the memorandum under discussion was squarely based upon the precedent of the Trieste case in which the Council assumed responsibility for the government of Trieste. As will be recalled from the discussion of the latter case in the preceding chapter, the general consensus of the Security Council in that case was that the necessary Charter power could be found in Article 24, which charges the Council with the primary responsibility for the maintenance of peace and security. The maintenance of peace and security is, in turn, one of the major purposes of the United Nations set forth in Chapter I of the Charter. It will be further recalled that a Secretariat memorandum in the Trieste case maintained that so long as the Council was acting in accordance with the broad purposes and principles of the United Nations, no more specific authorization for particular decisions or measures is required. The memorandum under discussion, in the Palestine case, seems to have followed that general line of thought.

For reasons advanced above in connection with the Trieste case, the view is herein maintained that a "constitutional approach" requires the development of a set of United Nations principles and procedures more precise than its general principles and purposes while, at the same time, it is recognized that such principles and procedures must be in more or less constant evolution. Consonant with this line of thought, it was considered that the Trieste case actually represented a first step in the development of a new United Nations power, namely that of governing or administering territory. From this point of view, the proposition that the Security Council was empowered to enforce the Plan of Partition with Economic Union would stand on an entirely different footing. With regard to the Trieste case, there was a reasonable prospect that the general membership could acquiesce in the proposition that the United Nations should, in principle, possess the right to govern or administer territory. With regard to the Palestine case, there was no practical prospect that the general membership would agree, in the foreseeable future, on the kind of power there under

[35] *Id.* at 23.

discussion, namely to make and enforce decisions as to the internal or external relations of states without the consent of states concerned. Not only were the Arab states firm in denying such a right in the Palestine case itself, but it is believed that states, generally, would reject the proposition whenever it came to be applied against themselves.

In the ensuing Council debate as to whether the Council should (on whatever constitutional grounds) apply tangible pressure in the Palestine case, the key statement was undoubtedly that made by the United States Representative on March 2, 1948, in which he stressed the discretionary power of the Security Council to determine whether a threat to the peace, breach of the peace or act of aggression existed such as would justify the application of enforcement measures.[36]

The Council terminated its discussion without acting and shortly thereafter a special session of the General Assembly was convened to consider the problem. In opening the session the Temporary Chairman could rightly say that "[United Nations] prestige had suffered rude shocks and the hopes founded upon it were now fraught with doubt and misgiving."[37] The point of the present discussion is that the setback sustained by the United Nations in this case resulted in part from the fact that the Organization itself, as well as some of the member states, had succeeded in creating the impression that the Plan was legally binding and enforceable as such. This was a factor in a mixed situation, in which another part was the creation of the impression that enforcement measures would be used if necessary to deal with a threat to peace or breach of the peace. Perhaps the most important factor was that, after the impression had been created that enforcement measures would be taken if necessary—whether for one or the other of these reasons, or both—they were not taken, notwithstanding the deterioration of the situation into one of war between Israel and the surrounding Arab states.

With regard to the constitutional issue here under discussion, there is no disposition to be critical of competent authorities if they felt that they had other and more important matters of concern in this case. Some of them evidently decided to throw the whole prestige of the United Nations into the balance, without regard to the Charter, in the effort to persuade the Arabs to accept the

[36] *Id.,* 260th meeting 398-401 (1948).
[37] U.N. Gen. Ass. Off. Rec. 2d Spec. Sess., Plenary 1 (1948).

Plan. Had this course of action been successful, damage to the Organization would have been greatly reduced. Even had the damage been considerable, however, it would be difficult to deny that it was acceptable in the interests of obtaining a peaceful solution of the case. However, the significant point to be noted, from the standpoint of the present discussion, is precisely that this effort was not successful. Had the majority been content to rest their efforts upon the Assembly's power of recommendation, fully recognizing the right of the Arabs to reject the proposals, they would have been equally as successful in gaining acceptance as they were in the actual event. The particular source of damage to the Organization with which we are here concerned—the confusion of public opinion as to whether the Organization is empowered to make and enforce changes in legal relationships—would have been eliminated. If, indeed, there had been a conscientious effort to find a solution based on relevant law and principles, and this effort had been fully explained and elucidated, some gain might have eventuated for the United Nations and the peaceful settlement process, notwithstanding the rejection of the recommended solution. However, since the course of action followed must have tended toward confusion in the public mind as to the powers of the Organization, any such opportunity was lost, and the prospects for advancing the rule of law to some extent set back.

The Suez "ships" case, certain aspects of which were considered above in Chapter 1, brings some new considerations into the discussion pertaining to the attribution to the United Nations of legislative and judicial powers.

It will be recalled that the case concerns the refusal of Egypt (later the United Arab Republic) to permit transit of the Suez Canal by Israeli-connected ships and cargoes. Egypt claimed to be still at war with Israel and contended that the actions complained of were therefore justified under the laws of maritime warfare and under the right of self-defense. The position was thus essentially based upon a claim of legal right. In the Council debate of 1951 some arguments seemed to contest the Egyptian legal position, while others seemed to assert that even if this position were correct in law, it ought to be changed in the interests of equity and justice. The resolution adopted by the Council on September 1, 1951, appears to the writer as susceptible of interpretation in accordance with either of these arguments, and as being, in fact, ambiguous. It provides in part:

5. *Considering* that since the Armistice regime, which has been in existence for nearly two and a half years, is of a permanent character, neither party can reasonably assert that it is actively a belligerent or requires to exercise the right of visit, search, and seizure for any legitimate purpose of self-defense;

6. *Finds* that the maintenance of the [Egyptian] practice . . . is inconsistent with the objectives of a peaceful settlement between the parties and the establishment of a permanent peace in Palestine set forth in the Armistice Agreement;

7. *Finds further* that such practice is an abuse of the exercise of the right of visit, search and seizure;

8. *Further finds* that that practice cannot in the prevailing circumstances be justified on the ground that it is necessary for self-defence;

9. *And further noting* that the restrictions on the passage of goods through the Suez Canal to Israel ports are denying to nations at no time connected with the conflict in Palestine valuable supplies required for their economic reconstruction, and that these restrictions together with sanctions applied by Egypt to certain ships which have visited Israel ports represent unjustified interference with the rights of nations to navigate the seas and to trade freely with one another, including the Arab States and Israel;

10. *Calls upon* Egypt to terminate the restrictions on the passage of international commercial shipping and goods through the Suez Canal wherever bound and to cease all interference with such shipping beyond that essential to the safety of shipping in the Canal itself and to the observance of international conventions in force.[38]

There were several later pronouncements which indicated that some states regarded this resolution as a decision binding on Egypt. In renewing Israel's complaint before the Council in 1953, the Israeli Delegation spoke of "the Council's rejection of the pretended claim of the Government of Egypt to the exercise of belligerent rights against Israel"[39] and the New Zealand Delegation introduced a draft resolution which, referring to the resolution of September 1, 1951, provided that the Council "Calls upon Egypt in accordance with its obligations under the Charter to comply

[38] U.N. Security Council Off. Rec. 6th year, 558th meeting at 2-3 (S/PV. 558) (1951).

[39] *Id.*, 8th year, Supp. July-Sept. 1953 at 73, 75 (S/3093) (1953). For other pronouncements indicating that Israeli ships and cargoes had a right to navigate the Suez Canal by virtue of the Council resolution of September 1, 1951, see *id.*, 9th year, 663d meeting at 3-4 (Denmark), 7-9 (France) (S/PV. 663) (1954); *id.*, 684th meeting, 6 (France) (S/PV. 684) (1954).

therewith."[40] This resolution would have passed except for a Soviet veto.[41]

The discussion contained several references to Article 25 of the United Nations Charter, and it would appear that this provision formed the basis upon which at least some states considered that the resolution was binding. It provides:

> The Members of the United Nations agree to accept and carry out the decisions of the Security Council in accordance with the present Charter.

Did, however, the resolution in the Suez case constitute a "decision" within the meaning of this provision? The French Delegation, which specifically declared that the relevant part of the New Zealand proposal was "manifestly based on Article 25 of the Charter,"[42] had said earlier during the same debate:

> The Security Council has not, under the Charter, any special competence to examine alleged infringements of obligations assumed under a particular treaty. The Council is not necessarily competent to deal with a case merely by virtue of the fact that an international treaty is involved. Its essential function is to remove threats to the peace. Its competence becomes operative only if such threats exist in the circumstances and under the conditions referred to in Article 33 et seq. of the Charter.[43]

However, as has been pointed out in the present chapter, the Charter stipulates positively that the United Nations power to deal with substantive issues of disputes and situations is the power of recommendation. This power is affirmatively set forth in Articles 36 and 37, in Chapter VI, and is carried over into Chapter VII through the inclusion of the power of recommendation in the introductory article of that Chapter, Article 39. As Goodrich and Hambro point out:

> It was made clear in the discussions in Committee III/2 at San Francisco that such recommendations have no binding force. It can hardly be supposed that Article 25, through the work of another Committee, was intended to reverse this asurance and the clear words of the Charter.[44]

---

[40] Id., 9th year, Supp. Jan.-March 1954, at 44 (S/3188 and Corr. 1).

[41] Id., 664th meeting 12 (S/PV. 664) (1954).

[42] Id., 9th year, 663d meeting 9 (S/PV. 663) (1954). For a Danish statement of similar import see id., 3-4.

[43] Id. at 8.

[44] Goodrich and Hambro, op. cit. supra note 8, at 209. Introduction to the Annual Report of the Secretary-General on the Work of the Organization

The San Francisco Conference, moreover, specifically refrained from expanding this power in cases constituting threats to peace.[45]

One of the ambiguous parts of the resolution of September 1, 1951, is that it "calls upon" Egypt to cease and desist the actions complained of. Because it was thus given something of the appearance of a "decision," some members of the Council may have been encouraged to conclude that it had binding force. However, the resolution of September 1, 1951, seemed plainly aimed at bringing about the permanent relinquishment of the relevant legal position which Egypt was claiming and enforcing, and to have therefore come within the Council's peaceful settlement function. The real power was therefore that of recommendation, and this power cannot, of course, be transmuted into a power of binding decision by a mere choice of phraseology.

Egypt therefore seems to have been on sound ground when it rejected the Council resolution of September 1, 1951, on the basis of its being a recommendation, and not binding.[46]

Apart from the position just referred to, however, the Egyptian argument shared the same basic fault as did that of the majority in attempting to assert for the Council a competence that that organ was never given and which states are generally unwilling to accept when applied to themselves. The Egyptian position in this respect differed from that of the majority mainly in that its representative seems to have been calling on the Council to perform a judicial, rather than a legislative, function. Thus, he said:

> This [New Zealand] draft resolution resembles the resolution adopted by the Security Council on 1 September 1951 in that it

---

16 June 1960-15 June 1961, U.N. Gen. Ass. Off. Rec. 16th Sess., Supp. No. 1A at 4 (A/4800/Add. 1) (1961); Bowett, *The Law of International Institutions* 32 (1963). The phrase "in accordance with the present Charter" in Article 25 is said to have been moved to the end of the Article by the Coordination Committee of the San Francisco Conference "so as to make clear that the members would be obligated to carry out only those Council decisions that were legally mandatory. Its 'recommendations,' under the Charter, would be precisely that, and therefore not obligatory." Russell and Muther, *A History of the United Nations Charter* 665 (1958). See Doc. WD 158, CO/79, 17 U.N. Conf. Int'l Org. Docs. 46-47 (1945); Doc. WD 44, CO/18, 18 *id.,* 63. The phrase "in accordance with the Charter" is similarly interpreted in *Charter of the United Nations: Report to the President on the Results of the San Francisco Conference,* by the Chairman of the United States Delegation, the Secretary of State 78-79 (1945). But see Kelsen, *The Law of the United Nations* 95-97, 293-95, 444-50 (1950).

45 Cf. p. 69 *supra.*

46 Cf. p. 67 *supra.*

takes no account of the legal character of the conflict submitted to the Council. Is a particular State a belligerent or is it not? Is the position one of armistice or of peace? Is a particular party exercising the sovereign right of legitimate self-defence or encroaching on the rights of others? These are all legal questions. As the 1951 documents of the Security Council themselves show, these legal issues were never studied in the conscientious manner worthy of a body like the Security Council.[47]

Thus, as already observed above in Chapter 1, there was an aspect of this case in which both sides advanced arguments based on differing interpretations of existing law; both were apparently appealing to the Security Council to decide on this basis; neither suggested a reference to adjudication notwithstanding that a judicial tribunal is the only type of organ competent to decide such questions.[48] Also there is little reason to doubt that both sides were equally prepared to reject the Council's decision if it did not conform to their wishes.

A later development in the case was a statement by the Secretary-General apparently assuming that the dispute had been adjudicated by the Security Council. This statement arose out of a request by the Security Council to the Secretary-General that he undertake a "survey of the various aspects of enforcement of and compliance with" the armistice agreements in the Palestine case.[49] The Secretary-General, in his report on this matter, noted that the Israeli Government had raised in this connection the question of Egyptian interference with Israeli shipping through the Suez Canal, as treated by the Security Council resolution of September 1, 1951, and he went on to say with reference to this Israeli suggestion:

> My attitude has been that the Suez question, as adjudicated by the Security Council, is not a question of compliance with the Armistice Agreement in the sense of my mandate. . . .
>
> . . . In an approach looking beyond the immediate problems which, as I understand the resolution of 4 April, 1956, the Security

---

[47] U.N. Security Council Off. Rec. 9th year, 662d meeting 11-12 (S/PV. 662) (1954).

[48] However, in the initial debate, the Indian and Chinese Representatives in the Council suggested that insufficient attention was being given the legal or Charter aspects of the case. *Id.,* 6th year, 553d meeting 10-11, 29-30 (S/PV. 553) (1951).

[49] Resolution of 4 April 1956, U.N. Security Council Off. Rec. 11th year, Supp. April-June 1956 at 1 (S/3575) (1956).

Council had in mind, it is obvious that the question raised by the Government of Israel should come under consideration in the light of the Council's finding in its resolution of 1 September 1951 that the blockade is incompatible with the Armistice regime, as this regime put an end to a state in which Egypt could avail itself of belligerent rights.[50]

Since, despite all the efforts to persuade Egypt that it was bound by the Council's decision of September 1, 1951, Egypt has persistently refused to abandon its position, and may have intensified it,[51] the impression must have been conveyed, at least to some parts of the interested world public, that Egypt has been successfully defying a binding order of the Security Council. In addition to the setback to United Nations prestige resulting from this impression, there must also have been some confusion as to the proper powers of the Organization in such matters, and resulting harm to the prospects of building up the Charter in terms of securing the necessary support and understanding of public opinion.

[50] "Report of the Secretary-General . . .," *id.* at 52-53. In the following year the United States Secretary of State said:

"We believe that under the Armistice Agreements there is not a right to exercise belligerent rights. We believe that is evidenced by the fact that that was the basis for the Security Council decision of 1951 with reference to the right of passage of cargo for Israel through the Suez Canal. And the basis for that decision was that under the Armistice Agreement Egypt did not possess belligerent rights. We voted for that resolution at the time and we adhere to the view which was then held." 36 Dep't State Bull. 596 (1957).

[51] Apparently the first actual seizure of a ship came only in the fall of 1954, after the matter had been twice debated in the Security Council. The ship in question was an Israeli vessel. Later, several ships of third-party nationality were seized and their cargoes confiscated. See *Yearbook of the United Nations 1954,* at 70-72; *id.,* 1959 at 35-36. In 1953 Egypt expanded the scope of its contraband list and may also have extended the geographical scope of its surveillance. Security Council Off. Rec. 9th year, Supp. Jan.-March 1954 at 5, 9 (S/3179) (1954); Gross, "Passage through the Suez Canal of Israel-Bound Cargo and Israel Ships," 51 Am. J. Int'l L. 530, 533-34 (1957).

Chapter IV

"Collective Measures" and "Peaceful Settlement" Functions

In the Congolese case the United Nations Force (ONUC) was several times engaged in combat with troops of the secessionist regime of Katanga Province and, in the end, the impression was probably fairly general that it suppressed this regime through military action. Contributing to this impression were, no doubt, consistent denials that ONUC was a "collective measure," as well as some affirmative statements to the effect that it was, in fact, deliberately engaged in putting down the secession. A problem is thus raised, by reason of what is believed to be the fact, as discussed in the preceding chapter, that neither the Charter itself nor the governments and peoples of the world have ever given the United Nations quasi-legislative or -judicial power; that is to say, power to make or enforce substantive decisions affecting the external or internal relations either of states or of other political entities, such as the secessionist regime of Katanga, without their consent.

Entering into the denial that ONUC was a "collective measure" there seems to have been a psychological factor which had been less apparent, or not applicable, in such earlier cases as those of Spain and Palestine. This factor appears to have been a major element in the Congolese case and in the Portuguese and South African cases to be discussed in the next chapter. Although it has evidenced itself most strongly in recent years, there is nothing new in the reason underlying it. It stems from the original supposition that "collective measures" would involve combat action for the prevention or suppression of aggressions such as had precipitated World War II. It is to be recalled, in this connection, that the authority of the United Nations to use force was emphasized from the outset as being the central element of strength of the new Organization—a new departure in collective security which would enable it to succeed where its predecessor, the League of Nations, had failed. Since Chapter VII of the Charter was usually regarded as the repository of this function, it was natural for action under this chapter to be associated with the probability of combat. Another psychological factor has been the inclination of states to give a major and exaggerated significance to the element of "accusation" implicit in findings that a threat to the peace or a breach of the peace exists. The political element prevalent in present-day international relations enables the sensitivity of states, on such matters, to supersede and take precedence over the objective and dispassionate approach which is plainly needed if the Charter is to function as an effective system.

More generally, it may have been felt that any United Nations action of the type contemplated by Chapter VII would raise the specter of war or other grave, if unforeseeable dangers.

This attitude is also understandable by virtue of the fact that, probably until the Lebanese-Jordanian crisis of 1958, no one envisioned the possibility that the United Nations might need to use force of a kind other than "enforcement action" directed against states. It is true that two years earlier, in the Suez crisis of 1956, the United Nations Emergency Force (UNEF) had been deployed to perform a necessary function; however, that operation was not envisioned at the time as involving the application of military force. Since it did not have to use overt force, and particularly since it was formed by the Assembly, which is not generally regarded as having any power to deploy military force, the question of the military role of this operation tended to be ignored. Later, however, when in connection with the Lebanese-Jordanian crisis, an armed force was proposed which would have been similar to UNEF in being directed against a situation, and not against a state, and when a force with such a mission was actually formed in the Congolese crisis of 1960 (this time by the Security Council), the questions concerning the powers and Charter authority of such operations could no longer be ignored. Since the prevailing interpretation was that all "collective measures" under the Charter were "enforcement measures" directed against states, since the forces in question were not actually directed against states and were not of the character which public opinion generally associated with such measures, and since troops for them had to be obtained by voluntary contributions of member states, it is only natural that the competent authorities attempted to stay as far as possible from the notion that these were "collective" or "enforcement" measures. The attempt to do so proved rather abortive, however, by virtue of developments in the Congolese case which seemed to bring that operation within the Charter definition of collective measures. Continued denials that it was of this character have tended to focus attention upon the question as to what the Charter category of these forces is. These denials have also tended to break down the barrier separating the major Charter concepts of "collective measures" and "peaceful settlement," which, it is believed, the "peoples of the world" incorporated in the Charter as essentially separate and distinct, if interrelated, powers which it was desired that the United Nations should exercise.[1]

The "collective measures" function, is defined in Article 1 (1) and Chapter VII of the Charter, relevant parts of which are set forth in Chapter 2 above.[2] It will be observed that Article 1 (1) gives the generic description "collective measures" to all forms of tangible pressure which the Organization might decide to be necessary "for the prevention and removal of threats to the peace, and for the suppression of acts of aggression or other breaches of the peace." In Chapter VII, where this function is spelled out in terms of the powers of the Security Council, Articles 41 and 42 again seem to embrace any measures that might be deemed necessary for the purpose indicated in Article 39 and, earlier, in Article 1 (1). The Charter thus seems to define "collective measures" comprehensively as authorizing the United Nations to apply any necessary degree of force, or any tangible pressures less than force, if deemed necessary to deal with threats to peace or breaches of the peace. On the other hand, the provisions authorizing "collective measures" are the only Charter authorization for the application of force as a factor in the handling of disputes and situations.[3] Uses of armed forces for this purpose should, then, conform to the Charter criteria governing "collective measures."

The framers of the Charter seem deliberately to have left a broad discretion to the competent United Nations organ to devise the type of measure deemed appropriate in a given case. A pro-

---

[1] Cf. pp. 76-77 supra.

[2] Cf. p. 38 supra.

[3] An exception to this statement which is, however, clearly defined and wholly irrelevant to the present discussion, is the provision made in Article 94 of the Charter for possible enforcement of decisions of the World Court. Another category of force which may be employed by the United Nations which, however, is not believed to conflict with the statement in the principal text, is mentioned in note 41 infra.

posal to contrary effect was made in Committee III/3 of the San Francisco Conference, which drafted Chapter VII, namely to incorporate in the Charter provisions which would assure that adequate measures of an "enforcement" character would be employed to deal with aggression. This proposal also, of course, involved the necessity of defining aggression. The Committee, however, believed that this distinction, although having the merit of clarity, might endanger the Council's free discretion as envisioned in the text of Dumbarton Oaks. "Too rigid a distinction between threats to the peace and attempts against the peace, or acts of aggression, appeared to the Committee to be in contradiction with the previous decision to avoid a definition of aggression and with the general spirit of the Charter."[4]

It being thus deliberately anticipated that the United Nations might decide that measures short of force, or recommendations, might be the most appropriate means of handling actual aggressions or other breaches of peace, there seems no logical reason to doubt that it would be equally within the intent of the Charter that actual force might sometimes be deployed to deal with threats which were not actual breaches of peace, and in which the action was not directed against a state, but against a "situation" as such. ONUC appears to have been an operation of this latter kind. Nevertheless, it is customarily excluded from the "collective measures" category, in part because of the continuing prevailing view that measures of this kind must be "enforcement" measures directed against states.[4a] Entering into this attitude are, no doubt, elements of the psychological factor referred to. It was evidently apprehended, in particular, that if an operation were to be designated as a "collective measure," governmental officials would assume that it was an "enforcement action" destined for combat, and would be correspondingly hesitant to contribute troops to its formation.[5]

---

[4] *The United Nations Conference on International Organization: Selected Documents* 764 (1946).

[4a] The Security Council's resolution S/RES/221 (1966) in the Rhodesian case would seem to make it difficult any longer to maintain that a collective measure or "enforcement action" must be directed against a state. *Cf.* pp. 183-86 *infra*.

[5] ". . . Message dated 24 February 1961 from the Secretary-General to certain African States concerning the need for troops and the Function of the Force," U.N. Security Council Off. Rec. 16th year, Supp. Jan.-March 1961, at 187 (S/4752, Annex VII) (1961); Schachter, "The Relation of

In this, as in other matters of Charter law, it is not believed necessary that the proper rule to be applied should be determined on the basis of Charter language, or such other possible pre-established factors as the intent of the framers, or prevalent notions of what the law is. A factor which certainly ought to be taken into account is the question of what rule or interpretation would best serve the interests of all concerned, which is one way of stating the basic intent and purpose of the Charter. If such a rule or interpretation does not appear to be in accord with Charter language or prevailing notions of what the Charter means, then attention should be given to ways of giving force and effect to the desired interpretation. The view may be reiterated that the Charter cannot remain static if it is to fulfill its purpose.

Functional Nature and Purposes of UNEF and ONUC

Under an objective view of the relevant Charter language, "collective measures" may be said to embrace any measures which fulfill the three requirements of being (a) applications of tangible pressure, (b) applied by the United Nations, and (c) applied to situations constituting threats to international peace, breaches of peace or acts of aggression.

The United Nations Emergency Force (UNEF) was organized and deployed by the United Nations as part of an agreement to bring about a cease-fire in the hostilities that broke out, in November 1956, between Israel, France and the United Kingdom, on one hand, and Egypt on the other. As to the three objective criteria just mentioned, it seems clear that the second and third were fulfilled, and the only remaining question would be as to whether this Force was an application of tangible pressure. Early pronouncements which bore on this question tended to be uncertain or negative. The original terms of reference for the Force as laid down by the General Assembly[6] instructed it "to secure and supervise the cessation of hostilities in accordance with all the terms of" the Assembly's earlier resolution calling for a cease-fire. The terms of reference were somewhat expanded by an Assembly Resolution of February 2, 1957[7] stating that:

Law, Politics and Action in the United Nations," 109 Academie de droit international, Recueil des Cours 165, 220-22 (1963-II).

[6] Res. 1000 (ES-I), U.N. Gen. Ass. Off. Rec. 1st Em. Spec. Sess., Supp. No. 1, at 2, 3 (A/3354) (1956).

[7] Res. 1125 (XI), *id.* 11th Sess., Supp. No. 17 at 62 (A/3572) (1957).

[T]he scrupulous maintenance of the Armistice Agreement requires the placing of the United Nations Emergency Force on the Egyptian-Israel armistice demarcation line . . . with a view to assist in achieving situations conducive to the maintenance of peaceful conditions in the area.

In an early report on the Force, the Secretary-General described its role and function in rather ambiguous terms, including the following passages:

While the General Assembly is enabled to *establish* the Force with the consent of those parties which contribute units to the Force, it could not request the Force to be *stationed* or *operate* on the territory of a given country without the consent of the Government of that country.

* * *

The Force obviously should have no rights other than those necessary for the execution of its functions, in co-operation with local authorities. It would be more than an observers' corps, but in no way a military force temporarily controlling the territory in which it is stationed; nor, moreover, should the Force have military functions exceeding those necessary to secure peaceful conditions on the assumption that the parties to the conflict take all necessary steps for compliance with the recommendations of the General Assembly.[8]

In regard to this last passage, the question suggests itself as to what the position would be if the Force encountered opposition from a force controlled by a hostile authority not prepared to comply with resolutions of the Assembly. Presumably, since UNEF was "in no way a military force temporarily controlling the territory in which it is stationed," it would have to give way.

Nevertheless, from the outset, this latter interpretation encountered a difficulty inherent in the mission of the Force. This difficulty was noted in the later Advisory Opinion of the World Court in the "Expenses" case where it is stated:

The verb "secure" as applied to such matters as halting the movement of military forces and arms into the area and the conclusion of a cease-fire, might suggest measures of enforcement, were it not that the Force was to be set up "with the consent of the nations concerned."[9]

---

[8] "Second and Final Report of the Secretary-General on the plan for an emergency international United Nations Force . . .," *id.* 1st Em. Spec. Sess., Plenary Meetings and Annexes: Annexes, Agenda Item No. 5, at 19, 20-21 (A/3302) (1956).

[9] *Certain Expenses of the United Nations (Article 17, paragraph 2, of the Charter)* 1962 I.C.J. Rep. 151, 170. The phrase "with the consent of

UNEF has, however, been able to fulfill its mission without the overt use of force, so that the question of its Charter status was not put to further test. In the circumstances, and considering particularly the fact that the Assembly was regarded as having no power in these matters beyond the power of recommendation, it seems probable that little thought was given to the possibility that this Force shared the basic objective criteria of "collective measures" as defined in the Charter.

With the Lebanese-Jordanian crisis of 1958 it became necessary, for the first time, to consider the possible need of the United Nations for armed forces which would have the right to employ force but would not be "enforcement measures" directed against states. The United States Representative proposed that the Council establish such a force, the members of which

> would not be there to fight unless they are attacked, but it should be fully clear also that they will have the authority to fire in self-defence in performance of their duties to prevent infiltration and to protect the integrity of Lebanon.[10]

Although it was defeated by the Soviet veto, this proposal was again mentioned by the Secretary-General in an oral statement before the Council on July 21, 1958, at which time he reiterated the above-quoted statement of the United States Representative concerning the proposed force and went on to say that it would have had limited rights "along the lines of [the] United Nations Emergency Force."[11] Consistently with this indication that UNEF had the right to use force as a part of its mission, the Secretary-General incorporated a corresponding description of its powers in his report on that force dated October 9, 1958:

> [M]en engaged in the operation may never take the initiative in the use of armed force, but are entitled to respond with force to an attack with arms, including attempts to use force to make them withdraw from positions which they occupy under orders. . . .[12]

This formulation received the implicit endorsement of the Gen-

the nations concerned" is from Assembly Res. 998 (ES-I), U.N. Gen. Ass. Off. Rec. 1st Em. Spec. Sess., Supp. No. 1, at 2 (A/3354) (1956).

[10] U.N. Security Council Off. Rec. 13th year, 829th meeting 4 (S/PV. 829) (1958).

[11] Id., 835th meeting 8 (S/PV. 835).

[12] "Summary Study of the experience derived from the establishment and operation of the Force . . .," U.N. Gen. Ass. Off. Rec. 13th Sess., Annexes, Agenda Item No. 65, at 8, 31 (A/3943) (1958).

eral Assembly and so appears as a definition of what UNEF was empowered to do in case of attack. The power thus defined is not that of self-defense against wrongful attack normally possessed by any individual or group; it is rather a statement that UNEF does not have to yield its positions to any other force with which it might come in contact. It appears to mean that UNEF was empowered, at least in some situations, to employ military force and was, consequently, an application of tangible pressure. Being deployed by the United Nations in a situation well known to constitute, at the least, a threat to peace, it thus appears to have met the objective criteria of a "collective measure" under the Charter. In limiting the use of force strictly to defense, the statement in question appears to have been carefully formulated to assure the "noninterventionist" nature of UNEF. Pursuant to this definition of function, it could be regarded as conforming to the Charter concept of "collective measures" but as being, at the same time, deployed to deal with a "situation" as such, and not, therefore, an "enforcement" measure directed against any state.

At approximately the time of the report on UNEF containing the passage just quoted, the Secretary-General promulgated his annual report on the work of the Organization for 1957-1958 which referred to UNEF, and forces of that character, as follows:

> It should, of course, be clear that any such Force, unless it were to be called into being by the Security Council under Chapter VII of the Charter, must constitutionally be a non-fighting force, operating on the territories of the countries concerned only with their consent and utilized only after a decision of the Security Council or the General Assembly, regarding a specific case, for those clearly international purposes relating to the pacific settlement of disputes which are authorized by the Charter. . . .[13]

In thus placing UNEF in the realm of the "peaceful settlement" function of the United Nations, this statement seems to have an import contradictory to that of the previously-quoted passage from the report of October 9, 1958, which seems to recognize UNEF as conforming to the objective characteristics of a "collective measure." UNEF thus seems to have been furnished with two parallel and basically distinct theories as to its character under the Charter.

---

[13] *Introduction to the Annual Report of the Secretary-General on the Work of the Organization 16 June 1957-15 June 1958, id.* Supp. No. 1A, at 2 (A/3844/Add. 1) (1958).

Mr. Schachter, Director of the General Legal Division of the United Nations, in a recent unofficial treatise, denies that UNEF was recognized, in the report of Ocober 9, 1958, as empowered to resist attack by the armed forces of states.[14] He points out that the Secretary-General "had taken the position that this could not be done under the authority of the General Assembly, and that it would require a decision of the Security Council under Chapter VII." He cites in support of this assertion, the Secretary-General's early report on UNEF of November 6, 1956. However, it also seems possible to suggest that the relevant parts of that report, emphasizing "permissiveness" as determinative of the constitutional character of the Force, were superseded by actual developments concerning the Lebanon in 1958 and by the resulting passage, quoted above, from the Secretary-General's report of October 9 of that year. These developments at least bring into view the possibility that future cases *might* arise in which it would be essential that the Assembly deploy a force sharing UNEF's "non-interventionist" characteristics but which would require, for the fulfillment of its mission, the authority to defend its positions against attacks by the military forces of a state. If the Assembly is to be regarded as prevented, by the Charter, from taking the necessary action, it would follow that not only the Security Council but the whole United Nations might be paralyzed in a given situation, and incapable of meeting its responsibility with respect to the maintenance of peace and security. This aspect of the problem is discussed more fully below, in Chapter 6. For purposes of present discussion it will be assumed that the Assembly possesses the residual power to initiate necessary action.

We then return to the major proposition that the nature of an operation should be determined on the basis of its objective characteristics. If an operation has the characteristics of a "collective measure," then the determination of its mission and terms of reference is properly a matter within the discretion of the principal United Nations organ (e.g. Security Council or General Assembly) seized with responsibility for the operation. It is within the discretion of such organ, for example, to give firm instructions that an operation should act only with the consent of some or all of the parties concerned in the case. As already observed in the present chapter, the framers of the Charter deliberately provided for such decisions to be made in this way. To attempt to eliminate this

---

[14] Schachter, *supra* note 5, at 210.

discretionary power on the part of the competent organ by attempting to say, for example, that a given armed force is in a category which forever forbids it from using its arms may, depending on developments, give rise to a difficult or impossible situation from the standpoint of basic Charter concepts. Conditions may arise in which adherence to such categorization would make action by the force impossible in circumstances where action was plainly required. Assuming, then, that the action were nevertheless taken, the resulting situation might make it difficult or impossible both to exclude the force from the category of "collective measures" and to include it within the other major Charter concept relevant to the handling of disputes and situations, that of "peaceful settlement."

The United Nations operation in the Congo (ONUC) is believed to furnish a practical example of the kind of difficulty under discussion. This Force was launched by the Security Council upon the request of the Congolese Government when a breakdown of internal security occurred in that country immediately following its independence in July 1960. By resolution of July 14, 1960,[15] the Security Council authorized the Secretary-General to furnish military assistance to the Congo until such time as its own security forces were in a position to fulfill their tasks. Troops were obtained through voluntary contributions by member states and the operation was, in this and other respects, similar to UNEF in its manner of establishment and organization.

The Secretary-General thus indicated the juridical basis of the Force in an early report which received the explicit approval of the Council:[16]

> I indicated as a "sound and lasting solution" . . . the re-establishment of the instruments of the Government for the maintenance of order. It was implied in my presentation that it was the breakdown of those instruments which had created a situation which through its consequences represented a threat to peace and security justifying United Nations intervention on the basis of the explicit request of the Government of the Republic of the Congo. Thus the two main elements, from the legal point of view, were on the one hand this

[15] U.N. Security Council Off. Rec. 15th year, Supp. July-Sept. 1960, at 16 (S/4387) (1960).

[16] However it is not considered that such explicit approval is necessary. The Secretary-General was given a broad authority in regard to these forces, and his reports embodying interpretations and policies concerning them are undoubtedly authentic statements of United Nations positions unless explicitly disapproved by the General Assembly or Security Council.

request and, on the other hand, the implied finding that the circumstances to which I had referred were such as to justify United Nations action under the Charter. . . .[17]

In a single sentence of the foregoing passage the operation is said to find its juridical base (a) in the consent of the Congolese Government, and (b) in being sent to deal with a threat to international peace in the Congo. In thus being accorded, simultaneously, the somewhat contradictory attributes of a "permissive" and of a "collective measures" type of operation, the Force had, from its inception, an ambivalent appearance as to its Charter status similar to that which had been acquired by UNEF.

With respect to its character as a "collective measure," such status would seem to be indicated by the assertion that the Congolese situation was, in its consequences, a threat to international peace. In the manner of its statement, moreover, the finding appeared as deliberately intended to invoke Chapter VII as a basis for the operation.[18]

Of outstanding importance in this connection would also seem to be the Secretary-General's description, in the same report, of ONUC's power to use force—e.g. as being forbidden to take initiatives, while having the recognized right to defend assigned positions —in identical terms, *mutatis mutandis,* as he had used in his report of October 9, 1958, with regard to UNEF. This application to ONUC of a particular language formula seems significant as the deliberate re-enactment of the terms of reference of UNEF, and as bringing this crucial definition of power to the forefront as a centrally important criterion of the nature of these forces, in contrast to its formerly rather obscure location in paragraph 179 of the Secretary-General's report of October 9, 1958, on UNEF. This description of its powers seems to underline the nature of ONUC as an application of tangible pressure. Since, in addition, it was deployed to deal with a situation specifically designated as a threat to peace, it seems to have fulfilled the objective criteria governing the Charter concept of "collective measures."

---

[17] First Report by the Secretary-General on the implementation of Security Council Resolution S/4387 of 14 July, 1960, U.N. Security Council Off. Rec. 15th year, Supp. July-Sept. 1960, at 16, 17 (S/4389) (1960).

[18] Schachter considers the Force to have been formed under authority of Chapter VII, but on different grounds. Schachter, "Legal Issues at the United Nations," in *Annual Review of United Nations Affairs 1960-1961,* at 143 (Swift, ed. 1961).

A course of historical development seems to sustain this notion of the proper role of ONUC. An incident occurred during its first year of operation when, as a result of what the United Nations referred to as "an inadmissible threat of the use of force,"[19] ONUC was compelled by Congolese authorities to evacuate Matadi, a main port of entry for its personnel and supplies. In protesting this incident, the Secretary-General said:

> United Nations, under the Security Council mandate, must keep complete freedom of decision as regards the deployment of national contingents in performance of the United Nations operation. . . . I am bound to consider unacceptable any attempt by force or otherwise to influence ONUC in this respect. . . . The forced withdrawal of the Sudanese detachment from Matadi today cannot be interpreted as derogating from this position of principle.[20]

A few days later, the United Nations Special Representative reported that in addition to conditions precedent for the return of troops to Matadi, he had received the following additional demands from the Congolese Acting Prime Minister:

> (a) No United Nations troopships may enter Matadi and river pilots have been forbidden to lend their services to such vessels;
>
> (b) All United Nations air traffic must be controlled by the Congolese authorities and subject to their permission;
>
> (c) Joint control must be established over all airfields and other strategic points now under the control of the United Nations Force;
>
> (d) All permanent movements of United Nations troops must be subject to the control of the Government and United Nations troops must obtain entry and exit permits;
>
> (e) All patrolling of United Nations troops with arms in Leopold-ville city must cease.[21]

In a message to the President of the Congo dated March 8, 1961, the Secretary-General referred to these demands and went on to say:

> We are, of course, strongly aware of the fact that the initial action of the United Nations was undertaken in response to a request of the Government of the Republic of the Congo. But I am certain that you, on your side, are also aware of the fact that this action was taken

---

[19] U.N. Security Council Off. Rec. 16th year, Supp. Jan.-March 1961, at 220, 221 (S/4758/Add. 4) (1961).

[20] *Id.* at 221.

[21] *Id.* at 239 (S/4761) (1961).

because it was considered necessary in view of an existing threat to international peace and security. Thus, in its resolution of 22 July 1960, and subsequent resolutions, the Security Council expressly linked the maintenance of law and order in the Congo to the maintenance of international peace and security, and made it clear that the primary basis of the Security Council decision was the maintenance of international peace and security. The considerations ruling the relationship between the Republic of the Congo and the United Nations, therefore, should not be seen solely in the light of the request of the Government and what flows from that request. The status, rights and functions of the United Nations are basically determined by the fact that the action was taken in order to counteract an international threat to peace.

* * *

[T]he relation between the United Nations and the Government of the Congo is not merely a contractual relationship in which the Republic can impose its conditions as host State and thereby determine the circumstances under which the United Nations operates. It is rather a relationship governed by mandatory decisions of the Security Council. The consequence of this is that no Government, including the host Government, can by unilateral action determine how measures taken by the Security Council in this context should be carried out. Such a determination can be made only by the Security Council itself. . . . It is of special importance that only the Security Council can decide on the discontinuance of the operation, and that, therefore, conditions which, by their effect on the operation, would deprive it of its necessary basis, would require direct consideration by the Security Council, which obviously could not be counted upon to approve of such conditions unless it were to find that the threat to peace and security had ceased.[22]

In this correspondence the United Nations was endeavoring to achieve an agreed settlement of the Matadi dispute, which it ultimately succeeded in doing. However, enough was said to make clear the official view that this Force was not dependent on the permission of the host state, but that it had both the legal power and the intent of defending its positions if necessary.

So long as ONUC continued to operate under its initial terms of reference, denials that it was a "collective measure" were made easier by its defensive and "non-interventionist" character. Under the prevalent theory which regards "collective measures" as limited to positive "enforcement" actions directed against states or other political entities, an operation with the characteristics of ONUC would be excluded. The defensive character of ONUC seemed to disappear, however, with the adoption of the Security Council's

---

[22] *Id.* at 262, 263 (S/4775) (1961).

resolution of February 21, 1961[23] authorizing that Force "if necessary" and "in the last resort" to use force for the prevention of civil
war in the Congo. This authorization may be paraphrased as meaning that ONUC was directed to use necessary force in order to
prevent, or deal with, a particular kind of breach of the peace,
namely civil war. It thus seems to have been brought, even more
clearly than formerly, within the objective Charter criteria governing the concept of "collective measures," and to have moved
away from its previously "defensive" and "non-interventionist"
character.

Also, in the same resolution, the Council authorized ONUC
to expel "mercenaries" from the Congo. This authorization was
supplemented and clarified by the Council resolution of November 24, 1961,[24] clearly authorizing the Force to expel mercenaries of the secessionist Katanga regime. In fulfilling its duties,
ONUC became several times engaged in combat, and these actions
were officially attributed, in part, to the carrying out of this last-
mentioned mission. Other aspects of the combat operations raise
questions somewhat apart from the present subject of discussion,
and will be considered further below, in the present chapter.

Official Denial that ONUC a "Collective Measure"

Notwithstanding the developments just referred to, the official
position has continued to be maintained that ONUC is not an
exercise of the "collective measures" function of the United Nations.

While the notions of "non-intervention" and "permissiveness,"
along with the restriction of the Force to defensive operations,
have no doubt entered into this position, they must have done
so as attributes of a larger notion that lay in the background, namely that of "peaceful settlement." Thus the basic underlying concept
of ONUC as something other than a "collective measure" may
have gone back to the idea of a "UNEF-type" force as elucidated
by the Secretary-General in his annual report on the work of the
Organization for 1957-1958. It will be recalled that it was there
said, in part:

> [A]ny such force, unless it were to be called into being by the
> Security Council under Chapter VII of the Charter, must constitution-

---

[23] *Id.* at 147 (S/4741) (1961).
[24] *Id.* Oct.-Dec. 1961 at 148, 149 (S/5002) (1961).

ally be a non-fighting force . . . utilized . . . for those clearly international purposes relating to the pacific settlement of disputes which are authorized by the Charter. . . .

Attention is invited to the phrase "called into being" and the word "constitutionally." Viewed in context with later developments, what the Secretary-General seems to be saying here is that unless the force is "called into being" as a "collective measure," it must, constitutionally, be an exercise of the "peaceful settlement" function. The constitutional nature of the force, in other words, is determined by the Charter concept invoked when it is established. The notion thus officially put forward is buttressed by bringing to its support the non-intervention principle of Article 2 (7) of the Charter, which provides that:

> Nothing contained in the present Charter shall authorize the United Nations to intervene in matters which are essentially within the domestic jurisdiction of any state . . .; but this principle shall not prejudice the application of enforcement measures under Chapter VII.

The resulting proposition was thus stated by the Secretary-General:

> The Council had never invoked Articles 41 and 42 of the Charter, which provided for enforcement measures and would override the domestic jurisdiction limitation of Article 2 (7).[25]

After the Council resolution of February 21, 1941, which appears to have removed the defensive, or "non-interventionist," limitation on the Force for a particular purpose, the position remained essentially unchanged:

> The function of the United Nations Force . . . was later expanded by the Security Council resolution of 21 February 1961 to include the objective of preventing civil war. The Security Council considered these measures necessary to counteract the threat to interna-

---

[25] *Annual Report of the Secretary-General on the Work of the Organization 16 June 1960-15 June 1961,* U.N. Gen. Ass. Off. Rec. 16th Sess., Supp. No. 1, at 27 (A/4800) (1961).

The last phrase of Article 2 (7), quoted in the principal text, seems to indicate that "enforcement measures" constitute an exception to the general rule against non-intervention in domestic affairs. This is not the case, however, since "enforcement measures" must always be directed to dealing with international situations, e.g., breaches of international peace, or threats to international peace. No questions of wrongful intervention in domestic affairs can arise in such situations. If this view is correct, there could be no question of enforcement measures "overriding" the domestic jurisdiction limitation of Article 2 (7). *Cf.* Ch. 7, note 64 *infra.*

tional peace, but the measures themselves did not constitute "sanctions" or enforcement action directed against a State as contemplated by Articles 42 and 43 of the Charter.[26]

Mr. Schachter notes that "for the Secretary-General, Article 42 appeared at times to be a touchstone of the degree to which the Council intended to intervene and apply military force;"[27] consequently the fact that the Council did not refer to Article 42 was taken as meaning that "the Council did not intend the measures to involve 'enforcement action' against any State."[28] Article 42 contains the Charter authorization for the use of force by the United Nations and is, of course, but one of several related provisions outlining the broad and basic "collective measures" or "police" function of the Organization.[29] Whereas it had been asserted that UNEF and the "UNEF-type" of force were not "collective measures" because not "called into being" under Chapter VII, the same cannot so readily be said in the case of ONUC, which is officially recognized as having been formed under Chapter VII. Reliance is therefore placed, instead, upon Article 42, notwithstanding that this forms part of Chapter VII.

However, the constitutional nature of an action is believed to depend less upon what it is called than upon its objective relationship to constitutional factors. As a second point it may be observed that, notwithstanding that an operation may be bound by certain constitutional limitations, it may not be impossible for the competent organ to change this status. When the operation being defined is, for example, an observation corps composed of military units, it is possible to say that it is not a collective measure, and that this description of its function is grounded in the Charter. However, assuming that the military unit is a suitable one for the purpose, the competent organ may change it to a "collective measure" at any time, for a *bona fide* purpose consistent with the Charter. After the change, the nature of the force may, again, be said to be grounded in the Charter. The point to be made, for purposes of present discussion, is that the framers of the Charter deliberately refrained from tying the hands of the competent

---

[26] "Statement by the Secretary-General at the 839th meeting of the Fifth Committee on 17 April 1961," *id.*, 15th Sess., Annexes, Agenda Items 49/50, at 36-37 (A/C. 5/864) (1961).

[27] Schachter, *supra* note 5, at 219-20.

[28] *Id.* at 220.

[29] Relevant provisions are set forth at p. 38 *supra.*

organs as to what they might do in particular situations and, by the same token, left it to the discretion of these organs, within the broad Charter limitations involved in such concepts as "collective measures," "provisional measures" and "peaceful settlement," to tailor particular operations to meet the requirements of particular situations.

In the case of ONUC, the United Nations, indeed, proceeded in the manner just indicated. Difficulty concerning the nature of the Force has arisen as a result of official insistence that, because it was not officially "called into being" as a "collective measure," it never had this character.

The official position just noted evidently became more difficult to maintain after ONUC had made overt uses of its force and, especially, after it had become engaged in combat. The first overt use of force appears to have been the taking over of major airports and the Leopoldville radio station on September 5 and 6, 1960. This action was officially said to have been taken to prevent an imminent breadown of law and order,[30] and thus could readily be placed within ONUC's initial mission of assisting the Government of the Congo until such time as its own security forces were ready to fulfill their missions. At the same time the Congolese situation had been officially recognized as a threat to international peace. Therefore the action, by the same token, can be described as an affirmative use of force to deal with a threat to peace, and as thus conforming to the Charter concept of "collective measures." The next such use of force appears to have been on August 28, 1961, when ONUC seized the Katanga radio, the Katangese gendarmerie headquarters and other key points and installations in Elisabethville. These actions were said to have been taken in the course of fulfilling the Force's mission of arresting and detaining mercenaries.[31] This operation, which involved combat, seems, again, to have fallen rather clearly into the "collective measures" or "police" category of United Nations activity. It was an employment of a particular kind of force (the expulsion of mercenaries) authorized as a means of dealing with the threat to peace represented by the Katangese secession. However, it was not, of course, recognized by the United Nations as having fallen

---

[30] *Annual Report of the Secretary-General . . ., op. cit. supra* note 25, at 10.

[31] *Annual Report of the Secretary-General on the Work of the Organization 16 June 1961-15 June 1962,* U.N. Gen. Ass. Off. Rec. 17th Sess., Supp. No. 1, at 3 (A/5201) (1962).

within that category. Further combat operations of September and December of 1961 were said to have been defensive in character.[32] However, as to the latter of these it was admitted by the United Nations authorities that it was not defensive in a strict sense. Katangese forces were establishing positions calculated to make ONUC positions untenable, and were manifestly planning to attack. The ONUC action which was then ordered was later officially said to have had the purposes of self-defense, of maintaining public order and of restoring the freedom of movement to which ONUC was entitled.[33]

These statements of motive seem to have been attuned to the narrow concept of "collective measures" as being limited to "enforcement" action and to have been designed in support of the proposition that ONUC did not fall into this category.[34] However, in the view of the present discussion, the only really relevant fact, so far as concerns the constitutional character of the Force, seems to be that the United Nations was, through ONUC, applying tangible military pressure in the dispute between the Government of the Congo and the secessionist regime of Katanga. Since the measure was directed to a situation recognized as a threat to international peace, its essential nature as a "collective measure" can hardly be mitigated by the adoption of flexible definitions of what is "defensive" and as to what is necessary to assure the Force's "freedom of movement."

Official Views of Affirmative Nature of UNEF and ONUC Under the Charter

An early official suggestion was that ONUC was a "provisional measure"[35] under Article 40 of the Charter.[36] While the sugges-

---

[32] *Id.* pages 4 and 14 respectively.

[33] *Id.* at 14. ONUC's "freedom of movement" in the Congo was assured by the Government of that country in an agreement with the United Nations concluded on July 14, 1960. U.N. Security Council Off. Rec. 15th year, Supp. July-Sept. 1960, at 27, 28 (S/4389/Add. 5) (1960). Bowett considers that a number of ONUC's actions went beyond what could be justified under the concept of self-defense; however, he regards them as justifiable assertions of the Force's right to freedom of movement. Bowett, *United Nations Forces* 200-205 (1964).

[34] See Schachter, *supra* note 5, at 226-28.

[35] *Annual Report of the Secretary-General . . .*, *op. cit. supra* note 25, at 27; Schachter, writing unofficially under the pseud. E. M. Miller, "Legal Aspects of the United Nations Action in the Congo," 55 Am. J. Int'l L. 1, 4-6 (1961).

[36] For text see p. 70 *supra*.

tion continues to be advanced by some authorities,[37] it seems to have been dropped by the United Nations. If this latter supposition is correct, the reason for the abandonment of the position may be that any resemblance between this Force and a "provisional measure" became very tenuous after the Force was authorized to use force, if necessary, to prevent civil war and to arrest and expel "mercenaries," and after it had become engaged in combat. The resemblance was, it is believed, always tenuous in fact. ONUC, as has been observed above, was an application of pressure by the United Nations in the Congolese situation, and seems to have conformed to the objective characteristics of a "collective measure" under the Charter. A "provisional measure," on the other hand, is a measure which the United Nations calls upon the parties to carry out in order to prevent the aggravation of a situation. A demand for a cease-fire is the typical manifestation of a "provisional measure" in past United Nations practice. Another example may have been the United Nations demand, early in the Congolese case, that Belgium withdraw its troops from that country.[38] A "provisional measure" would seem to differ from a "collective measure" in much the same way that a temporary injunction differs from a police measure in domestic law.

Another theory which has been officially advanced is that this operation was essentially internal in character. Thus the Secretary-General, in a statement to Committee 5 of the General Assembly, in April 1961, said:

> [O]ne must bear in mind the fundamental difference between the use of armed force under Article 43 or 42 of the Charter and the use of military personnel or contingents for essentially internal security functions in the territory of a Member State at the invitation of the Government of that State. The operation in the Congo is clearly of the latter type. . . .[39]

---

[37] Higgins, *The Development of International Law through the Political Organs of the United Nations* 235-36 (1963); Bowett, *The Law of International Institutions* 35 (1963); Bowett *op. cit. supra* note 33, at 177-78, 180. Regarding Article 40 as a possible basis for ONUC are Seyersted, "United Nations Forces: Some Legal Problems," 37 Brit. Yb. Int'l L. 351, 446 (1961); Franck in *The Legal Aspects of the United Nations Action in the Congo: Background Papers and Proceedings of the Second Hammarskjold Forum* 66 (Tondel ed. 1963).

[38] S/4387, *supra* note 15.

[39] "Statement by the Secretary-General . . ." *supra* note 26, at 36. Statements along this line have led to the suggestion that the United Nations operation in the Congo might be regarded (at least for purposes of finance)

No doubt ONUC, initially, had the appearance of an essentially internal operation. Its purpose was to take the place of the Congolese national security forces until the latter should be able to fulfill their function; the principal function was the preservation of internal peace and security. Nevertheless, the suggestion that ONUC was really an internal operation seems to be incompatible with the basic nature of the United Nations as an international organization having solely international functions. So far as ONUC was concerned, it was given an international character from the beginning, since it was officially declared to have been established and deployed to deal with a situation constituting a threat to international peace;[40] moreover, the finding of a threat to peace was declared to be one of the juridical bases of the Force.[41]

The International Court of Justice, in the "Expenses" case,[42] considered the legal status, under the Charter, of both UNEF and ONUC. In view of its coming to a conclusion as to the status of UNEF, the fact that it refrained from doing so with respect to ONUC may have some significance.[43]

---

as having had the juridical character of an agent of the Congo. Lee, "An Alternative Approach to Article 19," 59 Am J. Int'l L. 872 (1965).

Further development of "permissiveness" as a constitutional basis for ONUC is discussed at pp. 190-201 *infra.*

[40] In the oral presentation of his statement of April 17, 1961 (text accompanying note 39 *supra*), the Secretary-General was reported as saying that the ONUC operations "were essentially internal security measures taken by the Security Council at the invitation of the Government concerned to counteract the threat to international peace." U.N. Gen. Ass. Off. Rec. 15th Sess. (Pt. II), 5th Comm. 59 (A/C. 5/SR. 839) (1961).

[41] Text accompanying note 17 *supra.* An armed force giving a stronger appearance than ONUC of being an "essentially internal" operation was the force deployed to perform ordinary police functions in West Irian during the period of temporary United Nations administration of that territory. *Cf.* p. 34 *supra.* Unlike ONUC, this force does not appear to have been deployed to apply tangible pressure in a situation constituting a threat to peace; it does not, therefore, appear to have been a collective measure. It is rather believed to have been simply an adjunct of the larger United Nations operation entailed by the undertaking to administer this territory.

For further discussion of the argument that ONUC was an "essentially internal" operation see Halderman, "Legal Basis for United Nations Armed Forces," 56 Am. J. Int'l L. 971, 988-90 (1962).

[42] *Certain Expenses of the United Nations (Article 17, paragraph 2, of the Charter),* 1962 I.C.J. Rep. 151.

[43] Since the Opinion was in response to a question concerning the liability of member states to pay assessments for the costs of these forces, the Court's

As regards UNEF, the Court appears to have adopted the thesis of the Secretary-General which regards UNEF as a manifestation of the "peaceful settlement" function.[44] However, unlike the Secretary-General, the Court undertook to identify the specific Charter provisions under which the Force was established. It was thus inevitably brought to the Charter provisions which define the "peaceful settlement" function of the General Assembly:

Article 10
The General Assembly may discuss any questions or any matters within the scope of the present Charter . . . and . . . may make recommendations to the Members of the United Nations or to the Security Council or to both on any such questions or matters.

Article 11
* * *
2. The General Assembly may discuss any questions relating to the maintenance of international peace and security . . . and . . . may make recommendations with regard to any such questions to the state or states concerned or to the Security Council or to both.

Article 14
[T]he General Assembly may recommend measures for the peaceful adjustment of any situation, regardless of origin, which it deems likely to impair the general welfare or friendly relations among nations. . . .

It will be observed that the Assembly's basic power under these provisions, *vis-à-vis* the parties to disputes and situations, is the power of recommendation.

The Advisory Opinion indicated that UNEF might have been formed under Article 11 (2) or Article 14. As to the former it said:

[Article 11, paragraph 2], in its first sentence empowers the General Assembly, by means of recommendations to States or to the Security Council, or to both, to organize peace-keeping operations, at the request, or with the consent, of the States concerned.[45]

To say that UNEF was based, essentially, on the "recommendatory" power of the General Assembly is, however, awkward because, apart from the recruitment of troops which was, in effect,

discussion of their legal status under the Charter may be regarded as in the nature of *obiter dictum*. In separate concurring opinions several Judges, who concurred in the result on the main question, specifically refrained from expressing opinions as to the Charter bases of these forces.

[44] *Certain Expenses of the United Nations . . . supra* note 42, at 170-72.
[45] *Id.* at 164.

accomplished through recommendations to the member states, the Force was established and deployed by direct decisions of the United Nations, and not by virtue of recommendations.[46] Perhaps for this reason, the Secretary-General seems to have refrained from making unequivocal statements that UNEF was formed by recommendations of the Assembly.[47] Some authorities, however, place the Force on this basis.[48] The Judges concurring in the Advisory Opinion under discussion, since they had adopted the theory that UNEF was a manifestation of the "peaceful settlement" function, and since they desired to identify the specific Charter basis for the operation, had no choice but to place it under one or more of the provisions just quoted, and thus on a "recommendatory" basis.

In the case of ONUC, however, the Opinion went no farther in defining the nature of the operation than to say that it was not a "collective measure." In discussing this matter only in terms of "enforcement" action, it impliedly adopted the prevailing notion which limits "collective measures" to that category; moreover it defined "enforcement measures" so narrowly as to leave out of account measures designed to deal with threats to peace which are not actual breaches:

---

[46] Decisions such as the following led to the establishment, organization and deployment of the Force: Establishment of the U.N. Command for UNEF, Res. 1000 (ES-I), U.N. Gen. Ass. Off. Rec. 1st Em. Spec. Sess., Supp. No. 1, at 2-3 (A/3354) (1956); Appointment of the Chief of the Command, *ibid.*; Authorization of the Chief of the Command to recruit an officer corps, *ibid.*, and to proceed with the full organization of the Force, Res. 1001 (ES-I), *id.* at 3; Approval of the guiding principles and definitions of functions of the Force as expounded in a report of the Secretary-General, *ibid.*; Authorization of the Secretary-General to issue regulations and instructions for the Force and to take necessary executive and administrative measures, *ibid.*

[47] The Secretary-General did emphasize the "permissive" character of the Force which seems to be, like "recommendation," a notion seized upon as a means of identifying this kind of operation with the more basic "peaceful settlement" concept. The tendency to give independent force and effect to the concepts of "recommendation" and "permissiveness" as sources of authority for United Nations measures, believed to be one of the most confusing aspects of United Nations practice, is discussed more systematically, below, in Chapter 7.

[48] Bowett, *op. cit. supra* note 33, at 93-99, 289-90; Rosner, *The United Nations Emergency Force* 37-46 (1963); Hula, "The United Nations in Crisis," 27 Social Research 387, 418 (1960). To similar effect see Sohn, "The Authority of the United Nations to Establish and Maintain a Permanent United Nations Force," 52 Am. J. Int'l L. 229, 234 (1958).

[I]t can be said that the operations of ONUC did not include a use of armed force against a State which the Security Council, under Article 39, determined to have committed an act of aggression or to have breached the peace. The armed forces which were utilized in the Congo were not authorized to take military action against any State. The operation did not involve "preventive or enforcement measures" against any State under Chapter VII and therefore did not constitute "action" as that term is used in Article 11.[49]

Why did this Opinion not proceed to define the nature of ONUC under the Charter as it did in the case of UNEF? The answer may have been that, having excluded the "collective measures" concept, the concurring Judges were unable to find a category of United Nations activity within which it could satisfactorily be placed. True, ONUC shared with UNEF an important characteristic which seems to be officially regarded as an attribute of the "peaceful settlement" function, namely that it was deployed upon the request and with the consent of the Congolese Government. However, the existence of this factor was apparently not considered sufficient to overcome the obstacles which stood in the way of placing ONUC in that category. Among these obstacles were the facts (a) that ONUC was recognized as being formed pursuant to Chapter VII of the Charter, which imports quite a different character, (b) that it was, subsequently to its formation, authorized to use force, if necessary, to prevent civil war in the Congo and to arrest and expel "mercenaries" from that country, and (c) that it had actually engaged in combat. Also it may be questioned

---

[49] *Certain Expenses of the United Nations . . ., supra* note 42, at 177. Bowett cites this part of the Advisory Opinion as evidence that the Court did not consider Articles 41 or 42 to be the basis of ONUC. At the same time he concedes that the language of these provisions does not require that United Nations tangible pressures must be applied exclusively *against* states or other authorities. Bowett, *op. cit. supra* note 33, at 176. For this latter proposition he cites a statement of Schachter to similar effect, but in which that authority goes on to suggest that it was the intent of the San Francisco Conference that

"Article 42 would be resorted to for military action of an international character—that is to say, directed against the troops of a state or another governmental authority which bore responsibiliy for a breach of peace or act of aggression." Schachter, *supra* note 35, at 7-8.

It will be observed that this last statement resembles the passage quoted in the principal text in excluding "threats to the peace" as situations in which United Nations measures of the kind under discussion may be applied. Nevertheless, this category of situation is deliberately included in both Articles 1 (1) and 39 of the Charter. *Cf.* p. 38 *supra*.

that the element of "permissiveness" was actually present. The United Nations seemed prepared to act otherwise than by permission of the Government in the Matadi case, and certainly did not operate with the permission of the secessionist regime of Katanga Province, which formed one of the elements of the situation with which it was assigned to deal. This latter aspect of the Congolese case will be discussed below.

It is, of course, the view of the present discussion that the presence or absence of factors such as "permissiveness" and "recommendation" are really irrelevant to the problem under discussion. The two major Charter functions pertaining to the handling of disputes and situations are those of "collective measures" and "peaceful settlement," which are basically different in character, even though mutually dependant for their successful functioning. It is believed to be a disadvantage of the official position concerning ONUC—which emphasizes that the operation is not a collective measure while refraining from defining its affirmative character —that it tends to encourage the breaking down of the barrier between these major categories in the mind of the public, with resulting encroachment of the "collective measures" or "police" function into the proper realm of "peaceful settlement." This effect is believed to be concretely illustrated by the case of Katanga Province.

The Katanga Case

Katanga Province, the wealthiest part of the Congo because of its minerals and industrial development, announced its secession from and independence of the Congo shortly after the proclamation of independence of the latter country from Belgium in early July 1960. At about the same time, ONUC was sent into the Congo by the United Nations for reasons noted earlier in the present chapter. The Force was, in due course, authorized to use force, if necessary, to prevent civil war in the Congo, and to arrest and deport mercenaries of the Katanga regime. In the course of its duties it became several times engaged in combat with Katangese troops. Finally, in the period December 31, 1962-January 3, 1963, the Katangese secessionist regime collapsed coincident with the occupation by ONUC (virtually unopposed) of Jadotville and Kolwezi. The impression was thus strongly conveyed that ONUC had suppressed the secessionist regime by force.

The prevalence of this latter impression among the world public was furthered by other developments in the case. Among these was the consistent denial, by the United Nations itself and by some governments, that ONUC was an exercise of the "collective measures" (or "police") function of the United Nations. As observed at the conclusion of the preceding section, this denial, *per se,* had the tendency of suggesting that the purpose of the operation was to enforce a substantive United Nations decision concerning the internal regime of the Congo. This seeking of a permanent solution is, in fact, one element of the Charter concept of "peaceful settlement;" however, to the extent that it appeared to be seeking this end by force, rather than by persuasion, ONUC failed to give an impression of the "peaceful settlement" function as that concept was agreed to, in the Charter, by the peoples of the world. It is for these reasons that it can be said that ONUC tended to break down and confuse the distinction between the main Charter categories of "collective measures" and "peaceful settlement."

United Nations authorities also gave some positive indications that the Organization was, in fact, by this means attempting to enforce a substantive decision to suppress the secession. However, the indications on this latter point were far from consistent.

As an example, the United Nations Representative in Katanga indicated to the press that the hostilities which broke out in Elisabethville on September 13, 1961, were initiated by ONUC with the purpose of suppressing the secession;[50] however, the United Nations immediately superseded this statement by a pronouncement attributing the hostilities to an attack on United Nations forces while carrying out their duties.[51]

Conducive to the impression that the United Nations had decided the issues in dispute, and was enforcing the decision, was the Council resolution of November 24, 1961, providing, *inter alia,* as follows:

The Security Council
* * * *

1. *Strongly deprecates* the secessionist activities illegally carried out by the provincial administration of Katanga, with the aid of external resources, and manned by foreign mercenaries;

---

[50] N.Y. Times, Sept. 14, 1961, p. 1, col. 8.

[51] Report of the Officer-in-Charge of the United Nations Operation in the Congo to the Secretary-General . . . U.N. Security Council Off. Rec. 16th year, Supp. July-Sept. 1961, at 99 (S/4940) (1961).

* * * *

4. *Authorizes* the Secretary-General to take vigorous action, including the use of a requisite measure of force, if necessary, for the immediate apprehension, detention pending legal action and/or deportation of all foreign military and para-military personnel and political advisers not under the United Nations Command, and mercenaries. . . .

* * * *

9. *Declares* full and firm support for the Central Government of the Congo, and the determination to assist that Government, in accordance with the decisions of the United Nations, to maintain law and order and national integrity, . . . and to implement those decisions; . . .[52]

Paragraph 1 carries the import of a basic decision as to the status of the Katanga regime, since it declares it to be illegal. No indication is given as to the constitutional authority under which the Council was acting in making this declaration. The purpose of enforcing the decision is implied in paragraph 4, which gives clear and unequivocal authorization for the elimination by force of the foreign military personnel upon which the secessionist regime was dependent.

Later, on August 1, 1962, the Secretary-General said:

I have in mind economic pressure upon the Katangese authorities of a kind that will bring home to them the realities of their situation and the fact that Katanga is not a sovereign state and is not recognized by any government in the world as such. In the last resort and if all other efforts fail, this could justifiably go to the extent of barring all trade and financial relations.[53]

The indication here was, again, that the United Nations had the right to apply tangible pressures for the enforcement of a decision concerning the internal regime of the Congo. The supposed basis of authority for such a power may have been suggested by the Secretary-General in an interview on the American television on the following day, when he indicated that the United Nations might employ pressures against a secessionist regime simply on the basis of a request by the regime against which the secession is being attempted. There seems to be here involved the notion of "permissiveness" which, as has been observed above in the case of UNEF, seems to be invoked in such contexts as an attribute of the "peaceful settlement" function. However, as has been indicated

[52] *Id.* Supp. Oct.-Dec. 1961, at 148, 149 (S/5002) (1961).

[53] U.N. Doc. S/5053 Add. 11, Annex xxv; N.Y. Times, Aug. 2, 1962, p. 5, cols. 4-6. *Cf.* Bowett, *op. cit. supra* note 33, at 229-30.

above, the kind of action here being justified as "permissive" has no real relationship to the Charter function of "peaceful settlement." Nowhere has the United Nations been given the affirmative power to employ force or other tangible pressures for this purpose, nor can it be imagined that regimes of independent states which originated as secessionist movements would concede that the United Nations ever had the authority to attempt to suppress those movements.

In his annual report next following the collapse of the secessionist regime, the Secretary-General denied any interference in the dispute on the part of the United Nations:

> The Organization . . . had adhered closely to two fundamental principles laid down by the Council. First, it had respected the principle of non-interference in the internal political affairs of the Congo and had therefore refrained from intervening, beyond opposing secession in general, as required by the Council's resolutions. Secondly, it had also adhered to the principle of avoiding the use of force for political purposes. It was true, however, that the very presence and activity of the United Nations Force in the Congo had been an important factor in giving effective weight to United Nations opposition to secession. Not only had the United Nations never used the arms at its disposal to further the political aims of any group or to interfere with the country's political processes, but force had been used only in the most limited manner, with limited objectives, and no military initiative had ever been taken except as a last resort.

> The experience of ONUC has demonstrated the wisdom of the course originally ordered by the Security Council, namely, that the United Nations Force was not to be employed to regulate the internal political affairs of a country, even at the request of its Government.[54]

However, the annual report for the following year seems to give precisely the opposite indication:

> The United Nations operation in the Congo, having been directed by the Security Council to seek . . . to preserve the territorial integrity of the country, to prevent civil war and to eliminate mercenaries, was

---

[54] *Annual Report of the Secretary-General on the Work of the Organization 16 June 1962-15 June 1963*, U.N. Gen. Ass. Off. Rec. 18th Sess., Supp. No. 1, at 13 (A/5501) (1963). This report also states that a failure of communication occurred during the advance on Jadotville, as between the ONUC unit concerned and its headquarters, with the result that the advance was continued on the basis of plans improvised by officers on the spot. *Id.* at 9. Thus the United Nations may be said to have brought down the Katanga regime in a fit of absentmindedness, in so far as it might be thought that ONUC contributed immediately to this outcome.

inevitably opposed to the attempted secession of Katanga. While sparing no effort to achieve a peaceful solution, it did what it could, in collaboration with the Government of the Congo, to prevent the attempted secession from becoming an accomplished fact. It succeeded in its objective. . . . [T]he United Nations operation thwarted the Katanga secessionist effort. . . .[55]

Although the official indications, sketched above, seem to propound two opposing points of view as to whether ONUC was directed to the suppression of the Katanga regime, those suggesting an affirmative answer seem to be stronger than those which deny such a mission for the Force.

While the reasons underlying these various pronouncements are largely conjectural so far as the present writer is concerned, the arguments favoring the affirmative proposition just referred to would seem to follow logically from the basic United Nations position which denied that ONUC was a "collective measure." However, as a corollary to this latter denial, it had been asserted that the rule forbidding intervention in domestic affairs (Article 2 (7) of the Charter) was in force, and was the Charter provision which assured that the Force would not engage in combat. Therefore, any later indications that ONUC was attempting to put down the secession by force left the United Nations vulnerable to the objections that it was without power in the premises and that it was contravening the rule against intervention in domestic disputes. One of the factors in the United Nations positions under discussion consisted, perhaps, in the strong protests which were said to have emanated from several member states against any use of United Nations force against Katanga Province. This may be why the Secretary-General, in his annual report for 1962-1963, stressed the contention that ONUC had not been guilty of intervention in a domestic dispute.[56]

It is of further interest in this connection, however, that, in the same statement, he attributed the rule of non-intervention not to the Charter, but to a decision of the Security Council. The implication is thus given that the Security Council had the choice whether or not to apply the rule. In turn, the further implication would be that if the Council had not decided to apply it, that

---

[55] *Introduction to the Annual Report of the Secretary-General on the Work of the Organization 16 June 1963-15 June 1964, id.* 19th Sess., Supp. No. 1A, at 7 (A/5801/Add. 1) (1964).

[56] *Cf.* text accompanying note 54 *supra.*

organ could then have proceeded to the making and enforcement of a decision to suppress the secession. This implication, found in one of the strongest statements denying that ONUC was engaged in enforcing a substantive decision, is one reason for the conclusion, indicated above, that the conflicting pronouncements on this point in the Katanga case tend, on balance, to favor the proposition that the United Nations has the power to make and enforce such decisions as to the internal or external relations of states without their consent. The statement just referred to is also reminiscent of a statement of similar import, but of more general scope, contained in the Secretary-General's report on UNEF of October 9, 1958:

> Even in the case of UNEF, where the United Nations itself had taken a stand on decisive elements in the situation which gave rise to the creation of the Force, it was explicitly stated that the Force should not be used to enforce any specific political solution of pending problems or to influence the political balance decisive to such a solution. This precept would clearly impose a serious limitation on the possible use of United Nations elements, were it to be given general application to them whenever they are not created under Chapter VII of the Charter. However, I believe its acceptance to be necessary, if the United Nations is to be in a position to draw on Member countries for contributions in men and *matériel* to United Nations operations of this kind.[57]

This statement was obviously applicable to the Assembly, since that organ initiated UNEF. It seems somewhat surprising to find it thus suggested that the Assembly might, in its discretion, proceed to the enforcement of "any specific political solutions of pending problems or to influence the political balance decisive to such a solution" since the prevalent official view seems to be that that body's actions must be "recommendatory" and "permissive" in character.

However, and more basically, both of the two passages last-quoted are surprising in their suggestion that the Council and Assembly may enforce substantive decisions, in view of the lack of any such authorization to be found in the Charter and in view of the rule of non-intervention which *is* incorporated in that instrument.

One recalls, in this connection, the Secretariat memorandum in the Trieste case suggesting that the Security Council, in the exercise of its primary responsibility for the maintenance of peace

---

[57] "Summary Study . . .," *supra* note 12, at 29.

and security, is not limited to specific powers laid down in the Charter, but only by general purposes and principles of the Organization.[58] Does the above-quoted statement of 1958 have the purpose of advancing this concept and enlarging it to include powers of the Assembly comparable to those earlier cited as applicable to the Security Council? At first glance such a suggestion might seem to be contradicted by the simultaneous United Nations policy of denying that ONUC and, *a fortiori,* UNEF, were "collective measures," and the corollary invocation of the non-intervention rule of Article 2 (7) (here cited as a firm principle of the Charter)[59] in support of the proposition that ONUC was forbidden the use of force. However, the "collective measures" concept is restrictive of United Nations powers; its observance tends to restrict applications of United Nations pressure to cases of aggression, other breaches of peace and threats to peace. A move to narrow the applicability of the concept, then, tends to broaden the powers of the Organization. A move of this kind is, in fact, underway as appears from the case of ONUC. A parallel movement to broaden the decision-making and enforcement powers of the United Nations is also to be inferred, not only from the passages under discussion but from other developments which will be discussed below in Chapters 5 and 7.

"Collective Measure" or "Enforcement of United Nations Decision"?

The Katanga case, in another of its aspects, illustrates that situations may arise in which a United Nations military operation, even though it may be designated as a "collective measure," may require political guidance, and may be given a mission to perform which is indistinguishable from the enforcement of a substantive decision on the issue in dispute. The resulting question has thus been asked and answered, it is believed correctly, by Professor Eagleton:

> This distinction between enforcement of an Assembly resolution and the handling of a threat to the peace has been attacked as escapism, as "elaborate legal niceties," as a too finely drawn technical distinction; but it is much more than this. It signifies that proper respect is being paid to the constitutional law of the United Nations.[60]

---

[58] *Cf.* pp. 28-29 *supra.*

[59] *Cf.* pp. 104-05 *supra;* see also p. 123 *infra.*

[60] Eagleton, "Palestine and the Constitutional Law of the United Nations," 42 Am. J. Int'l L. 397, 399 (1948).

The correctness of this conclusion scarcely needs elaboration in the context of the present discussion, which has as its main thesis the proposition that it is desirable and necessary to build up the Charter in terms of world public opinion so that it can become the effective basis of a world legal order. This means, in turn, the building up of the major component Charter concepts which, so far as the present discussion is concerned, are mainly those of "peaceful settlement" and "collective measures." It is essential, in this view of the matter, that applications of tangible pressure by the United Nations have the *bona fide* purpose of dealing with threats to peace or breaches of peace, since these are the only purposes for which the world public has agreed, on a mutual and reciprocal basis, that such pressures may be used.[61] At the same time, one would not contend that such measures should be applied without guidance; nor can it be denied that such guidance might result, in effect, in the enforcement of substantive decisions affecting the relations of states or other entities without their consent.

A situation of the kind was in prospect during the Korean operation, when it appeared that forces under the United Nations command were going to advance to the northern boundaries of Korea. The General Assembly felt impelled in these circumstances to give some guidance as to what the objectives of the operation should be, and adopted resolution 376 (V)[62] which contained the following provisions, among others:

> *The General Assembly*
> * * *
> *Recalling* that the essential objective of the resolutions of the General Assembly referred to above was the establishment of a unified, independent and democratic Government of Korea,
> 1. *Recommends* that
> (a) All appropriate steps be taken to ensure conditions of stability throughout Korea;
> (b) All constituent acts be taken, including the holding of elections, under the auspices of the United Nations, for the establishment of a unified, independent and democratic government in the sovereign State of Korea. . . .

The Korean case was, no doubt, less conducive to confusion than was the Katanga case with respect to the true nature of the power

---

[61] See note 3 *supra* and accompanying text.

[62] U.N. Gen. Ass. Off. Rec. 5th Sess., Supp. No. 20, at 9 (A/1775) (1950).

being exercised by the United Nations since, in the former case, no one could have had any doubt that the United Nations operation had the essential purpose of dealing with an aggression. While the Katanga case is undoubtedly more difficult, still no reason is perceived why the world public should not have found the actions and policies of the Organization at least equally acceptable had they been represented as being basically designed to eliminate a threat to international peace in the Congo.

To pursue the argument by analogy, we may regard a given United Nations action, such as the Congolese military operation, as a potential building block in the structure of a world security system. In appearance, it may be regarded in either of two lights: as a "collective measure" designed to deal with a threat to peace in the Congo, or as an undertaking to enforce a United Nations decision as to what the internal regime of the Congo should be. If the operation is deliberately excluded from the former category, and placed in the latter, it tends, as between the two relevant major Charter concepts of "collective measures" and "peaceful settlement," to gravitate toward the latter. However, no real foundation in public opinion here exists, since the peoples of the world have recognized and accepted this function of the United Nations, on a full basis of reciprocity, only in terms of the basic power of recommendation. On the other hand, if this particular "building block" is treated as a "collective measure," it becomes a solid part of the structure because there is a foundation for it in the Charter with the concurrence—at least in principle—of public opinion. Thus used, in accordance with an accepted Charter principle, the block may serve to strengthen the whole structure.

"Practical" Reasons for Denial that ONUC Was a "Collective Measure"

It has appeared, in some other aspects of this discussion, that the long-range interests represented by law and Charter principle have been subordinated by governments to what they conceived to be their immediate and practical policy interests in particular disputes. Examination of some cases has suggested that policies better designed to serve the interests of law and principle would not always have been so detrimental to immediate and "practical" interests as seems to have been supposed.

In the case of ONUC, we can best consider this question in terms of the denial that the operation was a "collective measure," notwithstanding that no strong affirmative effort was made to prove that it *was* such a measure. In the Katanga phase of the case, it is true, another issue arose involving affirmations and denials that ONUC had made, and was enforcing, a decision as to the substantive issue in dispute; however, no clear-cut position emerged on this point.

The denial that ONUC was a "collective measure" seems, initially, to have been based upon the prevalent notion which equates "collective measures" with "enforcement action" against states and as therefore being likely to entail combat operations; the consequent apprehension was said to have been that if the measure were regarded as being in this category, states would have been reluctant to contribute troops.[63] To allay these fears, it has been suggested, it would not have been enough that the legal authority of the operation to use force should have been limited by the competent United Nations organ; it was essential that the limitation should have come from the Charter itself.[64] Otherwise, it is suggested, governments would have feared that they were being asked to contribute troops "on the basis of blank checks permitting the use of these troops in conflict with armed groups of Congolese."[65]

The Charter limitation desired to be invoked to allay these fears was the prohibition against intervention in domestic disputes, contained in Article 2 (7). The theory employed was that if an operation is not a "collective measure," then the rule of non-intervention is not overridden, and remains in force.[66] However, it is not believed that the applicability of the rule embodied in Article 2 (7) depends upon what an operation is called. The question is, rather, whether or not a given operation is dealing with an international situation; if it is, then the rule pertaining to domestic matters is, *ipso facto,* inapplicable. In the case under discussion, ONUC had the purpose, from the outset, of dealing with a threat to international peace, and the existence of such a threat in the Congo was officially regarded as one of its juridical bases.

For reasons noted above, ONUC appears to possess the objective characteristics of a "collective measure" under the Charter. This being so, there appears to be no other Charter category in which it could appropriately be placed. Within this category, the

---

[63] *Cf.* p. 94 *supra.*

[64] *Cf.* Schachter, *supra* note 5, at 223.

[65] *Ibid.*

[66] See note 25 *supra* and accompanying text.

framers of the Charter intended the competent organs (then regarded as being only the Security Council) to exercise all necessary discretion in tailoring particular measures to deal with particular situations. ONUC seems to prove that, at least in some complex situations, the application of appropriate measures cannot be
carried out in any other way. Notwithstanding official denials that
the operation was a "collective measure," the competent organ
proceeded to authorize it to use force in given contingencies and
for particular purposes, and the Force actually became several
times engaged in combat. At least by now, it would seem, as a practical matter, the world's statesmen must be aware of this relationship between official avowals and actual conduct. The history of
ONUC furthermore appears to furnish proof that the framers
of the Charter were right in vesting the decision of such matters
within the discretion of the competent organs of the United Nations. They obviously and necessarily considered that the decisions
of these organs would always be made with due discretion and
responsibility. Except on these bases it is difficult to see how, as a
general proposition, the Organization can ever be expected to fulfill its ultimate purpose. The recognition of the true source of
authority would therefore seem to entail nothing in the way of
"blank checks" to United Nations operations. Such recognition
would seem also to have positive advantages from the standpoint
of Charter development.

It may be argued against this view that, at the time the Charter
was drafted, it was contemplated that all such decisions would be
made by the Council with the concurrence of the permanent members; that there would accordingly have been little risk to the states
contributing forces. Notwithstanding that this was the case, it is
still only to be assumed that the responsible officials of the world's
governments are completely aware of the changes that have occurred. They necessarily must assess the risks involved in such
matters as troop contributions on the basis of the realities of given
situations more or less uninfluenced by what the operation may
officially be called.

The conclusion is then believed to be inescapable that member
states contributing troops to the Suez, Congolese and Cyprus operations did so with their eyes open, and thereby accepted risks of the
kind that have to be accepted if the United Nations is ever to
achieve the goal of becoming the framework of an effective system based on the rule of law.

In retrospect, therefore, it is not perceived that pronounced advantages necessarily attached to the policy of denying the status of a "collective measure" to ONUC, such as would compensate for the long-term disadvantage which this course of action is believed to have caused to the development of the rule of law in international relations.

Chapter V

"Decisions" and "Enforcement" In Human Rights Cases

The tendencies discussed in the two preceding chapters find their most important recent manifestations in cases concerning the Charter principle of "human rights" and the related principle of "self-determination." This discussion, being concerned with an essentially different subject—e.g., possibilities of advancing the rule of law through the handling of disputes and situations by the United Nations—does not purport to be comprehensive on the subject of human rights. At the same time it is pertinent to note that in so far as this, or any, discussion impinges on the Charter principle of human rights, it is dealing with a subject of unique importance representing, in an important sense, what the Organization is really about. By the same token it is true, as Professor Lauterpacht has said, that "the manner in which the acknowledgment and the safeguards of human rights as embodied in the Charter will be given effect will in itself be a powerful source of the political and moral strength of the United Nations."[1]

Human rights and the principle of self-determination are set forth as major purposes of the United Nations in Article 1 of the Charter:

> The Purposes of the United Nations are:
> * * *
> 2. To develop friendly relations among nations based on respect for the principle of equal rights and self-determination of peoples, and to take other appropriate measures to strengthen universal peace;
> 3. To achieve international cooperation in solving international problems of an economic, social, cultural, or humanitarian character, and in promoting and encouraging respect for human rights and for fundamental freedoms for all without distinction as to race, sex, language, or religion; . . . .

---

[1] Lauterpacht, "The International Protection of Human Rights," 70 Academie de droit international, Recueil des Cours 5-6 (1947-I).

The General Assembly is given the function of initiating studies and making recommendations for the purpose of "assisting in the realization" of human rights (Article 13). The promotion of human rights is made a particular task of the United Nations in the chapter of the Charter dealing with international economic and social cooperation and, in this connection, "All Members pledge themselves to take joint and separate action in cooperation with the Organization for the achievement of" these purposes (Articles 55 and 56). In particular, the Economic and Social Council is empowered (in Article 62 (2)) to:

> make recommendations for the purpose of promoting respect for, and observance of, human rights and fundamental freedoms for all.

It will be observed that the human rights provisions do not purport to impose specific obligations on states to observe particular rights, and that the powers of the Organization in the premises are recommendatory in character.

Human Rights

In the Universal Declaration of Human Rights,[2] adopted in 1948, the General Assembly undertook to define the particular rights which it considered to be embraced within the Charter concept. The legal nature of this Declaration is indicated in the following passages of the relevant Assembly resolution:

> *Whereas* Member States have pledged themselves to achieve, in co-operation with the United Nations, the promotion of universal respect for and observance of human rights and fundamental freedoms,
>
> *Whereas* a common understanding of these rights and freedoms is of the greatest importance for the full realization of this pledge,
>
> *Now, therefore, the General Assembly Proclaims* this Universal Declaration of Human Rights as a common standard of achievement for all peoples and all nations, to the end that every individual and every organ of society . . . shall strive . . . to promote respect for these rights and freedoms and . . . to secure their universal and effective recognition and observance. . . .[3]

At the same time the Assembly had under way a project for the incorporation of these particular rights, or as many of them as pos-

---

[2] Res. 217 (III), *Resolutions* 71, U.N. Gen. Ass. Off. Rec. 3d Sess., Pt. 1 (A/810) (1948).

[3] *Id.* at 72.

sible, in a "Covenant," or treaty, with provision for implementation. The rights thus specified would become legally binding as to states which accepted and ratified the Covenant. It was thus made clear that human rights under the Charter and the Universal Declaration were not officially regarded as representing rights of the kind which could be applied and enforced in specific concrete situations. The Covenant—a separate treaty—would have the purpose of giving them this character.

Although the proposed Covenant—now become two proposed Covenants—is not a matter of direct concern to the present discussion, it is pertinent, for background purposes, to invite attention to the difficulties that would appear to be inherent in this mode of approach to the subject. These difficulties are, no doubt, reflected to some extent in the fact that at the time of writing, in 1965, the Covenants have not yet been completed. By contrast with the more strictly international kind of Charter principles which form the general subject of the present discussion—e.g. principles which might be applied to the solution of international disputes and situations—human rights stand at a considerable disadvantage from the point of view of what can be accomplished through international action. This is because, first of all, progress in these matters frequently necessitates change in established social custom, and secondly, because the decisive action in such matters must, in the end, be taken by the states themselves. The best prospect of advancing this cause through international action might be suggested as lying in the kind of process under discussion in the present study, e.g. the gradual development of public opinion in support of the relevant international principles, and the simultaneous gradual bringing into alignment of this opinion with public opinion as it applies to individual state policies. The persuasive approach based on the recommendatory power of the United Nations is believed to be a valuable and, indeed, indispensable means of advancing the rule of law in general as well as those particular aspects of it which find expression in the Charter. Whether, in the human rights field, a better method can be found through treaties embodying specifically binding obligations and enforcement procedures, would seem to be problematical.

The Universal Declaration of Human Rights has been a powerful influence in promoting human rights.[4] It has served an im-

---

[4] McDougal and Bebr, "Human Rights in the United Nations," 58 Am. J. Int'l L. 603, 614-15, 637-40 (1964) and authorities there cited.

portant function in setting up standards agreed to in principle, but not yet achieved in practice, and has thereby served as a rallying point for the mobilization of public opinion for their further advancement. From this point of view, an element of strength of the Universal Declaration is its flexibility and readiness of adaptation to widely varying conditions among different peoples and in different parts of the world. Also, within the generally "recommendatory" spirit of the Charter and of the Universal Declaration, the United Nations, principally through its Human Rights Commission, has made valuable contributions to the advancement of human rights. Such progress has been made by means of studies, collection of information, conferences, the giving of advice when asked, and similar methods.

The writer is inclined to believe that, as between the Universal Declaration and the "Covenants," the former is likely to prove the more effective instrument for the advancement of human rights.[5]

Of a more peremptory character, in contrast to the Universal Declaration, is the United Nations Declaration on the Elimination of All Forms of Racial Discrimination, adopted by the General Assembly in 1963.[6] In language and general tone it gives the impression of a legislative enactment. The Assembly does not purport to "recommend," but rather "proclaims" the Declaration, the first articles of which provide in part:

---

[5] Richard Gardner, an official of the United States Department of State, in a recent unofficial publication, has ably argued the case for adherence to the covenants by the United States when they are completed. Gardner, *In Pursuit of World Order* 249-254 (1964). Admitting that such action would not, in itself, bring about automatic improvement in the observance of human rights (p. 252), this authority argues that adherence by the United States would increase that country's influence in future efforts to improve such observance. This line of thought raises a question as to whether the "covenants" could bring about progress in securing human rights (over and above that accomplished by the Universal Declaration) which would compensate for the damage that might be assumed to accrue to the over-all role of law in international relations through concluding treaties that are expected *not* to be observed by some states for some time to come. Such practice would seem to conflict with the widely held proposition which is incorporated in the preamble of the Charter, that the observance of treaties—*pacta sunt servanda*—is one of the essential foundations of the rule of law.

[6] Res. 1904 (XVIII), U.N. Gen. Ass. Off. Rec. 18th Sess., Supp. No. 15, at 35 (A/5515) (1963).

Article 1

Discrimination between human beings on the ground of race, colour or ethnic origin is an offence to human dignity and shall be condemned as a denial of the principles of the Charter . . ., as a violation of the human rights and fundamental freedoms proclaimed in the Universal Declaration of Human Rights, as an obstacle to friendly and peaceful relations among nations and as a fact capable of disturbing peace and security among peoples.

Article 2

1. No state, institution, group or individual shall make any discrimination whatsoever in matters of human rights and fundamental freedoms in the treatment of persons, groups of persons or institutions on the ground of race, colour or ethnic origin.[7]

One does not question the rightness of the principles underlying such statements, but one may question whether this mode of stating them contributes to practical progress in any way comparable to the more modestly worded Universal Declaration. It seems equally reasonable to suggest that the adoption of peremptory language, giving the impression of legislative enactments, represents an attempt to compensate for the absence of power in the United Nations to make such enactments. It seems highly doubtful that the desired result can be obtained in this way.

Turning from such general pronouncements to specific situations, there has been a point of view from the beginning which maintains not only that the human rights provisions of the Charter contain legal obligations, but also that there ought to be international procedures for promoting the observance of these obligations in particular situations. Possible procedures for realizing these rights in concrete situations, such as were suggested by Lauterpacht and others *vis-à-vis* the United Nations,[8] and such as have achieved fruition in the limited context of the European Convention on Human Rights of the Council of Europe,[9] are beyond the scope of

---

[7] *Id.* at 36.

[8] For proposals made in the United Nations and certain proposed measures of implementation, see United Nations *Yearbook on Human Rights.* See generally, Lauterpacht, *An International Bill of Rights of Man* (1945); Lauterpacht, *supra* note 1; Lauterpacht, *International Law and Human Rights* (1950); Green, *The United Nations and Human Rights* (1956); Moskowitz, *Human Rights and World Order* (1958); McDougal and Bebr, *supra* note 4.

[9] Council of Europe, *European Convention on Human Rights: Collected Texts,* Section 1 (1963); 45 Am. J. Int'l L. Supp. 24 (1951).

present discussion. Within the scope of this discussion might be the observation that in this, as in other aspects of the United Nations, public opinion is obviously not yet prepared to give effect to the Charter principle through international action.[9a] Moreover, some of the uses made of the United Nations, to be noted below, in connection with disputes and situations involving human rights questions, are not very conducive to the achievement of the relevant capability on the part of the Organization.

From the early years of the United Nations there have been disputes on human rights issues which have been handled by the General Assembly and Security Council. Resulting resolutions were, at first, recommendatory in character, but have later taken on the appearance of binding decisions. A resolution of the latter kind, adopted by the General Assembly on November 28, 1961,[10] provides in part as follows:

> *The General Assembly.*
>
> * * *
>
> *Considering* that in its resolutions 616 B (VII) of 5 December 1952, 917 (X) of 6 December 1955 and 1248 (XIII) of 30 October 1958 the General Assembly has declared that racial policies designed to perpetuate or increase discrimination are inconsistent with the Charter of the United Nations and with the pledges under Article 56 of the Charter,
>
> * * *
>
> 2. *Strongly deprecates* the continued and total disregard by the Government of South Africa of its obligations under the Charter. . . .

Taken by itself, such a resolution could be interpreted as being no more than an expression of opinion on the part of the Assembly and therefore as action concerning which no constitutional question would arise. However, as this quoted passage indicates, there has been a series of resolutions along this general line, and there has also been a tendency to regard them, increasingly, as embodying binding judgments as to compatibility of state actions with Charter obligations. Dr. Higgins says in this connection:

> An examination of practice shows that . . . most resolutions which are concerned with a situation that is primarily a denial of human rights refer to breach of Articles 55 and 56, which are unequivocal and clear, and call upon the particular state; moreover, resolutions addressed to specific states nearly always have been based on a report or finding by a committee of a breach of these particular articles on

[9a] Compare Falk in chapters cited *supra* Ch. 3 note 5.
[10] Res. 1663 (XVI), U.N. Gen. Ass. Off. Rec. 16th Sess., Supp. No. 17, at 10-11 (A/5100) (1961).

human rights. In other words, action by the United Nations in human-rights areas, where such action consists of a finding against an individual state, is invariably based on a *prior legal consideration* of whether there has been a breach of the Charter provisions on human rights.[11]

Maintaining that the Charter provisions on human rights do constitute specific obligations binding on individual states, this authority says:

> If one accepts this view, it is possible to look at the practice of the United Nations on human rights in a new light: namely, that the jurisdiction which the United Nations had undeniably asserted is based on the right to condemn, and to demand rectification of, breaches of specific articles of the Charter which give rise to legal obligations.[12]

There is thus probably reflected a general point of view. A question to be raised concerning it takes into account the notable lack of results which this approach has obtained. No reason is perceived, in relation to these matters, for altering the general view maintained in the present discussion that if the Charter is to be used as the instrumentality for advancing the rule of law in international relations, it is necessary, first of all, to increase the weight of moral force behind the Charter.

There are, meanwhile, several relatively detailed points that might be considered. One is the fact that under Article 6 of the Charter the General Assembly, on the recommendation of the Security Council, may expel a state for persistent violation of Charter principles. Thus, for this particular purpose, these organs are given conjointly what amounts to a judicial power to determine when a state has breached the principles of the Charter, including, of course, the Charter principle of human rights. Expulsion procedures on the ground of persistent violation of human rights would require a minimum of explanation to the world public in view of this provision. The provision would, however, hardly bear interpretation as conferring competence on these organs enabling them to pass judgment on the general observance of human rights by member states.

The other consideration to be mentioned at this point concerns the facts that allegations that states have violated the human rights

---

[11] Higgins, *The Development of International Law through the Political Organs of the United Nations* 119 (1963).

[12] *Ibid.*

clauses of the Charter necessarily involve questions of Charter interpretation, and that such questions are recognized as generally falling within the competence of the organ seized of the particular situation in which the question arises. However, the competence of the Assembly and Council in such matters is not so comprehensive as to empower them to impose a given interpretation upon a state against its consent, much less to hold that state in violation. Committee IV/2 of the San Francisco Conference, which considered this problem, stated in its report that "It is to be understood, of course, that if an interpretation made by any organ of the Organization or by a committee of jurists is not generally acceptable it will be without binding force."[13] There appears to be here no derogation of the general rule that a state cannot be bound to a new rule of law without its consent.

The United Nations powers just referred to—the power to adjudicate in connection with the expulsion procedure, and the power of Charter interpretation—could conceivably be made to contribute to the development of a rule of law under which the Assembly or Security Council might be recognized as having the power to make binding decisions with respect to the compliance of states with the human rights provisions of the Charter. Such a development seems distant, however, in view of the apparent probability that neither the major states nor the generality of states are prepared to recognize a power of this kind in the sense that it might be directed against themselves.

Not only has the United Nations been caused to appear as making binding decisions as to substantive issues in dispute involving human rights, but it has also apparently undertaken to enforce decisions of this kind. Among several resolutions to this effect in the case concerning *apartheid* in the Republic of South Africa, that of the General Assembly, dated November 6, 1962,[14] is, perhaps, most far reaching. It provides in part:

The General Assembly,
* * *
1. *Deplores* the failure of the Government of the Republic of South Africa to comply with the repeated requests and demands of

---

[13] Report of Rapporteur of Committee IV/2 to Commission IV, *The United Nations Conference on International Organization: Selected Documents* 880 (1946).

[14] Res. 1761 (XVII), U.N. Gen. Ass. Off. Rec. 17th Sess., Supp. No. 17, at 9 (A/5217) (1962).

the General Assembly and of the Security Council and its flouting of world public opinion by refusing to abandon its racial policies;

2. *Strongly deprecates* the continued and total disregard by the Government of South Africa of its obligations under the Charter of the United Nations and, furthermore, its determined aggravation of racial issues by enforcing measures of increasing ruthlessness involving violence and bloodshed;

3. *Reaffirms* that the continuance of those policies seriously endangers international peace and security;

4. *Requests* Member States to take the following measures, separately or collectively, in conformity with the Charter, to bring about the abandonment of those policies:

 (a) Breaking off diplomatic relations with the Government of the Republic of South Africa or refraining from establishing such relations;

 (b) Closing their ports to all vessels flying the South African flag;

 (c) Enacting legislation prohibiting their ships from entering South African ports;

 (d) Boycotting all South African goods and refraining from exporting goods, including all arms and ammunition, to South Africa;

 (e) Refusing landing and passage facilities to all aircraft belonging to the Government of South Africa and companies registered under the laws of South Africa;

* * *

8. *Requests* the Security Council to take appropriate measures, including sanctions, to secure South Africa's compliance with the resolutions of the General Assembly and of the Security Council on this subject and, if necessary, to consider action under Article 6 of the Charter.

It will be observed that this resolution undertakes, in paragraph 4, to initiate a wide range of diplomatic and economic pressures against the Republic of South Africa and makes it clear that these have the purpose of compelling that country to change its internal racial policies. While some question of mixed motive of the kind that has been mentioned in previous chapters might be suggested by paragraph 3, in which the situation in South Africa is said to endanger international peace, any implication that this is an application of the "collective measures" function seems to be overruled by the plain statement that the measures have the purpose of enforcing substantive decisions of the United Nations.

Why did the Assembly, at the same time, consider it appropriate to ask the Council to apply "sanctions" having, apparently, the same objective? What would the Council be expected to do which would be different in kind from what the Assembly was doing in

this resolution? The answer to this last question is obscure. As to
the first question however, it seems fairly clear that the Assembly
did not regard its own action as being in the nature of "enforcement measures" or "sanctions." This opinion probably derived,
first of all, from the prevailing view that the Assembly is without
Charter power to initiate such measures. Secondly, it was apparently felt that, since the Assembly was merely "recommending" that
member states take the desired action, the whole operation was
thereby placed in the "permissive" or "peaceful settlement" category. This view of the matter was evidenced by the Security Council when, some months later, it took up the case. Although it had
been asked by the Assembly to apply measures in the nature of
"sanctions," or "enforcement measures," the Council in initiating
an arms embargo against South Africa, used language intended to
have a recommendatory effect with respect to the participation of
states in the measure, with the evident purpose of indicating that
the measure was not to be regarded as of the "collective" or "enforcement" variety.[15]

The Representative of the United States in the Council, apparently speaking for himself and some other representatives, stated
that the changes in language had this purpose, and indicated, further, that the Council's measure was to be regarded as an exercise of the "peaceful settlement" function of the United Nations.[16]

There is thus recalled the effort of the Secretariat, referred to
in the preceding chapter, to establish that UNEF and UNEF-type
forces would fall within the "peaceful settlement" function of the
Organization. In both cases this attempted designation is believed
inappropriate to the measures, since they were not persuasive in
character, but were rather applications of tangible pressure.

By virtue of the plain statement of intent which has been noted
in the Assembly resolution referred to above, the resolution must
have tended to give the impression of attempting to enforce United
Nations decisions as to what South Africa's internal policies should
be. The language of the Council Resolution of August 7, 1963,
not reproduced here, contained indications of "mixed motives,"
permitting interpretation as being intended either to deal with a
threat to peace or to enforce substantive decisions. However, the

[15] U.N. Security Council Off. Rec. 18th year, Supp. July-Sept. 1963, at
73 (S/5386) (1963).
[16] U.N. Security Council Off. Rec. 18th year, 1056th meeting 6-7 (S/PV.
1056) (1963). *Cf.* p. 146 *infra.*

evident intent of the Council to place the measures outside the "collective measures" category must have tended to create the impression that they did have the purpose of attempting to enforce substantive decisions of the United Nations. Any tendency of this kind would have been strengthened by statements of several delegations asserting that the Organization had the right to make binding and enforceable decisions in such matters.[17]

Self-Determination of Peoples and Nations

With respect to the International Covenants on Human Rights, the Assembly, in 1952, decided:

> to include in the International Covenant or Covenants on Human Rights an article on the right of all peoples and nations to self-determination in reaffirmation of the principle enunciated in the Charter of the United Nations. This Article shall be drafted in the following terms: "All peoples shall have the right of self-determination," and shall stipulate that all States, including those having responsibility for the administration of Non-Self-Governing Territories, should promote the realization of that right, in conformity with the Purposes and Principles of the United Nations, and that States having responsibility for the administration of Non-Self-Governing Territories should promote the realization of that right in relation to the peoples of such Territories.[18]

---

[17] The Nigerian Delegation said that "if the major countries of the world were prepared to go along with us and apply economic sanctions to South Africa, Dr. Verwoerd, Dr. Louw and their associates would mend their ways." U.N. Gen. Ass. Off. Rec. 17th Sess., Plenary 667 (A/PV. 1164) (1962). The Tunisian Representative in the Security Council said:

> "The South African Government, which is now evading the obligations it has accepted under the Charter, particularly under Articles 4 and 25, cannot disregard our decisions indefinitely. The time has come for the Security Council to take positive, firm and immediate action to dispel any doubts as to the determination of the United Nations to ensure that the aims of the Charter are achieved without delay in the Republic of South Africa." U.N. Security Council Off. Rec. 18th year, 1050th meeting 18 (S/PV. 1050) (1963).

The reference to Article 4 in this passage doubtless has regard to the requirement, as a condition of membership in the Organization, that states accept the obligations of the Charter. As to the relevancy of Article 25 cf. p. 86 supra.

[18] Res. 545 (VI), U.N. Gen. Ass. Off. Rec. 6th Sess., Supp. No. 20, at 36 (A/2119) (1952). In 1955 the Assembly's Third Committee adopted a specific article designed to carry out the Assembly's directive. Id. 10th Sess., 3d Comm. 261-62 (A/C. 3/SR. 676) (1955); Yearbook of the United Nations 1955, at 153-58 (1956).

The Assembly thus, by implication, recognized that the Charter principle of self-determination did not, in itself, constitute a specifically binding legal obligation, and that its further elaboration by treaty would be necessary for it to achieve this status. Subsequently, there has been a gradually increasing tendency to maintain that the principle has acquired legally binding force, in relation to concrete situations, notwithstanding that the Covenants embodying the statement of the right remain unfinished and, of course, unratified.

Assertions along this line sometimes cite a series of resolutions, principally of the General Assembly, which "recognize" the right as applicable to particular situations. Resolutions of this kind with respect to Morocco and Tunisia were passed in committee in 1953, but failed of the necessary two-thirds for adoption.[19] After several efforts in the Algerian case, the General Assembly, in 1960, recognized the right of the Algerian people to self-determination.[20]

Also adopted in 1960 was the Assembly's important resolution 1514 (XV) incorporating its "Declaration on Granting Independence to Colonial Countries and Peoples,"[21] in which that body:

Declares that:

1. The subjection of peoples to alien subjugation, domination and exploitation constitutes a denial of fundamental human rights, is contrary to the Charter of the United Nations and is an impediment to the promotion of world peace and co-operation.

2. All peoples have the right to self-determination; by virtue of that right they freely determine their political status and freely pursue their economic, social and cultural development.

3. Inadequacy of political, economic, social or educational preparedness should never serve as a pretext for delaying independence.

4. All armed action or repressive measures of all kinds directed against dependent peoples shall cease in order to enable them to exercise peacefully and freely their right to complete independence, and the integrity of their national territory shall be respected.

---

[19] *Annual Report of the Secretary-General on the Work of the Organization 1 July 1953-30 June 1954,* U.N. Gen. Ass. Off. Rec. 9th Sess., Supp. No. 1, at 22-24 (A/2663) (1954) (Morocco); *id.* at 21-22 (Tunisia).

[20] Res. 1573 (XV), *id.* 15th Sess., Supp. No. 16, at 3 (A/4684) (1960). The development referred to is traced in Higgins, *op. cit. supra* note 11, at 95-97, citing, as to part, Alwan, *Algeria before the United Nations* 67 (1959).

[21] U.N. Gen. Ass. 15th Sess., Supp. No. 16, at 66 (A/4684) (1960).

5. Immediate steps shall be taken, in Trust and Non-Self-Governing Territories or all other territories which have not yet attained independence, to transfer all powers to the peoples of those territories, without any conditions or reservations, in accordance with their freely expressed will and desire, without any distinction as to race, creed or colour, in order to enable them to enjoy complete independence and freedom.

6. Any attempt aimed at the partial or total disruption of the national unity and the territorial integrity of a country is incompatible with the purposes and principles of the Charter of the United Nations.

7. All States shall observe faithfully and strictly the provisions of the Charter of the United Nations, the Universal Declaration of Human Rights and the present Declaration on the basis of equality, non-interference in the internal affairs of all States, and respect for the sovereign rights of all peoples and their territorial integrity.

The language is peremptory in tone, giving the impression of a legislative enactment,[22] like the later Declaration on the Elimination of All Forms of Racial Discrimination, for which it may have served, in this respect, as the model. Some have maintained that it is indeed legislative in character, making the right of self-determination legally binding and obligatory,[23] and it has at least had the effect of fortifying opinions which tend toward according it this status.[24]

The Iranian Delegation said of the Declaration, in 1961:

From the legal standpoint, this resolution may be said to have introduced new elements into international law. The declarations of States have always been regarded as one of the sources of the rules of international law. What differentiates the Declaration from the declarations of States of former times is that, instead of representing the wishes of a few Powers from a limited geographical region, it is an expression of the will of nearly all the members of

[22] "How strong the wording of this resolution is needs no underlining. In it the right of self-determination is regarded not as a right enforceable at some future time under indefinite circumstances, but as a legal right enforceable here and now." Higgins, *op. cit. supra* note 11, at 100.

[23] The Liberian Delegation to the General Assembly stated that it was "a decision of this Assembly and thereby imposes immediate juridical and moral obligations on Member States." U.N. Gen. Ass. Off. Rec. 16th Sess., Plenary 639 (A/PV. 1054) (1961).

[24] Dr. Higgins states that the Declaration, "taken together with seventeen years of evolving practice by United Nations organs, provides ample evidence that there now exists a legal right of self-determination." Higgins, *op. cit. supra* note 11, at 104.

the existing international community. Moreover, it is endowed with special force and value because, in it, the wishes of States square entirely with the aspirations of the peoples.[25]

This statement may be compared with that of the Secretary-General that the Declaration "may be regarded as a comprehensive re-statement in elaborated form of the principle laid down in the Charter."[26] The two statements are not necessarily contradictory since a declaration which restates and elaborates a Charter principle such as this, which has the nature of a goal, may represent a step in the evolution of the principle into a rule of law applicable in concrete cases. However, before a new rule can be said to have come about in this way there must be evidence of its general acceptance in practice.

The practice of states does not appear to give the necessary support to the proposition that the principle of "self-determination" has achieved the status of a binding and applicable rule of law. For instance, in the Algerian case, while France had, by 1959, announced that the principle of self-determination would be applied,[27] its representative continued to claim that the case was essentially within its domestic jurisdiction and that the Assembly, in consequence, was not even entitled to discuss it.[28] Such a position is hardly compatible with a recognition on the part of France that the subject matter is governed by a rule of international law, either under the Charter or otherwise. Another example may be found in the British assertion that the Assembly was acting in an essentially domestic matter, and was thereby *ultra vires,* in adopting, in June 1962, a recommendatory resolution on the Southern Rhodesian question.[29] In the case of the Portuguese colonies, to be discussed below, it is well known that Portugal has repeatedly denied any right on the part of the United Nations to consider this question.

A related difficulty in recognizing the right of "self-determination" as having binding force in specific concrete situations concerns the definition of "self-determination." Recent efforts by countries of "anti-colonial" persuasion to treat it as a legal right

---

[25] U.N. Gen. Ass. Off. Rec. 16th Sess., Plenary 770 (A/PV. 1061) (1961).

[26] *Introduction to the Annual Report of the Secretary-General on the Work of the Organization 16 June 1960-15 June 1961, id.* Supp. No. 1A, at 2 (A/4800/Add. 1) (1961).

[27] N. Y. Times, Sept. 17, 1959, p. 1, col. 1; *id.* Oct. 16, 1959, p. 1, col. 5.

[28] U.N. Gen. Ass. Off. Rec. 15th Sess., Gen. Comm. 4-5 (A/BUR/SR. 127) (1960).

[29] *Id.* 16th Sess., Plenary 1533 (A/PV. 1120) (1962).

involves a particular concept of "self-determination" quite distinct from the traditional notion which would seem to be reflected in the Charter phraseology "self-determination of peoples." It is doubtful that any consistent definition of the modern "anti-colonialist" concept of "self-determination" is possible, but it is certain (notwithstanding the title of the "Declaration on Granting Independence to Colonial Countries and Peoples") that it does not apply to "peoples" as such. Indeed, it rules out the whole classical notion of self-determination as expounded by President Wilson, which gave the strongest impetus to the generic concept of "self-determination" as we have it today. The attitude of the Asian and African states on this point is understandable since no state containing distinct ethnic groups occupying well-defined territories (as does India, for example) could agree to this concept of "self-determination" without conceding, at the same time, the necessity for its own partial dissolution upon the request of such groups.[30]

While the "Declaration on Granting Independence to Colonial Countries and Peoples" therefore does not apply to "peoples," it also does not apply to "countries" except in the sense that governments want it to apply in particular cases. What is meant by a "country"? To say that the principle applies to "the majority within a generally accepted political unit," as has been suggested,[31] would presumably not have been acceptable to India, a leading exponent of the current concept, in regard to its claim to Hyderabad in 1948 or, indeed, to its claim to Kashmir today. These were Indian states (as distinguished from those parts of India directly under British rule) which were, at the time of independence, "generally accepted political units" and which were, in principle, recognized as having the right of self-determination. Thus the Indian Representative in the Security Council said, on January 15, 1948:

> On 15 August, when the Indian Independence Act came into force, Jammu and Kashmir, like other States, became free to decide whether it would accede to the one or the other of the two Dominions, or remain independent.[32]

It is not unusual for countries of "anti-colonialist" sentiments to reject the principle of "self-determination" when it is proposed

[30] Emerson, *From Empire to Nation* 297-301 (1960).

[31] Higgins, *op. cit. supra* note 11, at 104.

[32] U.N. Security Council Off. Rec. 3d year, 227th meeting 13 (1948).

to be applied against themselves or other members of the group. Thus twenty-five Asian and African countries, apparently voting on what they considered "anti-colonialist" grounds, opposed a proposal that the Assembly should recognize the principle as applicable in the West Irian case. These votes, together with those of the communist countries, were enough to defeat the proposal for lack of the necessary two-thirds majority.[33] In that case, Indonesia was vigorously opposed to a Netherlands proposal that the people of West Irian be accorded the right of self-determination before being placed under Indonesian control. When Communist China took steps to deprive the peoples of Tibet of their right of self-determination, the Soviet Union claimed that the matter lay wholly within the jurisdiction of the Chinese regime, and that the United Nations had no right even to discuss it.[34] Similarly the Soviet Union refuses to countenance any claims of the right of self-determination on behalf of peoples incorporated within her own boundaries, such as the Baltic states, or held in subjection under puppet regimes.[35] As an example in this latter category, the people of East Germany would seem to fall clearly within the scope of the "Declaration on Granting Independence to Colonial Countries and Peoples" and have given evidence of their wishes in the matter by attempting to revolt.

There are thus two reasons for venturing the opinion that the Charter principle of "self-determination" does not have the status of a legally binding obligation or right in specific situations: (a) the required degree of general acquiescence in such a rule has been lacking, and (b) a satisfactory or generally acceptable definition of the concept is also lacking.

The United Nations has, nevertheless, given the appearance, in the case concerning Portuguese overseas territories, of attempting to enforce this kind of right. The Assembly resolution of December 14, 1962[36] on this matter provides *inter alia:*

---

[33] U.N. Gen. Ass. Off. Rec. 16th Sess., Plenary 873 (A/PV. 1066) (1961).

[34] *Id.* 14th Sess., Plenary 448 (A/PV. 826) (1959).

[35] *Id.* 15th Sess., Plenary 982-83 (A/PV. 925) (1960). To similar effect see *id.* 16th Sess., Plenary 683-84 (A/PV. 1056) (1961). See also the candid statement by Trotsky *vis-à-vis* the Soviet takeover of Georgia, quoted by Emerson, *op. cit. supra* note 30, at 306-07, citing Trotsky, *Between Red and White* 86 (London: Communist Party of Great Britain, 1922).

[36] Res. 1807 (XVII), U.N. Gen. Ass. Off. Rec. 17th Sess., Supp. No. 17, at 39-40 (A/5217) (1962).

The General Assembly

* * *

Noting with deep concern that the policy and acts of the Portuguese Government with regard to the Territories under its administration have created a situation which constitutes a serious threat to international peace and security.

* * *

2. *Condemns* the attitude of Portugal, which is inconsistent with the Charter of the United Nations;

3. *Reaffirms* the inalienable right of the peoples of the Territories under Portuguese administration to self-determination and independence and upholds without any reservations the claims of those peoples for their immediate accession to independence;

4. *Urges* the Portuguese Government to give effect to the recommendations contained in the report of the Special Committee on Territories under Portuguese Administration, in particular those set out in paragraphs 442 to 445 of that report, by taking the following measures:

(a) The immediate recognition of the right of the peoples of the Territories under its administration to self-determination and independence;

(b) The immediate cessation of all acts of repression and the withdrawal of all military and other forces at present employed for that purpose;

(c) The promulgation of an unconditional political amnesty and the establishment of conditions that will allow the free functioning of political parties;

(d) Negotiations, on the basis of the recognition of the right to self-determination, with the authorized representatives of the political parties within and outside the Territories with a view to the transfer of power to political institutions freely elected and representative of the peoples, in accordance with resolution 1514 (XV);

(e) The granting of independence immediately thereafter to all the Territories under its administration in accordance with the aspirations of the peoples;

* * *

7. *Earnestly requests* all States to refrain forthwith from offering the Portuguese Government any assistance which would enable it to continue its repression of the peoples of the Territories under its administration and, for this purpose, to take all measures to prevent the sale and supply of arms and military equipment to the Portuguese Government;

8. *Requests* the Security Council, in case the Portuguese Government should refuse to comply with the present resolution and previous General Assembly resolutions on this question, to take all

appropriate measures to secure the compliance of Portugal with its obligations as a Member State.

Here we find intermixed, once again, the two motives for action which have been previously encountered in other connections. In the first paragraph the situation being dealt with is said to constitute a threat to peace. A resemblance to the Charter definition of "collective measures" may be noted since this resolution undertakes to initiate a form of tangible pressure—e.g. an arms embargo—against Portugal with at least the partial purpose of dealing with this threat. Also the resolution may be read as an attempt to enforce the policy decisions concerning the right of the peoples in question to self-determination, and other matters. In the final paragraph, this latter motivation is made clear, since the Council is asked to take requisite measures, if necessary, to enforce these decisions. A parallel may be observed between this resolution and Assembly resolution 1761 (XVII) in the South African case, parts of which were quoted above.

A parallel may also be observed between the Portuguese and South African cases in respect of Security Council actions taken subsequent to the Assembly resolutions just mentioned. The Council action of July 31, 1963,[37] in the Portuguese case, was like that of August 7 of the same year in the South African case in imposing an arms embargo, and was also similar in that certain modifications were made in the language of the resolution to make clear that the measure was not intended to be an "enforcement action."[38] As in the South African case, the result must have been to give the impression that the measure was designed to enforce a substantive decision as to Portugal's internal and/or external affairs without that country's consent.[39]

---

[37] U.N. Security Council Off. Rec. 18th year, Supp. July-Sept. 1963, at 63 (S/5380) (1963).

[38] U.N. Security Council Off. Rec. 18th year, 1048th meeting 6-7 (S/PV. 1048) (1963); id. 1049th meeting 6-7.

[39] Also as in the South African case, any such impression would have been strengthened by statements of some delegations asserting the right of the Organization to make such decisions. See e.g., id. 1041st meeting 8 (S/PV. 1041) (Sierra Leone): id. 1046th meeting 4-8 (S/PV. 1046) (Tunisia). The Soviet Representative argued that once the decision was taken by the Council, as distinct from the Assembly, it became mandatory and enforceable. Id. 1049th meeting 8-9 (S/PV. 1049).

Some Policy Considerations

The reason, or reasons, for the denial that the measures in question were "collective measures" are, in the first place, conjectural so far as the present writer is concerned. It seems reasonable, however, to assume that they form part and parcel of the "political" approach that has dominated the handling of disputes and situations in the United Nations.

A possible reason for the denial might be that governments regard "collective measures" as involving binding orders upon states to participate, whereas they would prefer the freedom of decision and action which is provided if the United Nations decision is merely recommendatory. This latter approach may, then, in turn be regarded, in the prevailing view, as throwing the measure in question outside the "collective measures" category.

It would obviously be preferable if the participation of member states in United Nations measures should always be determined by the United Nations, as the framers anticipated, and not by the states themselves. However, present-day conditions do not make this possible. In such cases as Spain, Korea, Katanga Province, Portuguese colonies, and South African *apartheid* we find measures being decided upon by majority decision of the United Nations, and then being implemented by those members, only, which choose to take part.

In seeking ways and means of enabling such United Nations activities to contribute to the development of the Charter and of law as the basis of international relations (and thus bringing the measures themselves within a better legal framework), the suggestion naturally presents itself of regularizing the situation just referred to by making a distinction between the basic United Nations decision pertaining to the application of measures, and the decision of states as to participating in those measures.

The former category of decision is the more basic, from the Charter point of view. The application of force or other tangible pressures in international situations involves the highest risks that the United Nations is authorized to assume, and the framers necessarily anticipated that the competent organ would always act in such matters in accordance with United Nations principles and with all due discretion. If, for example, some governments were to agree upon the application of pressures in order to avoid antagonizing one faction in a case, and then deny that the measure in question was a "collective measure" for the purpose of avoiding participation in its application, the whole Charter would tend to be subverted.

While it is, no doubt, erroneous to think that governments might act, even in part, by virtue of such motives, there is, at the same time, no doubt that the long-range interests reflected by the Charter have carried little weight in relation to what states have considered to be their interests in light of immediate situations. It is this problem that we are concerned to deal with.

There is also no doubt that incongruities exist in practice. For example, one does not question the *bona fides* of the United States Representative in the Security Council, apparently speaking for his own government and others, in denying that the South African situation constituted a threat to peace:

> [T]he United States is most gratified that the sponsors have seen fit to change their original formulation from "is seriously endangering international peace and security" to "is seriously disturbing international peace and security." In making this change they clearly recognize that a number of Council members are not prepared to agree that the situation in South Africa is one which now calls for the kind of action appropriate in cases of threats to the peace or breaches of the peace under Chapter VII of the United Nations Charter.[40]

It seems rather contradictory, however, that the same resolution proceeded to initiate a "kind of action appropriate in cases of threats to the peace or breaches of the peace under Chapter VII," namely an arms embargo. The states adopting the position described in the above-quoted passage no doubt considered the measure to be outside the latter category because the resolution merely "recommended" that member states apply it against South Africa; however, so far as the Charter is concerned, the mode of initiating the measure does not enter into the definition of its constitutional nature.

A second difficulty arising from the Council resolution in the South African case—and such statements as that above-quoted in connection with it—is that while a tangible pressure is applied against South Africa, its affirmative nature under the Charter is not defined. For reasons which have been indicated, this measure then gives the impression of being intended to enforce a change in the internal regime of South Africa, a kind of action for which authority is generally understood not to exist, exercise of which

---

[40] *Id.* 1056th meeting at 6.

seems bound to be confusing to the world public and therefore detrimental to the development of law.

A factor which may furnish at least partial motivation for denials, by governments, that measures of the kind under discussion are "collective measures" might be the fear of offending states by voting for the application of such measures against them. This is admittedly a doubtful factor in cases such as those pertaining to Portugal and South Africa. Tangible pressures were initiated in these cases and it must be the measures themselves, not what they are called, that is decisive as to the reaction of the target state. Nevertheless, the matter of giving offense may be a factor in some cases, as it undoubtedly was, for example, in the failure of some major powers to implement League of Nations measures against Italy, in the Abysinnian case of 1935. In the politically charged atmosphere which has prevailed in international relations since World War II, the hostile reaction of a state to an adverse vote in the United Nations may be enough to give pause to the state casting the vote. The problem is purely political; like other aspects of the over-all problem, it can only be overcome gradually.

The main suggestion to emerge out of this discussion of the Portuguese and South African cases is that—at least in the interests of the long-range development of law and the Charter—governments should endeavor to restrict the application of tangible pressures to situations in which such measures are deemed necessary for the maintenance of peace and security, and then to designate them properly as "collective measures." If it is necessary, for practical reasons, to initiate such measures through recommendations to member states (instead of binding orders) that they participate, this procedure should not be regarded as derogating from the true character of the measures in question as "collective measures."

Gradually, through well directed efforts, it might reasonably be hoped that the general understanding might emerge that states usually act in accordance with their own concepts of right and justice; that the United Nations does not engage in condemning states for alleged wrongful acts, but rather seeks to act in the general interest, taking the course best calculated to prevent clashes and to maintain peace and security. The gradual development of public opinion along this line ought to contribute to the dulling, and gradual elimination, of the sharp edges of conflict that frequently now prevail between states as to what "justice" and "principle" demand in particular situations.

Chapter VI

Powers of Assembly and Security Council to Apply Collective Measures

The three preceding chapters, and the ensuing one, are largely concerned with tendencies which (a) cause the United Nations to appear in some cases as if it were making binding decisions on substantive issues in international disputes and situations, (b) cause applications of tangible pressure by the Organization to appear as attempts to enforce such decisions and (c) deny that such applications are in the "collective measures" category notwithstanding that this appears to be the only Charter concept which authorizes the application of such pressures in the handling of disputes and situations.

One basic factor in the problem is undoubtedly that the state of international relations since the Charter was adopted has prevented the Organization from applying "collective measures" in the manner originally intended by the framers, e.g. on the basis of legally binding orders by the Security Council that member states carry out that body's decisions in the premises. Under this concept of "collective measures" there was, in the first place, no role for the General Assembly. The Council, however, has also apparently felt that it was not in a position to act in the manner originally anticipated and has either invoked measures by means of recommendations to member states, or has denied that its measures were in the "collective measures" category.

Before proceeding with the discussion, it has become necessary to take up a factor which, though sometimes unspoken, has undoubtedly entered into some of these denials, namely the question of competence of the given organ, under the Charter, to do what it appeared to be doing. The major factor in this connection is, of course, the prevalent opinion that the General Assembly is wholly without power to apply "collective measures," or tangible pressures generally. No corresponding question, of course, exists as to the

149

Council. Certain questions concerning that organ's Charter powers are, however, believed relevant to the present phase of the discussion, and will be touched upon toward the end of the chapter.

The basic Assembly powers in the handling of disputes and situations, as specifically set forth in the Charter, are found in Articles 10, 11(2) and 14.[1] The powers thus defined are those of discussion and recommendation. The corollary that "collective measures" are the monopoly of the Security Council is not only a generally prevalent view, but is supported by the fact that, apart from Article 1(1) which states the general purpose of the Organization in this respect, all the provisions spelling out the nature of the power and the mode of its exercise refer explicitly to the Council.

That the problem of the Assembly's power in the premises is, nevertheless, a real one, becomes clear upon consideration of the fact that this organ has, on a number of occasions, initiated measures which apparently fulfill the requirements for "collective measures" under an objective reading of the Charter. Mentioned above, in Chapter 4, was the United Nations Emergency Force (UNEF) deployed in the Suez crisis of 1956 with power to defend its assigned positions, if necessary, in the event of attack. As was there observed, an armed force with such power seems to be an application of tangible pressure; since it was deployed by the Organization in a situation known to the world as a flagrant breach of international peace, it appears to have conformed to the Charter definition of "collective measures."

The Assembly has also initiated applications of diplomatic and economic pressures such as are set forth in Article 41[2] of the Charter as forming part of the definition of "collective measures." As we have seen, the Assembly, in 1946, asked the member states to withdraw their ambassadors and ministers from Spain as a means of pressure against the Franco regime.[3] In 1949, in the Greek case, it recommended that members apply an arms embargo against Albania and Bulgaria.[4] A similar recommendation, directed against Communist China, was made in 1951 in connection with

---

[1] Relevant parts quoted p. 111 *supra.*

[2] *Cf.* p. 38 *supra.*

[3] *Cf.* p. 65 *supra.*

[4] Res. 288 (IV), *Resolutions* 9, U.N. Gen. Ass. Off. Rec. 4th Sess. (A/1251) (1949).

the Korean case.[5] The Greek and Korean measures were applied to situations constituting breaches of peace known to the world, and so fulfilled this particular requirement for the application of collective measures under the Charter. As observed in the preceding Chapter, the Assembly, in 1962, initiated a wide range of economic measures against the Union of South Africa, and an arms embargo against Portugal. Whether or not they were proper applications of "collective measures," these actions raise questions as to the Assembly's constitutional powers.

Another aspect of the Korean case provides proof that resort to the Assembly may sometimes be unavoidable if necessary action is to be taken by the Organization. After the Council had initiated measures to deal with the original aggression, a new factor came into the case when the People's Republic of China entered the conflict as an ally of the North Korean aggressors. It was decided by the United Nations that the regime was an aggressor, and that the United Nations measures already underway to meet the aggression from North Korea should be directed to meet this new situation. These decisions were taken by the Assembly because the Council was prevented by lack of unanimity among the permanent members from doing so. The Assembly's resulting resolution of February 1, 1951[6] appears to have been just as clearly in the "collective measures" category as was the Council's original initiation of measures. It might be thought, indeed, to have been even more clearly in that category since it explicitly affirmed that the measures were being taken by the United Nations, whereas the original Council resolution,[7] *recommending* that member states furnish assistance to the Republic of Korea, had left some doubt as to whether this was the case or whether the measures were being taken by individual states.

A glance at the Suez and Congolese operations gives ground for apprehension that situations might well arise in the future requiring Assembly action. The veto actually occurred in the Suez case, leading to the setting up of UNEF by the General Assembly. Since that Force was not required to use overt force, no question has been openly precipitated as to whether or not it is a collective

---

[5] Res. 500 (V), *id.* 5th Sess., Supp. No. 20A, at 2 (A/1775/Add. 1) (1951).

[6] Res. 498 (V), *id.* at 1.

[7] S/RES/83 (1950), Doc. S/1511.

measure. ONUC was, shortly after its creation by the Council, authorized to use force, if necessary, to prevent civil war in the Congo. At about the same time, a veto occurred in connection with a related proposal which dealt with unlawful arrests, assassinations and other outrages in certain parts of the Congo and which, in its original form, called for the use of United Nations force, if necessary, to prevent or deal with such occurrences. The veto in question was cast by the Soviet Representative against a United States proposal to expand the geographic scope of the resolution to include Stanleyville, which was then controlled by the Communist leader Gizenga.[8] The ensuing situation was not such as to make it necessary that this issue be taken up in the Assembly. However, the case illustrates how readily a situation requiring such treatment might arise in future cases.

In the Uniting for Peace resolution of November 3, 1951,[9] the Assembly asserted the right to recommend collective measures, including the possible use of force, when the Council is prevented, by lack of unanimity, from exercising its primary responsibility in a situation constituting a threat to peace, breach of the peace or act of aggression. This resolution followed shortly after the Korean aggression of June, 1950, and resulted from the realization that Council action in that case had been possible only because of the temporary absence of the Soviet Representative. When that Representative returned, shortly thereafter, he proceeded to veto further Council action in the case. The Uniting for Peace resolution was a manifestation of the determination of the general membership of the United Nations, frequently expressed in the debate on the resolution,[10] not to allow the entire Organization to be paralyzed by the use of the veto in the Security Council.

Charter authority for necessary applications of collective measures by the General Assembly may, it is believed, be derived from Article 1(1) of the Charter and a theory of interpretation—or possibly of Charter modification—generally consistent with a theory outlined in the preamble of the Uniting for Peace resolution just mentioned.

---

[8] U.N. Security Council Off. Rec. 16th year, 942d meeting 19-20, 24-25, 27 (S/PV. 942) (1961). For original draft proposal see *id.* Supp. Jan.-March 1961, at 142 (S/4733/Rev. 1) (1961).

[9] Res. 377 (V), U.N. Gen. Ass. Off. Rec. 5th Sess., Supp. No. 20, at 10 (A/1775) (1950).

[10] For the debate see *id.* 1st Comm. 63-174 (A/C. 1/SR. 354-371) (1950); *id.* Plenary 292-347 (A/PV. 299-302).

Article 1(1) of the Charter, it will be recalled, declares it to be a major purpose of the United Nations to maintain international peace and security and, to that end:

> to take effective collective measures for the prevention and removal of threats to the peace, and for the suppression of acts of aggression or other breaches of the peace . . .

It is to be observed that this statement of major "Purpose" pertains to the Organization as a whole, not just to the Security Council. Also relevant is the specification that collective measures are to be "effective" for the purpose of maintaining peace and security. It seems thus to be suggested that the Organization's major purpose in this respect is not of a kind to be frustrated by the inability of the Security Council to fulfill its primary responsibility in a particular situation; the intent might rather be thought to be indicated that adequate measures are to be applied at all cost when needed to maintain or restore peace and security.

The existence of a residual authority in the Assembly to apply necessary measures, when the Council is prevented from doing so, is suggested in the preamble of the Uniting for Peace resolution, which begins by quoting from Article 1 of the Charter, just referred to. It proceeds to recognize the primary responsibility of the Council for the maintenance of peace and security, as provided in Article 24 of the Charter. It then goes on to suggest that this responsibility is not sole and exclusive:

> *The General Assembly* . . . *Recognizing* in particular that . . . failure [of the Security Council to discharge its primary responsibility] does not deprive the General Assembly of its rights or relieve it of its responsibilities under the Charter in regard to the maintenance of international peace and security. . . .

The main operative provision of the resolution then goes on to provide that in the event of a failure on the part of the Council, due to lack of unanimity among the permanent members, the Assembly may make recommendations to members for collective measures, including, if necessary, the use of force. As will be discussed more fully in the ensuing chapter, most of the delegations supporting the resolution in the Assembly apparently regarded that organ's substantive power of recommendation as the basis for the resolution. It is not herein maintained that the resolution, including the preamble, cannot be read in a way to sustain this interpretation.[11] However, it also contains the outline of the theory here under discussion, which is believed to be more conducive to Charter development along lines which might enable the Organization to become the basis of an effective rule of law in international relations. Under this theory, "recommendation" is not of the essence; it is merely the procedure chosen in the Uniting for Peace resolution for implementing more basic decisions which form the main subject matter of the resolution. These latter decisions pertain to the application of tangible pressures for which Charter authority is to be found only in the provisions applicable to "collective measures" and particularly, insofar as concerns the Assembly, in Article 1(1).

For the recognition of a secondary power of "collective measures" in the General Assembly it is not herein considered essential to identify Article 1(1) as the positive source of this authority. A more essential factor is that a process of Charter development has taken place, resulting in the existence of this power in the Assembly, where it was not recognized as existing at the time the Charter was adopted. It may be possible to regard this development as one of Charter interpretation focused upon Article 1(1) or, on the other hand, it may be preferable to regard it as having the nature of Charter modification. Again, in this case, such modification might be said to depend, in part, upon the fact that Article 1(1) makes "collective measures" a major purpose of the Organization. Of greater importance, however, would be the fact that peoples and governments generally seem to have acquiesced in the exercise of relevant powers by the General Assembly.

In a recent treatise, Dr. Bowett objects to the use of Article 1(1) as the basis of the Assembly's powers in the premises, on the ground that this provision does not identify the power in question with the General Assembly. He would accord to the Organization a broad power to effectuate the basic purposes and principles of the Charter, and considers that, at least so far as the establishment of United Nations forces is concerned, the principal limits upon this power lie "in the principle that the doctrine of implied powers cannot be divorced from the question of which organ chooses to exercise powers which may be legitimately implied for the Organization."[12]

---

[11] *Cf.* p. 181 *infra.* Wright, "Domestic Jurisdiction as a Limit on National and Supra-National Action," 56 Nw. U. L. Rev. 11, 30 (1961).

[12] Bowett, *United Nations Forces* 311 (1964).

Thus the power to establish a Force for particular purposes cannot be implied for a particular organ except upon the basis of construction of the general and express powers of *that* organ.[13]

With respect to the Assembly's power to establish UNEF, he finds the authority in Articles 10, 11(2) and 14.[14] He thus seems to be in accord with the official United Nations position, and that of the Advisory Opinion in the "Expenses" case as noted above in Chapter 4.

While it is true that the articles just mentioned pertain to the General Assembly, it is also true that they pertain, substantively, to the exercise of the "peaceful settlement" function. As suggested above in Chapter 4, there is reason to apprehend that the use of these provisions as the basis for an armed force such as UNEF entails the danger of confusing the "peaceful settlement" and "collective measures" functions of the United Nations.

It is herein believed, on the other hand, that the substantive principles just mentioned—"collective measures" and "peaceful settlement"— reflect the nature of the powers which the "peoples of the world" are agreed that the Organization should exercise in the handling of international disputes and situations. As such, they are capable of being built upon. By building them up in their proper relationship as separate, though interdependent, concepts, the Charter is developed in a constructive direction. In contrast to the view of Dr. Bowett, just referred to, it is herein considered that the building up of such substantive principles should be the first consideration in seeking solution of constitutional problems such as that under discussion; the question as to which organ should carry out a particular function is believed, in principle, to be of secondary importance. Further, while it is true that Article 1(1) does not identify the General Assembly as possessed of the function of "collective measures" which it describes, governments and peoples of the world are believed to have recognized that organ as being, in fact, possessed of residual powers of this essential character, and, indeed, to have employed it in practice for the exercise of such powers. Thus a real constitutional development has been in progress which identifies the residual power for the application of collective measures with the General Assembly and with no other organ.

---

[13] *Ibid.*
[14] *Id.* 296.

The question to be considered is, then, whether there has been such general acquiescence as would bring this development to fruition.

It may be objected that the major affirmation of this power was in connection with the Uniting for Peace resolution, since which time there has been a great influx of new states into the Organization. However, governments of the latter states, and successor governments, have been well aware of the Assembly's assertion of authority in that resolution, and have not objected to it. On the contrary, it was largely these states of Asia and Africa which were behind the Assembly actions, outlined in the preceding Chapter, initiating tangible pressures against Portugal and the Republic of South Africa in 1962 and 1963. While the Charter basis of these measures is rather unclear, the measures at least indicate that the states in question have no objection, in principle, to the initiation of tangible pressures by the Assembly in international situations.

The principal objection to the course of development under discussion has been on the part of the Soviet Union and associated states on grounds that the Charter endowed the Security Council with the monopoly of power with respect to the application of collective measures. This objection was voiced with respect to the Uniting for Peace resolution[15] and is, at the time of present writing, being advanced with respect to all kinds of so-called peace-keeping measures (whether involving tangible pressures or not) on the ground that all such measures are within the exclusive province of the Council. The present Soviet objections have grown out of the controversy concerning liability to pay assessments on account of the costs of such operations, particularly those of Suez and the Congo.[16]

It is true that, as a general rule, the adherence to a given Charter interpretation by a majority is not binding on a minority which disagrees.[17] There are nevertheless believed to be reasons for denying that the Soviet and other communist objections in this case

---

[15] U.N. Gen. Ass. Off. Rec. 5th Sess., 1st Comm. 80-86 (A/C. 1/SR. 357) (1950); *id.* Plenary 324-35 (A/PV. 301) (1950).

[16] The position is summarized in *Annual Report of the Secretary-General on the Work of the Organization 16 June 1962-15 June 1963, id.* 18th' Sess. Supp. No. 1, at 137-38 (A/5501) (1963). *Cf.* ch. 7, note 82 *infra.*

[17] *The United Nations Conference on International Organization: Selected Documents* 880 (1946).

are sufficient to overcome the development of the Assembly's residual power to apply collective measures.

The first argument along this line might be based upon the proposition that the intent of the Charter is, as evidenced in Article 1(1), that *effective* measures must be taken at all costs when necessary for the maintenance or restoration of peace. It is obvious that the fulfillment of this function could be a matter of survival of life on earth, to say nothing of being a precondition of the ability of the United Nations to fulfill any of its other purposes. The argument might then proceed along the line that the "police" function is a function of the Organization as such, and not within the exclusive province of the Security Council. Again as a matter of survival, it cannot be permitted to be disrupted by constitutional objections of a minority. A somewhat analogous proposition was debated and adopted at San Francisco on the basis of an Egyptian proposal that, in the drafting of Article 1(1) of the Charter, the reference to "the principles of justice and international law" should be made to apply not only to the "peaceful settlement" function, but should be so placed as to apply to the whole paragraph, including the "collective measures," or "police," function. The Rapporteur of Committee I/1, in describing the debate in committee on this motion, said:

> The situations that may arise may be conceived this way. Peace is threatened by disputes or by situations that may lead to a breach of the peace. A breach of the peace may ensue. At the first stage, the Organization should insist and take measures that states do not threaten or cause a breach of the peace. If they do, the Organization should, at the second stage, promptly stop any breach of the peace or remove it. After that, it can proceed to find an adjustment or settlement of that dispute or situation. When the Organization has used the power given to it, and the force at its disposal to stop war, then it can find the latitude to apply the principles of justice and international law, or can assist the contending parties to find a peaceful solution.[18]

Applications of collective measures are likely to be controversial, and states objecting may find constitutional arguments to support their contentions. If operations were to be stopped on this account, the Organization might be prevented from taking steps vital to the prevention of general war.

The most basic part of this argument—e.g., that the United

---

[18] *Id.* 534.

Nations cannot be prevented by the paralysis of the Security Council from doing what is necessary to maintain peace and security— is, in essence, the argument advanced by the generality of members in support of the Uniting for Peace resolution. The principal difference was that these members did not consider that the Assembly was seeking to exercise the right of "collective measures." The general theory was that the Assembly was to exercise some other—and vague—kind of power based on the substantive power of "recommendation." This part of the case will be considered further in the ensuing Chapter.

Even though a certain validity has to be recognized in Soviet objections that, from the outset, it only agreed to the Organization's "police" function on the condition that it was to be exercised with the consent of all the permanent members of the Security Council, it is also necessary to take account of actions of the Organization, inconsistent with this rule, which have persisted almost since its founding, and of the fact that Communist objections to this course of action have by no means been consistent. It was, in fact, a member of the Communist bloc, Poland, which gave the Assembly its initial push in the direction of engaging in this kind of activity. This initiative occcurred in the Spanish case, in the Organization's first year. The Polish Representative, having brought the case before the Security Council,[19] later moved that that body relinquish it so that it could be taken up in the Assembly.[20] The Polish Delegation in the Assembly then moved the resolution which, as amended, recommended the withdrawal by member states of their ambassadors and ministers from Spain.[21] The Soviet Union strongly supported these moves by Poland.[22]

Later, when the Soviet Delegation was vigorously objecting to the legality of the Uniting for Peace resolution on the ground that the Assembly had no power in the premises, it was challenged on the ground of its earlier support of action by that organ initiating diplomatic measures in the Spanish case. Mr. Vyshinski responded with a rather involved argument, the gist of which seems to have been that:

---

[19] Letter dated April 9, 1946, from the Representative of Poland addressed to the Secretary-General, U.N. Security Council Off. Rec., 1st year, 1st ser. Supp. No. 2, at 55 (S/34) (1946).

[20] Id. 79th meeting 498 (1946).

[21] U.N. Gen. Ass. Off. Rec. 1st Sess., Pt. 2, 1st Comm. 352 (A/C. 1/24) (1946).

[22] See, e.g., id. Plenary 1212-14 (1946).

> We are asked whether the severance of diplomatic relations is not in fact enforcement action. Of course it is enforcement action, but you forget that when we speak of enforcement action, we connect it with the possibility of using armed forces.[23]

The distinction thus suggested is not found in the Charter definition of collective measures, which applies equally to measures of force and to measures short of force. The same is true of the Uniting for Peace resolution, which, in its main operative paragraph, asserts the right of the Assembly to initiate "collective measures, including . . . the use of armed force when necessary." In other words, it embraces the whole range of collective measures as outlined in the Charter. Mr. Vyshinski's statement is certainly not a disavowal of the right of the Assembly to apply diplomatic pressures. As to whether such measures are "enforcement measures," he said that they were, but suggested in the same sentence that they were not. A decade later, however, in connection with the imposition of similar measures by the Organization of American States against the Dominican Republic, the Soviet Representative strongly maintained that they were "enforcement measures":

> As is known, the measures provided for in Article 41 of the Charter are, of their nature, enforcement measures because they are employed by the Security Council for the very purpose of forcing an aggressor to cease acts of aggression against another State and of preventing the recurrence of aggression. How, in the light of this, can one assert that the breaking of diplomatic relations and the interruption of economic relations do not constitute enforcement action?[24]

In 1962 the Soviet Union supported Assembly recommendations initiating a broad range of economic measures against the Republic of South Africa,[25] and an arms embargo against Portugal.[26] While most Members may have felt that these were not United Nations measures, since they were initiated by recommendation to the member states, it is more doubtful that this view was held by the Soviet Union. In the Vyshinski statement of 1950, concerning the diplomatic measure taken against Spain in 1946, there was no disposi-

---

[23] Id. 5th Sess., Plenary 334 (A/PV. 301) (1950).

[24] U.N. Security Council Off. Rec. 15th year, 894th meeting 11-12 (S/PV. 894) (1960).

[25] Resolution quoted in part, p. 134 supra. For a record of the vote see U.N. Gen. Ass. Off. Rec. 17th Sess., Plenary 679 (A/PV. 1165) (1962).

[26] Resolution quoted in part, p. 143 supra. For a record of the vote see id. 1148 (A/PV. 1194) (1962).

tion to rely on this argument, even though the action in the Spanish case was instituted by recommendation. Rather, Mr. Vyshinski referred to the measure in question as an enforcement measure.

Turning, then, to consideration of the Soviet attitude toward the use of actual armed force, it is to be observed that, notwithstanding strenuous objections made in connection with the Uniting for Peace resolution to the initiation of such measures by the General Assembly, that country's Delegation to the Assembly subsequently abstained from voting on the establishment and deployment of UNEF by that Organ.[27] True, the Delegation *said* that it considered the action illegal on the ground that only the Security Council had the right to establish international armed forces.[28] However, on the actual vote, where it could have made its objection count, it abstained and thereby indicated its acquiescence in the action taken.[29] The Soviet Delegation, moreover, said that it regarded UNEF as an armed force, and a police operation, of the kind which, in its view, was within the exclusive competence of the Security Council. In this it was unlike the delegations which actively supported the Force, since these seemed generally to regard the operation as essentially non-military in character, and as partaking of the nature of an observer corps. The Soviet Delegation, therefore, in abstaining, seems to have given some degree of acquiescence to the proposition that the Assembly has the authority to apply collective measures involving armed force.[30]

In conclusion, then, as to the powers of the General Assembly to apply tangible pressures in international situations, it may be observed, first of all, that that organ has initiated such pressures in a number of cases. In some cases the Assembly action took the

---

[27] U.N. Gen. Ass. Off. Rec. 1st Em. Spec. Sess., Plenary Meetings and Annexes 89 (A/PV. 565) (1956) (re Resolution 1000 (ES-I) establishing the Command of UNEF); *id.* 126 (A/PV. 567) (re Resolution 1001 (ES-I) requesting the Chief of the Command to proceed with full organization of the Force).

[28] The Soviet Delegation said that it refrained from opposing the resolutions because the victim (Egypt) had agreed to UNEF as a means of halting the alleged aggression. *Id.* at 127-28.

[29] See Ch. 2, note 38 *supra* and accompanying text.

[30] It will be recalled that the clearest example of actual Charter modification, through practice acquiesced in by the member states, involved the recognition of the proposition that abstention from voting has the effect of acquiescence. *Cf.* pp. 23-25 *supra*.

form of recommendations that member states apply the desired measures. In the case of UNEF, where the action was clearly that of the United Nations itself, Charter authority has been sought in the "peaceful settlement" function and the partially related notions of "permissiveness" and "recommendation." The applicability of these concepts, which seem somewhat unrelated to the objective nature of the measures, will be considered in the ensuing Chapter. So far as concerns what is being done in fact—e.g. the application of tangible pressures by the United Nations—the Assembly's power so to act seems to have, in principle, the general acquiescence of the governments and peoples of the world. Some degree of Charter development thus seems to have taken place.[31] Whether this development has been in the nature of Charter interpretation or of Charter modification might be a matter of disagreement; however the question would not seem to be of the essence. In either case, the development in question must be regarded as uneven. Some of the precedents—as in the Spanish, Portuguese and South Africa cases—take the form of apparent "quasi-legislative" actions which are believed to represent a Charter concept incapable of realization, since governments and national populations seem certain to reject its reciprocal application to themselves. The valid element of Charter development in these cases would be the recognition of the Assembly's power to apply tangible pressures in principle, and in proper situations. It would then be the view of the present discussion that "proper" situations would consist of those which conform to the Charter concept of "collective measures." Contributing to the full development of this last-mentioned power on the part of the General Assembly would be the arms embargoes initiated by that organ in the Greek and Korean cases, by the Assembly's finding of Communist Chinese aggression in the Korean case, by its directing of United Nations measures to meet that aggression, and by UNEF.

While the framers did not anticipate that the "collective measures" function would be carried out in this way, there is believed little doubt that they considered fulfillment of the function to be

---

[31] Although the Uniting for Peace resolution was not alone in bringing about the development under discussion, Benjamin Cohen is believed correct in calling it "a great constitutional landmark in the development of the Charter comparable to Marshall's decision in *McCulloch v. Maryland*." Cohen, *The United Nations: Constitutional Developments, Growth, and Possibilities* 18 (1961).

of vital importance to the maintenance of peace, and thus to the achievement of all the purposes of the United Nations.

There has been a somewhat similar problem pertaining to the Security Council. It did not, of course, arise from any lack of explicit Charter provision authorizing that organ to apply collective measures. One source of the problem is believed to lie in the widespread, if not prevalent, belief that whenever the Council desires to apply such measures, it should decide what should be done and then "order" the member states, with legally binding effect, to carry out the decision. Although the Council has, several times, initiated measures of tangible pressure, it has never done so by means of binding orders on member states; there has been some impression, as a consequence, at least until the Rhodesian case of 1966, that it has never initiated "collective" or "enforcement" measures.

The first case of the kind was that of Korea. The Council could not make binding orders in that case because of the absence of the agreements which were supposed to have been concluded between the member states and the Security Council under Article 43 of the Charter. These agreements were to "govern the numbers and types of forces, their degree of readiness and general location, and the nature of the facilities and assistance to be provided" by the member states in particular situations on the "call" of the Council. Because the agreements were never concluded, the Council could not then, nor can it now, "order" states to take part in measures of military force. Probably for this reason the Council decided, in the Korean case, to "recommend" that the member states take steps to meet the aggression. The impression also apparently prevailed that the resulting measures were not United Nations "collective measures."[32]

If it was then thought that the Council was without legal authority to apply "collective measures" in the absence of "Article 43 agreements," this notion is no longer generally prevalent.[33] The following statement in the Advisory Opinion of the World Court in the "Expenses" case would probably have general acquiescence at present:

---

[32] The prevalent opinion appears to have been voiced by the British Representative in the Council. U.N. Security Council Off. Rec. 5th year, 476th meeting 3 (S/PV. 476) (1950).

[33] Bowett, *United Nations Forces* 276-77 (1964); Seyersted, "United Nations Forces: Some Legal Problems," 37 Brit. Yb. Int'l L. 351, 438-39 (1961).

[A]n argument which insists that all measures taken for the maintenance of international peace and security must be financed through agreements concluded under Article 43, would seem to exclude the possibility that the Security Council might act under some other Article of the Charter. The Court cannot accept so limited a view of the powers of the Security Council under the Charter. It cannot be said that the Charter has left the Security Council impotent in the face of an emergency situation when agreements under Article 43 have not been concluded.[34]

That the Korean operation was a United Nations "collective measure" was, indeed, recognized by the Secretary-General as early as 1951,[35] a view affirmed by the incumbent of that office in 1963.[36]

Nevertheless, the notion that binding "orders" of the Council are prerequisite to "collective" or "enforcement" action is unhesitatingly invoked when this course is deemed to serve a useful purpose. Thus, as noted in the preceding Chapter, it was maintained that measures initiated by the Council against Portugal and South Africa were not "collective measures" because they were initiated by recommendations to member states, and not by binding orders. This supposed effect of "recommendation" will be considered further in the next Chapter.

Meanwhile, it is a matter of interest that up to the time of writing (May 1966) the Security Council has never initiated measures by means of binding orders on member states[36a]—not even measures short of force as to which the supposed obstacle of the nonfulfillment of Article 43 is not applicable. The reason is, of course, that the Council has preferred to act by recommendation; some possible reasons for the preference have been suggested in preceding chapters. It may, however, be pertinent, in the context of a discussion of basic Charter powers, to suggest that, in point of constitutional realities, the Council, like the Assembly, is limited to recommending that member states carry out such measures as may be determined upon.

---

[34] *Certain Expenses of the United Nations* . . . [1962] I.C.J. Rep. 151, 167.

[35] *Introduction to the Annual Report of the Secretary-General on the Work of the Organization 1 July 1950-30 June 1951,* U.N. Gen. Ass. Off. Rec. 6th Sess., Supp. No. 1A, at 3 (A/1844/Add. 1) (1951).

[36] Address by Secretary-General, June 13, 1963, U.N. Press Release SG/1520, 12 June 1963.

[36a] The Security Council resolution of April 9, 1966 in the Rhodesian case does not appear to be an exception to this statement. *Cf.* pp. 183-86 *infra.*

The development of the Assembly practice of initiating tangible pressures, and the recognition of its power to do so (notably by means of the Uniting for Peace resolution) came about as the result of an even more important development, or more properly a non-happening, the failure of the new world security system represented by the Charter to come into being. Although states had formally agreed in the Charter to carry out the orders of the Security Council with respect to the application of collective measures, it may be surmised that when governments and peoples saw that the anticipated collaboration of the major powers was not to be forthcoming, they tacitly withdrew this consent. As events have proved, this does not mean that governments decided, in principle, to withhold their collaboration in such matters. However, since the collaboration of the major world powers, among themselves, proved not to be forthcoming, and the risks involved for smaller states thereby became of an entirely different order from what had been anticipated, it is only reasonable to suppose that the smaller powers decided to continue, as in the past, to determine such questions on a case-by-case basis, and not on the basis of an advance blanket commitment. The resulting factual situation is believed to constitute the underlying reason why the Council has refrained from "ordering" that states participate in measures decided upon.

The true nature of the Council's powers in these matters may have been demonstrated by the decision of several states to withdraw their troop contingents from ONUC in the midst of the Congolese crisis, and the apparent inability of the Council to do anything to deter them.[37] It may be argued to the contrary that, in the absence of "Article 43 agreements," the Council is without legal power to make binding orders in such a case. However, if the Council possessed any degree of genuine authority, as distinct from authority on paper, one might justifiably expect it to become perceptible in such a situation, with a resulting effective "order" that states continue the participation of their troops, at least until a favorable opportunity for their withdrawal presented itself.

If conditions of insecurity have caused states to draw back from the advance commitment to participate in United Nations measures, the same conditions have, no doubt, brought about a height-

---

[37] N. Y. Times, Feb. 1, 1961, p. 13, col. 3. See also *Annual Report of the Secretary-General on the Work of the Organization 16 June 1960-15 June 1961,* U.N. Gen. Ass. Off. Rec. 16th Sess., Supp. No. 1, at 33, 37 (A/4800) (1961).

ened desire to see the Organization acquire the capability of fulfilling its security function. Thus, as the Council has proved incapable of fulfilling its primary responsibility for the maintenance of peace and security, the "peoples of the world" have moved in the direction of recognizing a secondary authority in the Assembly. The effect of the two tendencies has been to bring the General Assembly and Security Council onto a basis of approximate equality, in that both organs may initiate measures while, at the same time, both are obliged to secure the requisite degree of voluntary support and backing to assure the success of those measures. Both seem also to share, in about equal measure, the responsibility and opportunity of using their powers in ways that will contribute to bringing into existence such degree of moral force and prestige behind their decisions as will assure them real force and effect in international relations.

Chapter VII

Major Sources of Confusion: "Recommendation," "Permissiveness," "Peace-Keeping Operations"

Substantive Power of Recommendation

The substantive power of recommendation, as it applies to the handling of international disputes and situations in the United Nations, is the power to recommend procedures of settlement, or actual terms of settlement, of the substantive issues involved.[1] It is a means by which the United Nations may bring moral pressure on states, looking to such adjustments or interpretations of existing situations as seem to be required in the interests of maintaining peace and security. As between this recommendatory power and a binding power of decision as to substantive issues, the former was the more appropriate for inclusion in the Charter for the simple reason—if for no other—that the peoples and governments of the world were willing that the United Nations should exercise it, and were unwilling that it should exercise the latter, at least as against their own countries. This basic disposition on the part of the "peoples of the world" appears to remain unchanged, notwithstanding various attempts, such as have been discussed in the preceding chapters, to cause Assembly and Security Council decisions concerning the permanent relations of states to appear as if they had binding force. Such attempts have not included admissions by states that such decisions might be made with binding or enforceable effect as against themselves.

Efforts of the kind just mentioned have included the use by the United Nations of language other than that of "recommendation" in situations in which "recommendation" was, neverthless, the proper course of action under the Charter, the apparent purpose being to create the impression that the action in question was

---

[1] Cf. pp. 68-70 supra.

stronger than a recommendation. Thus, in the Suez "ships" case, the Council "called upon" Egypt to adopt a certain course, and apparently succeeded in causing some governments to consider the resolution as binding on Egypt.[2] In other cases (e.g. the Assembly resolution embodying the Plan of Partition with Economic Union of Palestine), resolutions have used the language of recommendation, but have coupled this with intimations that they are binding and enforceable.[3]

A related problem deserving of mention is illustrated by paragraph (c) of the Assembly's partition resolution:

> *The General Assembly . . . Requests that . . .*
>
> (c) The Security Council determine as a threat to the peace, breach of the peace or act of aggression, in accordance with Article 39 of the Charter, any attempt to alter by force the settlement brought into effect by this resolution.[4]

The last phrase: "the settlement brought into effect by this resolution," is misleading since the resolution was nothing more than a recommendation to the parties to the dispute. Later, the United States Representative in the Security Council said in regard to this case:

> Attempts to frustrate the General Assembly's recommendation by the threat or use of force, or by incitement to force, on the part of States or people outside Palestine, are contrary to the Charter.[5]

The French Delegation, in the same connection, spoke of "open revolt" against the General Assembly resolution and asserted that armed action contrary to the resolution in question was contrary to the Charter.[6]

In a somewhat different form, the view under discussion received expression by Kelsen:

> The legal effect of the recommendations made by the General Assembly is the same as that of the recommendations made by the Security Council. They are not binding unless the Security Council

---

[2] *Cf.* pp. 84-87 *supra.*

[3] *Cf.* p. 76 *supra.* The Cuban Delegation maintained that the partition resolution was illegal because, since it implied coercion, it was not a simple General Assembly recommendation. U.N. Gen. Ass. Off. Rec. 2d Sess., Plenary 1383-84.

[4] See Chapter 3, note 23 *supra.*

[5] U.N. Security Council Off. Rec. 3d year, 253d meeting 265 (1948).

[6] *Id.* 262d meeting 23.

considers non-compliance with a recommendation made by the Assembly as a threat to the peace under Article 39.[7]

The present writer is inclined to disagree with these statements in so far as they seem to be saying that a recommendation may become enforceable. The correct rule is believed to be that, notwithstanding the moral force attaching to United Nations recommendations, states are within their legal rights in rejecting them. To attach legal consequences to such rejections, particularly such consequences as result in the use of enforcement measures against the states in question, would seem to negate the right of rejection.[8] This point of view is well illustrated by the Palestine case itself. The Arab states there rejected the recommendation that Palestine be partitioned, and proceeded to use force in what they, in good faith, considered to be defense of Arab territory. The United Nations had the right to judge whether or not this use of force constituted a wrongful breach of peace such as would warrant collective measures. However, the matter should not be regarded as prejudged by the fact that the Arab states had rejected the partition resolution. The same act may amount to a rejection of a recommendation, and, at the same time, a threat to peace; however, the determination of the latter fact should be made independently of the former. The correct rule is believed to have been stated by the United States Representative in the Security Council in the meeting of March 2, 1948. Speaking in connection with the above-quoted paragraph (c) of the Assembly's resolution recommending the Plan of Partition with Economic Union of Palestine, he reiterated the earlier statment of the United States Delegation in the Assembly that:

[Paragraph (c)] does not ask the Security Council to act on a hypothetical situation, but requests that it act in the event that a situation which constitutes a threat to international peace and security should arise. This, at best, can only be an admonition to the Security Council. The Security Council by its own constitution has the duty to exercise surveillance over such situations and to determine when a threat to international peace and security exists.[9]

and went on to say:

---

[7] Kelsen, *The Law of the United Nations* 459 (1950).

[8] Hearings before the Committee on Foreign Relations, U.S. Senate on the Charter of the United Nations . . ., 79th Cong., 1st Sess., pp. 274-79 (1945).

[9] U.N. Security Council Off. Rec. 3d year, 260th meeting 401 (1948).

[T]he acceptance of request (c) requires determination of the question of fact of threat to international peace and, if such threat is found, action under Chapter VII.[10]

Finally, among the methods employed by the United Nations in efforts to exceed its basic power of recommendation with respect to the substantive issues of international disputes and situations, we have observed, in connection with the cases of Spain, Portugal and South Africa, measures of tangible pressure initiated with the apparent purpose of enforcing substantive decisions, notwithstanding that the proper powers of the Organization seem to be those of recommendation only.

While some governments and peoples are willing to see such methods employed by the United Nations against other countries, they are believed to be generally unwilling to see them employed against themselves. So long as the "peoples of the world" continue to refuse to concede to the Organization the relevant powers, with any requisite degree of mutuality of obligation, repeated efforts to make the United Nations appear as if it has such powers cannot lead to a development of law along the lines indicated; it can only lead to confusion among the world public as to what the true powers of the Organization are in such matters. Such confusion is, in turn, detrimental to the building up of the rule of law in international relations.

A second consequence, more pertinent to the present stage of the discussion, is that developments of the kind under discussion tend to eliminate the substantive power of recommendation, and with it, the essentially persuasive nature of the "peaceful settlement" function of the United Nations. The accompanying tendency is to substitute peremptory demands, and voting victories imposed by *ad hoc* majorities derived on a basis of politics rather than principle. Notwithstanding these trends, however, the essential nature of international relations, which was in the minds of the framers when they placed the power of recommendation at the center of the peaceful settlement function, still remains. This essential nature is manifested by the readiness of states to reject solutions proposed by the United Nations, whether made in the form of recommendations or something stronger. From this point of view, the power of recommendation has a valuable flexibility by virtue of the very fact that it is not binding. A greater facility

---

[10] *Ibid.*

is thereby accorded to competent authorities to incorporate such elements as "principle" and "reason" in United Nations resolutions—elements which are of the essence when it comes to developing the rule of law. The fact that a state may reject a recommendation does not, by any means, deprive the recommendation of its force and effect in this respect. Of course the effect is enhanced if the recommendation *is* accepted. However, if the United Nations were, in relevant situations, to designate its pronouncements candidly as "recommendations" and to strive conscientiously to base these on principle and reason, the result would seem most likely to be an evolution in the direction of a stronger United Nations and an improved role for law in international relations.

However, the probable effectiveness of this line of approach is discounted by Falk:

> Even in domestic society, threats and symbolic eruptions of violence are the motive force behind a successful social protest on a fundamental issue. Any claim that social and political change are the products of merely persuasive processes is a most inaccurate observation; at best, it represents a slogan uncritically built into democratic ideology.[11]

The present writer would only go so far as to suggest that the introduction of efforts at persuasion through the United Nations, based on principle, accompanied by efforts to cause the United Nations to act in accordance with principle in other respects, is an effort worth making. It would not be expected that such efforts would bring about immediate solutions of serious disputes; the hope would rather be to bring about an evolution in the thinking of the governments and peoples of the world in the direction of developing effective constitutional principles. Any such development of public opinion should logically lead to increased effectiveness of the United Nations and an increasing tendency toward acceptance of United Nations recommendations as bases of solution of international disputes and situations.

The use and misuse of the substantive power of "recommendation" as just outlined has been of a character that must have led to public confusion as to the true powers of the United Nations in the relevant areas of its activity. We must now turn to consider other uses of the substantive power of "recommendation" which

---

[11] Falk, "The Adequacy of Contemporary Theories of International Law—Gaps in Legal Thinking," 50 Va. L.R. 231, 247 (1964).

are not authorized by the Charter at all—uses which, taken in conjunction with the distortions of its proper purpose just referred to,
makes the notion of "recommendation" a leading source of confusion as to the true powers of the United Nations and a major
hindrance to any prospects of developing the Charter as the basis
of a constitutional system capable of maintaining peace and
security.

United Nations Recommendations of Measures to be Applied by Member States

The use of "recommendation" now to be considered is that in
which the United Nations recommends that member states apply
tangible pressures in international disputes and situations. An example is the recommendation of the Security Council that member
states afford assistance to the Republic of Korea in repelling the
aggression from North Korea in 1950.[12] Speaking of this resolution, Vallat points out that "the intention that the Security Council
should take enforcement action only upon a decision under Article
39 and by the use of armed forces in accordance with Article 42
has been completely frustrated by the failure of any Member to
negotiate a special agreement"[13] under Article 43, and goes on to
say:

> The intention of the founders having been frustrated, the Mem-
> bers of the Organisation have naturally re-examined the Charter to
> see how, in accordance with other provisions, its basic Purposes and
> Principles can be fulfilled. Whatever may have been the original
> intention, as Kelsen concedes, the wording of Article 39 does not
> exclude an interpretation according to which the Security Council
> may, under that Article, recommend Members to use armed force.[14]
> . . . [I]t may be concluded that such a recommendation, being
> necessary to fulfill the purposes of the Organisation, should not
> be regarded as unconstitutional.[15]

---

[12] Cf. ch. 6, note 7.

[13] Vallat, "The Competence of the United Nations General Assembly," 97
Academie de droit international, Recueil des Cours 203, 259 (1959-II).

[14] Citing Kelsen, *Recent Trends in the Law of the United Nations* 932
(1951). Kelsen's own view is that "Article 39 distinguishes between 'recommendations' and 'measures . . . taken in accordance with Articles 41 and
42,' which Articles provide enforcement measures," and that "If the Council
wants to make recommendations under Article 39, it cannot recommend
enforcement measures; it can recommend only peaceful means for the
adjustment of a situation. . . ." *Ibid.* This view seems to correspond to
the original intent of the framers. *Cf.* p. 69 *supra.*

[15] Vallat, *supra* note 13, at 259-60.

In regard to this use of "recommendation" the question suggests itself as to whether the contemplated action is to be regarded as taken by the United Nations through the member states, or by the member states on their own responsibility. In the view maintained in the present discussion, the action should properly be regarded as taken by the United Nations, in which case the "recommendation" is merely a procedural device by which it chooses to act. It will be observed, however, that Professor Vallat, in the above-quoted passage, attributes Council action to the *substantive* power of recommendation found in Article 39 of the Charter. He appears to be consistent, then, in indicating that the contemplated action would be taken by the states. The "recommendation" must, in this view, be regarded as constituting a substantive authorization to states, and the only purpose of this recourse would seem to be to initiate action by states which the United Nations either considered itself legally unable to take, or was unwilling to take. A fundamental question is at once raised as to whether such a use of the substantive power of "recommendation" is warranted by the Charter, or would represent a useful course of Charter development.

Professor Wright, also, asserts the right of the United Nations to make such recommendations, but with the proviso that "An Assembly recommendation would hardly justify states in forcible intervention against another state unless there was a threat to, or breach of, the peace or an act of aggression."[16] In thus limiting the range of permissible action to that which would be open to the United Nations itself, a contradiction seems to be suggested as respects the indication, in the same sentence, that the action would be taken on the responsibilities of the states. Recognition of the limitation would seem to imply that the Charter authority is to be found in the parts of the Charter which authorize tangible pressures to deal with these kinds of situations. If this is so, the recommendation must be nothing more than a mode of procedure.

So long as measures initiated in this way are limited to situations constituting threats to peace, breaches of peace, and acts of aggression, no serious question need arise as to the exact nature of

---

[16] Wright, "Domestic Jurisdiction as a Limit on National and Supra-National Action," 56 Nw. U. L. Rev. 11, 30 (1961). Professor Wright is here referring to the Assembly, rather than the Security Council. However, the rule stated would seem to be based in the Charter and equally applicable to either body. Accord, Bowett, *United Nations Forces* 293 (1964).

the "recommendation" being employed. Such questions naturally become subordinated to the dominant fact that the United Nations is fulfilling a function which the "peoples of the world" conferred upon it and continue to recognize as essential to the maintenance of peace and security. In a case such as that of Korea, where the action is taken against clear-cut aggression, a disputation as to whether it is taken by the United Nations directly, or by individual states on the basis of a United Nations recommendation, would not seem to have major significance.[17] The real problem arises only when the notion of "recommendation" is used to initiate measures for purposes not to be found in the Charter.

The earliest illustration of this latter kind of case may be found in the recommendation by the Assembly, in 1946, that the member states withdraw their ambassadors and ministers from Spain as a means of pressure to bring about the replacement of the Franco Government by a more democratic regime.[18] This measure was a modified form of diplomatic sanction, one of the forms of pressure authorized by Article 41 of the Charter for dealing with aggressions, other breaches of peace, or threats to the peace. However, in the Spanish case there was no finding of a threat to peace; on the contrary a Subcommittee of the Security Council concluded that there was no such threat.[19] This Subcommittee went on to say:

> The Subcommittee finds that the present situation in Spain, though not an existing threat within the meaning of Article 39, is a situa-

---

[17] Thus, regarding the Korean case by itself, one would not necessarily disagree with Bowett that:

"The better view is to regard the Korean action as enforcement action authorized by recommendations under Article 39. In terms of the actual content of the Resolutions, their validity rests on the broader basis that the action taken by Members was fully consistent with the Purposes and Principles of the Charter and was authorized by Resolutions of a competent organ of the United Nations." Bowett, *op. cit. supra* note 16, at 34 (1964).

That this authority regards the operation as enforcement action undertaken by the United Nations, notwithstanding its initiation by recommendation to the member states, is confirmed *id.* at p. 267. On the use of the power of recommendation under Article 39, see *id.* 276-78.

[18] Res. 39(I), *Resolutions* 63, U.N. Gen. Ass. Off. Rec. 1st Sess., Pt. 2 (1946). *Cf.* p. 65 *supra.*

[19] "Report of the Sub-Committee on the Spanish Question," U.N. Security Council Off. Rec., 1st year, 1st ser., Spec. Supp., Rev. ed. 8 (S/75) (1946).

tion the continuance of which is in fact likely to endanger the maintenance of international peace and security. The situation in Spain thus falls to be dealt with by the Security Council under Chapter VI of the Charter, which covers measures of peaceful settlement and adjustment.[20]

As to the importance of maintaining the distinction, the Subcommittee said:

> A very sharp instrument has been entrusted to the Security Council by the United Nations under Chapter VII of the Charter, and the Security Council must be careful that this instrument is not blunted nor used in any way which would strain the intentions of the Charter or which would not be applicable in all similar cases.[21]

Yet the Subcommittee went on immediately to suggest that the General Assembly recommend that the member states withdraw their diplomatic representation from Spain as a means of pressure on that country to secure the desired change of government. As to the Assembly's authority to act in this way, the Subcommittee said:

> The General Assembly has power under Article 14 to make recommendations as to the peaceful adjustment of any situation . . . Furthermore, the General Assembly's powers of recommendation under Article 10 cover all matters within the scope of the Charter, including the purposes of the Charter set out in paragraph 2 of Article 1, which is to take appropriate measures to strengthen universal peace.[22]

The Subcommittee, plainly acutely aware of the limitations upon the use of tangible pressures by the United Nations as such, apparently did not feel that these limitations were applicable or relevant when taken by states pursuant to United Nations recommendation. In maintaining that the Assembly might recommend, and that member states might impose diplomatic measures pur-

[20] *Id.* at 10.

[21] *Id.* at 8.

[22] *Id.* at 10. With regard to this invocation of Article 1, paragraph 2, it may be observed that the preceding paragraph of the Charter (Article 1 (1)), sets forth the specific function of applying tangible pressures, and in doing so limits the use of such measures to situations constituting threats to peace, breaches of peace and acts of aggression. Text quoted p. 76 *supra.* The use of Article 1 (2) here suggested by the Subcommittee would amount to a *carte blanche* enabling the Assembly to apply such measures for any purposes which were deemed to strengthen international peace. No further attempt to use Article 1(2) in this way has been observed by the present writer.

suant to that recommendation in the Spanish case, which was found in the same report not to constitute a threat to peace, the Subcommittee evidently felt that the Assembly recommendation would be without juridical significance and that the resulting action would be entirely upon the responsibilities of the states. A striking difference will be noted as between this view and that of Professor Wright, referred to above, in which the latter authority, while maintaining that the Assembly may recommend action, and that the resulting measures will be taken by the states (rather than by the United Nations), holds that the measures can be legally justified only in situations constituting aggression or other breaches of peace, or threats to peace.

When the proposal came before the General Assembly, a relatively few states supported the Subcommittee's apparent position that action taken pursuant to Assembly recommendation would be taken by the member states and not by the Organization.[23] The discussion turned mainly on the question whether or not the proposed action would constitute wrongful "intervention" by the United Nations in the affairs of Spain.[24] Most states which supported the measure argued that it would not, but on grounds which did not deny that the proposed action would be taken by the United Nations as such.[25] Among these was the Soviet Union.[26]

A number of states, including the United States and the United Kingdom, opposed the proposed measure in the Spanish case on the ground that it would involve wrongful intervention by the

[23] A proposal incorporating this view was introduced by the delegations of Chile, Guatemala, Mexico, Panama and Venezuela. U.N. Gen. Ass. Off. Rec. 1st Sess., pt. 2, 1st Comm. 358 (A/C. 1/108) (1946). See statements of France and Panama in plenary session, id., Plenary 1193, 1220.

[24] This point is discussed infra this chapter at p. 199.

[25] The Venezuelan and Panamanian Delegations, in arguing that the rule of "non-intervention" did not apply to situations such as the Spanish case, seemed to assume that the action would be taken by the United Nations. U.N. Gen. Ass. Off. Rec. 1st Sess., pt. 2, 1st Comm. 229, 240-41 (1946). Thereby they seemed to contradict the position noted in note 23 supra.

[26] That Delegation and some others maintained that the Franco regime of Spain was fascist and therefore, automatically, a threat to international peace. This can be said to constitute one argument in the mixture of arguments advanced in support of the Assembly resolution. The Assembly could readily have overruled the Subcommittee's finding that the situation was not a threat to peace; however, no concerted move in this direction developed.

United Nations in the affairs of Spain.[27] These delegations must have considered that the proposed action would be taken by the United Nations as such. This position, as it bore on the fact that the action would be initiated by "recommendation" of the United Nations, was thus explained by the Delegation of El Salvador:

> While each state had the right to decide on its relations with another, when the United Nations recommended that its Members break off diplomatic relations with Spain, it was a clear case of collective intervention . . .[28]

The mixed arguments advanced in this case must have created a mixed impression on the part of the world public as to the Charter basis for the action. Most people no doubt consider that a concerted move by states to apply pressures against another state, with a view to forcing a change in its internal regime, would be wrongful intervention. In this case, the action was concerted through the United Nations and had the sanction of the Organization; however, it must also be equally clear to most informed people that the United Nations itself was never given the power to apply tangible pressures against states for such purposes. Conversely, it is forbidden to intervene in the domestic affairs of states. How, then, could the United Nations, by "recommending" that states act, give its sanction for doing something that it could not do itself? The most reasonable answer is, perhaps, that it was drawing from the substantive concept of "recommendation" an entirely new meaning enabling it, in conjunction with member states, to make and enforce substantive decisions concerning the internal and external relations of states. However, it could hardly be expected that the "peoples of the world" would readily comprehend and adopt such a thesis. Only the previous year, at San Francisco, they had had the opportunity of conferring such far-reaching powers on the Organization had they desired to do so; however, such a possibility had scarcely been discussed. It was, by the same token, hardly reasonable to expect that they would suddenly become willing to accept, as against their own states, the right of the

---

[27] In the Plenary session the United States Delegation did not pursue this argument but, at the same time, did not indicate that it had changed its opinion. It voted for the resolution which, by then, had been modified so as to recommend only the withdrawal of ambassadors and ministers from Madrid, instead of a complete breach of diplomatic relations. *Cf.* ch. 3, note 2 *supra.*

[28] U.N. Gen. Ass. Off. Rec. 1st Sess., pt. 2, 1st Comm. 231 (1946).

United Nations to apply measures for purposes similar to those being pursued in the Spanish case.

Notwithstanding that the theory presently under discussion—that the measure was being taken by the member states and not the United Nations—was only one of several advanced in the Spanish case, it may have made a disproportionate impact on the informed world public. This would seem possible because of the generally prevailing impression that the United Nations—and particularly the General Assembly—could not legally act to overturn the government of a state, and the resulting impression that the action in this case must have been intended to be taken by states acting independently of the Organization.

To the extent that any such impression was created, it was probably strengthened by the Assembly's recommendation of 1949 that states apply an arms embargo against Albania and Bulgaria, on account of those countries' threats to the independence of Greece.[29] The Security Council was obstructed from acting in this case by the Soviet veto. Since the Assembly was generally regarded as being unable to take such action as an arms embargo, the general opinion was, no doubt, that it was going no further than to "recommend" action which would then be taken by the member states. However, this measure clearly had the purpose of dealing with a threat to—indeed an actual breach of—international peace, so that there was no question of the United Nations going beyond its prescribed powers.

The Korean case was similar in this respect. The prevailing view at the time was, apparently, that the Council, in recommending that member states go to the assistance of the Republic of Korea, was acting on the basis of the substantive power of "recommendation" found in Article 39 of the Charter.

While this view of the matter may, to some extent, have strengthened the impression that the resulting action by states is outside the Organization, the case may also have had a countervailing impact in demonstrating that this use of "recommendation" is nothing but a device for taking action which, for some reason, the Organization is not deemed capable of initiating in the "normal" manner. In this case the disability was considered to lie in the failure to conclude the agreements contemplated by Article 43 of the Charter, so that the Security Council was not in a position to "order" member states to provide troops and other assist-

---

[29] Res. 288 (IV) *Resolutions 9, id.* 4th Sess. (A/1251) (1949).

ance to the Republic of Korea. In such case, it might seem a logical recourse to "recommend" that states take the desired action, and viewed in this light, the recommendation would appear as nothing more than an alternate mode of procedure.

There were also other reasons for considering that this operation was, from a constitutional standpoint, a United Nations operation.[30] A question pertinent in this connection is: if it is desired that a given measure be carried out by individual states, outside the United Nations, why undertake to secure a United Nations "recommendation" at all? The interested states could make the necessary arrangements outside the Organization, which is largely what was done in the Korean case. The answer is, rather obviously, that it is hoped, by obtaining United Nations sanction of the proposed measures, to gain public support for them, and to make them more effective. In the Korean case, this motivation was clearly spelled out by the Assembly's Collective Measures Committee, which also recommended that efforts be made to stress the United Nations connection in any future operations of the kind, in order to mobilize public support behind them.[31] Among measures taken by the Council for this purpose, in the Korean case, was the authorization of the use of the United Nations flag and United Nations decorations by forces in the field. The command of the operation, though organized by the United States, was frequently referred to (particularly by the United States) as the "United Nations Command."[32]

However, there are more fundamental reasons for regarding such an operation as a United Nations operation. By recommending an operation, the United Nations sanctions it and, inescapably, commits to it its prestige and responsibility. It seems inconsistent that the United Nations should take such a step and, at the same time, be considered as absolved from responsibility for it. By the

---

[30] It can be said to have been, in actual political reality, an operation of the United States with assistance from some other United Nations members. However, we are here speaking of its constitutional nature viewed from the standpoint of the United Nations. It may also be observed that the United States was foremost in desiring to have the operation covered by the U.N. "umbrella."

[31] *Report of the Collective Measures Committee,* U.N. Gen. Ass. Off. Rec. 6th Sess., Supp. No. 13, at 28 (A/1891) (1951).

[32] For a comprehensive compilation of indications that this was a United Nations operation, see Weissberg, *The International Status of the United Nations* 78-105 (1961). See also Bowett, *op. cit. supra* note 16, at 45-47.

same token, it seems to involve a contradiction that the United Nations should be able to recommend that states apply force, or other tangible pressures, for the pursuit of aims which it could not pursue itself. The result of this line of thought is that the United Nations may recommend that states apply such tangible pressures only for purposes which are within its own powers. The further result then emerges that the power of recommendation thus being employed is merely procedural—a legitimate device to be employed by the United Nations for the achievement of its legitimate purposes.

That the Korean operation was a collective measure of the United Nations has, in fact, been indicated by Secretaries-General of the United Nations,[33] by some other authorities[34] and by the General Assembly in its resolution of February 1, 1951.[35] Some authorities hold otherwise.[36] Vallat, upholding the view that the operation was carried out by member states on the recommendation of the United Nations, thus explains the Assembly resolution of February 1, 1951:

> Once it is conceded that the General Assembly is competent to recommend that Members of the United Nations should take steps to meet aggression, it follows that the Assembly must be regarded as competent to make a finding of aggression as the basis for such a recommendation. This is an excellent illustration of the organic interpretation of the Charter, which is justified if one views it as a

---

[33] Ch. 6, notes 35 and 36 *supra* and accompanying text.

[34] Bowett, *op. cit. supra* note 16, at 59; Taubenfeld, "International Armed Forces and the Rules of War," 45 Am. J. Int'l L. 671, 675, note 22 (1951). Professor Leo Gross considers that it was an action of the United Nations at least to the extent of obliging members, under Art. 2(5), to "give the United Nations every assistance in action it takes in accordance with the present Charter." Gross, "Voting in the Security Council: Abstention from Voting and Absence from Meetings," 60 Yale L. J. 209, 254-55 (1951).

[35] *Cf.* p. 151 *supra.*

[36] Professors Stone and Lacharrière consider that the operation took place outside the United Nations and had the legal nature of war. Stone, *Legal Controls of International Conflict* 234 (1954); Lacharrière, "L'Action des Nations Unies pour la Sécurité et pour la Paix," 18 Politique Étrangère 307, 333-34 (1953). That it was not a United Nations operation is the view of Baxter, "Constitutional Forms and Some Legal Problems of International Military Command," 29 Brit. Yb. Int'l L. 325, 335-36 (1952). That the action was taken by member states, outside the United Nations, is the view of Seyersted, "United Nations Forces: Some Legal Problems," 37 Brit. Yb. Int'l L. 351, 430-31 (1961). To similar effect, Kelsen, *op. cit. supra* note 14, at 936-37 (1951), but see *id.* 937-38.

constitution designed to give effect to certain purposes and principles rather than as a contract to be construed strictly.[37]

With reference to the Assembly's designation of the operation as a United Nations action, this authority simply states that, notwithstanding the application of this "label," "military action to restore the peace in Korea was taken by Members of the United Nations and not by the Organization itself."[38] To the present writer it appears that, notwithstanding this last assertion by Professor Vallat, his statement quoted just previously tends to support the view that the Korean operation was, in fact, from a constitutional point of view, a measure of the United Nations. If the action is by the member states, why is the "finding of aggression" regarded as the basis for it, or even relevant? If it is relevant, it would seem to follow that the Organization is acting under its power to apply "collective measures." Again, in this light, the "recommendation" falls into place as a procedural device for carrying out the basic decision.

The Korean case inspired the Uniting for Peace resolution which, perhaps, more than the Korean case itself, tended to build up the notion that "recommendation," in the sense under discussion, is used as a substantive source of authority and not in a merely procedural sense. Before proceeding to consider the basis for this opinion, reference may be made to the description of the resolution in Chapter 6, and the opinion therein expressed that it should properly be regarded as based on a substantive, residual, power on the part of the General Assembly to apply collective measures.

However, in the Assembly debate on the resolution, the generality of states supporting it sought to base it upon an entirely different theory of Charter interpretation. Following the then prevalent view of the Korean case, they were disposed to regard the power of "recommendation" as forming the substantive basis of the contemplated measures, and consequently identified the Charter basis as being those provisions—herein generically cited as Articles 10, 11(2) and 14—which confer a substantive power of "recommendation" on the Assembly in connection with its handling of disputes and situations.[39]

---

37 Vallat, *supra* note 13, at 269.

38 *Id.* at 270.

39 Provisions quoted at p. 111 *supra*. This general view was exemplified in the statements of the United States, Chile, France, Peru and Cuba. U.N. Gen. Ass. Off. Rec. 5th Sess., 1st Comm. 64, 67, 70, 75, 79-80 (A/C. 1/ SR. 354-357) (1950).

The Soviet Delegation opposed the resolution on the ground that it represented an assertion on the part of the Assembly of power to take action, whereas Article 11(2) of the Charter provides that "any such question on which action is necessary shall be referred to the Security Council by the General Assembly."[40]

In attempting to meet this argument, delegations cited the proposition stated in the preamble of the proposed resolution that the Council's responsibility in such matters is "primary" and not exclusive. However they did not go on to make what would seem to be the logical inference that the Assembly therefore had a residual authority to take the same kind of "action" as may be taken by the Council, e.g. "collective measures." The tendency was rather to agree with the Soviet Union that the Security Council had the monopoly of such measures and then to argue that, by acting under its power of "recommendation," the Assembly was taking a different kind of action than that referred to in Article 11(2). The Canadian Delegation, for example, after strongly asserting the power of the General Assembly to take measures to safeguard peace and security when the Council is prevented from doing so, went on immediately to say that "actions" under Article 11(2) are not to be confused with recommendations which the Assembly is empowered to make to member states.[41] The Philippine Delegation expressed the view that the proposed resolution "did not substitute one body for another, but established a second line of defense in case the first failed."[42] These pronouncements seem to have reflected the general view held by those who supported the resolution. The necessary consequence seems to have been that these delegations considered that action to be taken under the resolution would be by member states acting on their own responsibility and outside the Organization.

There is in this case an understandable reason, stronger than that in the Korean case, for the desire to have the contemplated action taken outside the United Nations, namely the generally prevailing view that the Assembly is without power in the premises. The theory maintained by the delegations supporting the resolution had the dual purpose (a) of enabling the Organization to act in the event that the Security Council is prevented from doing so,

[40] *Id.* at 80-86 (A/C. 1/SR. 357).

[41] *Id.* at 90 (A/C. 1/SR. 358).

[42] *Id.* at 92. See also statement of Pakistani Delegation, *id.* at 127 (A/C. 1/SR. 363).

and, at the same time, (b) of leaving undisturbed the prevailing impression that the Council has the monopoly of true United Nations collective measures as contemplated by the Charter.

Reasons for considering this theory untenable, and, particularly, for considering that operations instituted in this way should be regarded as United Nations operations, have been advanced above, in connection with the Korean case. The view may also be reiterated that so long as the resulting measures are plainly in accord with a well-understood United Nations function—that of "collective measures"—the constitutional issue does not achieve great significance. Nevertheless, continued insistence upon the use of the substantive power of recommendation in such matters has a tendency to break down the distinction between the "collective measures" function and that of "peaceful settlement" (to which the substantive power of recommendation normally pertains), and real harm is done when, aided by this tendency, states cause the Organization to sponsor applications of tangible pressures against other states, without their consent, with the ostensible purpose of enforcing changes in their internal or external relations. Such harm—which is conceived in terms of resulting public confusion detrimental to the development of law and the Charter—is believed inevitably to have been caused by United Nations measures in the Spanish, Portuguese and South African cases. The responsible authorities considered, of course, that the advantages of the courses pursued in those cases outweighed any disadvantages. Pros and cons involved in particular cases are discussed elsewhere in this book.

Rhodesian Case

Recent developments in the Rhodesian case, at the time this study was completed, indicate that the theory advocated in the preceding section may be in accord with a policy currently being followed by the Security Council.

Following Rhodesia's unilateral declaration of independence from Great Britain on November 11, 1965, the Security Council took the following decisions, *inter alia,* in its resolution of November 20, 1965:[42a]

   1. *Determines* that the situation resulting from the proclamation of independence by the illegal authorities in Southern Rhodesia is ex-

---

[42a] S/RES/217 (1965) Nov. 20, 1965, 2 U.N. Monthly Chronicle, No. 11, at 25 (December 1965).

tremely grave, that the Government of the United Kingdom . . .
should put an end to it and that its continuance in time constitutes a
threat to international peace and security;

* * *

4. *Calls* upon the Government of the United Kingdom to quell
this rebellion of the racist minority;

* * *

8. *Calls upon* all States to refrain from any action which would
assist and encourage the illegal regime and, in particular, to desist
from providing it with arms, equipment and military material, and
to do their utmost in order to break all economic relations with Southern Rhodesia, including an embargo on oil and petroleum products;

9. *Calls upon* the Government of the United Kingdom to enforce
urgently and with vigour all the measures it has announced, as well
as those mentioned in paragraph 8 above; . . . .

Although the British Government, in early April, 1966, desired
to use force on the high seas to prevent the carriage of oil destined
for Rhodesia, that Government and others were evidently of the
opinion that the above resolution did not contain the necessary
authorization. Consequently the British Government requested the
Council to enact a new resolution, which that body did on April
9, 1966.[42b] In this resolution the Council, *inter alia*:

1. *Determines* that the . . . [Rhodesian] situation constitutes a
threat to the peace;

2. *Calls upon* the Portuguese Government not to permit oil to be
pumped through the pipeline from Beira to Rhodesia;

3. *Calls upon* the Portuguese Government not to receive at Beira
oil destined for Rhodesia;

4. *Calls upon* all States to ensure the diversion of any of their
vessels reasonably believed to be carrying oil destined for Rhodesia
which may be en route for Beira;

5. *Calls upon* the Government of the United Kingdom to prevent
by the use of force if necessary the arrival at Beira of vessels reasonably
believed to be carrying oil destined for Rhodesia, and empowers the
United Kingdom to arrest and detain the tanker known as the Joanna
V upon her departure from Beira in the event her oil cargo is dis-
charged there.

This last paragraph was accepted by all concerned as placing
the British action in question in the category of United Nations
"collective measures," and the British Government proceeded to
utilize the authority by stopping and diverting, on the high seas,
a tanker heading for Beira.

[42b] S/RES/221 (1966) April 9, 1966.

It is to be observed that the phrase "calls upon" introduces relevant paragraphs of both resolutions. Since paragraph 9 of the earlier resolution, and paragraph 5 of the later, both introduced by this phrase and both apparently authorizing British authorities to stop vessels carrying oil for Rhodesia, have been given opposite interpretations as to the nature of the authority thus granted under the Charter, it may be inferred that the phrase in question is not regarded as having more than procedural importance. While this view, on the particular point, is believed to be correct, it would seem that, at least for the benefit of public opinion, some clearer indication than is to be found in these resolutions, concerning the nature of the action being undertaken, is needed. The formulations of these resolutions, taken as a whole, scarcely seem calculated to lessen the general state of public confusion as to the true nature of the relevant powers of the United Nations which is believed to exist, and which forms the subject of the present chapter.

While the phrase "calls upon" is found in Charter provisions relating to "collective measures," it has also been used in contexts which have left its meaning in resolutions ambiguous. Statesmen have tended to juxtapose "binding orders" versus "recommendation," and these notions give a clearer idea of the alternative approaches involved in the discussions. A binding order of the Council has sometimes been regarded as a prerequisite to the initiation of collective measures, while the "recommendation" of a measure has sometimes been regarded as signifying that the measure is not in the "collective measure" category. As between "binding orders" and "recommendations," it seems clear that the Council, by paragraph 5 of its resolution of April 9, 1966, was not intending to "order" the United Kingdom to take the specified action in the sense of legally obligating it to do so regardless of its wishes in the premises. Indeed, it seems doubtful that the Council possesses the authority to order the use of force by a state in the absence of an agreement with that state concluded pursuant to Article 43. In the Rhodesian case, the British Government was not only prepared to take the action in question, but itself initiated the request for United Nations authority to do so. Thus, in point of practical fact, the resolution of April 9, 1966, appears, in this respect, more to resemble a "recommendation" than a "binding order."

The use of the phrase "calls upon" instead of "recommends" to introduce the paragraph in question might be interpreted as reflecting a desire to avoid the latter phraseology because of the precedents of the recent Portuguese and South African cases, wherein the initiation of measures by recommendation was taken to mean that the resulting measures were not in the "collective measures" category of the Charter. This line of thought would lead to the conclusion that the phrase "calls upon" in the Rhodesian resolution had substantive import *vis-à-vis* the categorization of the resulting measure as a "collective measure." One difficulty of this interpretation is that paragraph 9 of the earlier resolution of November 20, 1965, also used this phrase, but with different effect.

On the other hand, a precedent for the initiation of force by recommendation is to be found in the Korean case. Since that operation has been officially recognized as a collective measure, it would seem that the use of "recommendation" is there regarded as having been merely procedural. To give a similar interpretation to the use of "calls upon" in the Council resolutions of November 20, 1965, and April 9, 1966, would seem to be reasonable.

"Recommendation" and "Permissiveness" as Authority for United Nations Measures

Recommendation by the United Nations to Itself

The development of the official theory which places the United Nations Emergency Force (UNEF) within the "peaceful settlement" function of the United Nations has been outlined in Chapter 4, above. The Force, it will be recalled, was established and deployed pursuant to decisions of the General Assembly. The official view that this operation is of the "peaceful settlement" variety was affirmed by the World Court's Advisory Opinion in the "Expenses" case,[43] which then went on, logically enough in view of this theory, to hold that the Force was formed pursuant to the substantive power of "recommendation" found in Articles 11 or 14 of the Charter. As to Article 11, paragraph 2, the Opinion states:

> This paragraph . . . in its first sentence empowers the General Assembly, by means of recommendations to States or to the Security Council, or to both, to organize peace-keeping operations, at the request, or with the consent, of the States concerned.[44]

---

[43] *Certain Expenses of the United Nations* . . . [1962] I.C.J. Rep. 171-172.
[44] *Id.* at 164.

A question may be suggested as to whether it is either desirable or necessary to give to the word "recommendation" such a new meaning as this, in which the Assembly recommends to itself and thereby finds the authority to undertake an action. The Advisory Opinion justifies this use of the word as follows:

> Whether the General Assembly proceeds under Article 11 or under Article 14, the implementation of its recommendations for setting up commissions or other bodies involves organizational activity—action—in connection with the maintenance of international peace and security. Such implementation is a normal feature of the functioning of the United Nations. Such committees, commissions or other bodies or individuals, constitute, in some cases, subsidiary organs established under the authority of Article 22 of the Charter. The functions of the General Assembly for which it may establish such subsidiary organs include, for example, investigation, observation and supervision, but the way in which such subsidiary organs are utilized depends on the consent of the State or States concerned.[45]

There have been a number of cases in which the Assembly and Security Council have appointed mediators, conciliation commissions, commissions of investigation, observer corps and similar organs and individuals, and it has never been considered necessary to bring up the substantive power of recommendation as a basis for doing so. The Assembly and Security Council would seem to possess the capability, either as spelled out in the Charter or by necessary implication, to adopt appropriate methods not inconsistent with the Charter for carrying out their functions. These are procedural matters, not of the essence. The more fundamental question is always whether the substantive function in question is possessed by the Organization, or the particular organ. In the Suez case, this question was: did the Assembly have the authority to set up an armed force with the powers of UNEF? It is difficult to perceive how the substantive power to make recommendations as part of the "peaceful settlement" function has anything to do with this question.

In the Security Council resolution of March 4, 1964, concerning the Cyprus case,[46] the following two paragraphs provide for the establishment and terms of reference of the United Nations Force to serve in the Cypriot crisis of that year:

---

[45] *Id.* at 165.

[46] U.N. Security Council Off. Rec. 19th year, Supp. Jan.-March 1964, at 102 (S/5575) (1964).

The Security Council,

* * *

4. *Recommends* the creation, with the consent of the Government of Cyprus, of a United Nations peace-keeping force in Cyprus. The composition and size of the force shall be established by the Secretary-General, in consultation with the Governments of Cyprus, Greece, Turkey and the United Kingdom. The commander of the force shall be appointed by the Secretary-General and report to him. The Secretary-General, who shall keep the governments providing the force fully informed, shall report periodically to the Security Council on its operation;

5. *Recommends* that the function of the force should be, in the interest of preserving international peace and security, to use its best efforts to prevent a recurrence of fighting and, as necessary, to contribute to the maintenance and restoration of law and order and a return to normal conditions; . . .

The actual establishment of the Force, in the constitutional sense, would appear to be the kind of act which should be carried out on behalf of the Organization by the Security Council or General Assembly. In such basic policy matters, the Secretary-General is generally subject to the instructions of these two bodies. The first sentence of the above paragraph 4 would, therefore, be expected to contain an appropriate declaration establishing the Force, after which the remainder of the paragraph, instructing the Secretary-General to carry out the decision, would be logical. Actually, however, what we find in the first sentence is a mere recommendation that the Force be established. Nor is it made clear to whom the recommendation is directed. On a first reading of the paragraph it might appear to be directed to the Secretary-General; however, this would be illogical for reasons just indicated. Although the resolution contemplates that member states would supply the necessary troops, equipment, etc., for the force by voluntary contribution—e.g. pursuant, in effect, to "recommendation" of the Organization—there is no intimation in the resolution that the Force would be formally established by these states.

The correct solution of the problem is, no doubt, that the recommendation is directed to the United Nations itself. It was perhaps considered that this formulation would be the logical outcome of the theory that the Force was not intended to be a collective measure, but fell rather in the "peaceful settlement" category of United Nations activity.

The same theory was doubtless desired to be officially maintained in the case of UNEF and, at least initially, in that of ONUC.

In neither of these cases, however, was the word "recommends" used as the operative word in establishing the forces. In the case of UNEF, the Assembly established the United Nations Command, appointed the Chief of the Command, issued instructions to competent authorities subject to its jurisdiction, and made other appropriate decisions.[47] With respect to ONUC, the Secretary-General was given a blanket instruction to organize and deploy the Force.[48] The use of "recommends" would have been inappropriate and confusing, in either of these cases, as it appears to be when used as the operative word in establishing the Cyprus Force. Used in this sense, it means "establishes," whereas its ordinary meaning is quite different.

As to paragraph 5 of the Cyprus resolution, quoted above, there may be a somewhat more cogent reason for casting the terms of reference of the Force in terms of a "recommendation." The desire was, no doubt, to do everything possible to reassure states contributing troops that the Force would not become engaged in combat while, at the same time, leaving some doubt in the minds of the parties to the dispute as to what the Force might do in urgent circumstances. Reference is made to the discussion of some factors believed relevant in this connection toward the end of Chapter 4 above. Also relevant is believed to be the suggestion ventured in the present chapter that, so long as the operation in question is obviously discharging a major and agreed purpose of the United Nations, questions of detail as to the exact Charter basis of what is being done are relatively inconsequential. So far as Cyprus is concerned, the world knows that it is a threat to peace, and also is aware that the United Nations is fully empowered to apply tangible pressure if necessary to deal with such a threat. A United Nations Force, in such a case, may act as long as possible in pursuit of the United Nations peaceful settlement function, and may then, if conditions necessitate, and if duly authorized, assume the role of a collective measure. In such a case no serious questions are to be anticipated as to the constitutional basis of what is being done.

Public confusion would seem to be the likely result, however, when the United Nations purports to establish an armed force by recommendation, but leaves it unclear to whom the recommendation is directed.

---

[47] *Cf.* Ch. 4, note 46 *supra*.

[48] U.N. Security Council Off. Rec. 15th year, Supp. July-Sept. 1960, at 16 (S/4387) (1960).

"Intervention," "Non-Intervention" and "Permissiveness"

An important aspect of the type of recommendatory action under discussion is the apparently general opinion that any measures resulting from this source of authority must have the consent of the state or states affected by them. "Permissiveness" was, from the outset, an element of the official United Nations position as to the nature of UNEF,[49] which position was confirmed by the Advisory Opinion in the "Expenses" case.[50]

The concept of "permissiveness" was accorded the status of a positive source of authority for such measures when the Secretary-General said that the situation in the Congo "represented a threat to the peace and security justifying United Nations intervention on the basis of the explicit request of the Government of the Republic of the Congo."[51] That permission may play a role as a source of authority is also suggested in the following statement of the Legal Adviser of the United States Department of State in his oral argument before the World Court in the "Expenses" case:

> A State, or group of States, would be free, if the necessary consents were obtained, to use its forces to maintain the peace, as the Middle East and Congo forces are now being used. The United Nations Charter does not limit that right. And surely what States might band together to do outside the United Nations, it is not forbidden that they do through the mechanism of that Organization . . .[52]

These statements differ somewhat from each other in scope, but seem to give to the element of "permissiveness" an affirmative force and effect as a source of authority which is quite indefinite, and contrary to the proposition that the United Nations is an organization of limited and delegated powers. It is, indeed, sometimes asserted that the United Nations is not of this latter character.[53] This is, however, in the view of the present discussion, an opinion that has to be controverted simply on the ground that if an effective system is to be built up, it has to be built on the basis of principle, Charter and otherwise. The idea that permission

---

[49] *Cf.* p. 96 *supra.*

[50] *Cf.* pp. 111-12 *supra.*

[51] Passage quoted p. 100 *supra.* See also discussion at that point concerning the dual nature of the authorization.

[52] *Certain Expenses of the United Nations . . . — Pleadings, Oral Arguments and Documents* 423 (I.C.J. 1962).

[53] Seyersted, "United Nations Forces: Some Legal Problems," 37 Brit. Yb. Int'l L. 351, 447-48 (1961).

of states concerned may serve, wholly or in part, as the basis for United Nations action appears to invoke a criterion quite divorced from any basis in principle.[54]

The notion of "permissiveness" is undoubtedly linked with the rule which prohibits United Nations intervention in the domestic affairs of states. This rule is set forth in Article 2(7) of the Charter as follows:

> Nothing contained in the present Charter shall authorize the United Nations to intervene in matters which are essentially within the domestic jurisdiction of any state or shall require the Members to submit such matters to settlement under the present Charter; but this principle shall not prejudice the application of enforcement measures under Chapter VII.

If the United Nations is an organization of delegated powers, as is believed to be the case, the rule stated in Article 2(7) is but one of three interrelated propositions. Two of them could have been stated in terms similar to the tenth amendment of the United States Constitution, e.g. by saying that the powers not conferred upon the Organization by the Charter are reserved to the member states. This would amount to a formulation, in positive terms, of the propositions that the United Nations has the powers which the members have agreed to in the Charter, and that all other powers continue to reside in the member states. The third proposition is, then, that negatively formulated in Article 2(7), stating that the Organization must not intervene in those matters as to which it has not been given any power and which, consequently, remain in the states.

Article 2(7) is, therefore, merely one way of stating a basic proposition inherent in the fact that the United Nations is an organization of limited and delegated powers. However in this respect, as in others pertaining to Charter law, practice has diverged from sound theory. The tendency has been to treat Article 2(7) as a criterion of Charter powers rather distinct from the various provisions laying down such powers in affirmative terms elsewhere in the Charter. So strongly, indeed, has attention been concentrated upon the issue of "intervention" versus "non-intervention" in various cases that it is sometimes possible to discern the outline of an emergent rule under which particular measures would be held to be within the powers of the Organization on the sole basis

---

[54] Bowett, *op. cit. supra* note 16, at 180, 231-32, 311-12.

of findings that they would *not* constitute intervention. The notion of "permissiveness" has an obvious relevance in this theory.

The tendency under discussion, in so far as it involves the rule of non-intervention in domestic affairs, may have had its origins as early as the San Francisco Conference. One of the features of the corresponding clause of the Dumbarton Oaks Proposals was that, following the precedent of the League Covenant, it referred only to the handling of disputes and situations. At San Francisco, a change in this formulation was felt to be necessary as a result of the decision to incorporate in the Charter provisions on social and economic matters—subjects traditionally within the domestic jurisdictions of individual states. In explaining the revised draft provision introduced by the Sponsoring Powers, the United States Delegate, Mr. Dulles, delineated the main issue as follows:

> [T]he question has been raised as to what would be the basic relation of the Organization to member states: Would the Organization deal with the governments of the member states, or would the Organization penetrate directly into the domestic life and social economy of the member states?[55]

He went on to explain that the proposal under discussion, pertaining to the non-intervention clause, would require the Organization to deal with governments. On the same point, the United States Delegation to the Conference, in its Report to the President, said:

> To extend this principle [e.g. non-intervention in domestic affairs] to the activities of the Organization as a whole, instead of limiting it to the pacific settlement of disputes as had been proposed at Dumbarton Oaks, seemed desirable because of the amplification of the power and authority given to the Assembly and, particularly, to the Economic and Social Council. Without this general limitation, which now flows from the statement of the principle in Chapter I, it might have been supposed that the Economic and Social Council could interfere directly in the domestic economy, social structure, or cultural or educational arrangements of the member states. Such a possibility is now definitely excluded.[56]

There seems to be here implied a discontinuity as between the positive powers of the United Nations, and the rule of non-inter-

---

[55] Doc. No. 1019, I/1/42, 6 U.N. Conf. Int'l Org. Docs. 508 (1945).

[56] *Charter of the United Nations: Report to the President on the Results of the San Francisco Conference* by the Chairman of the United States Delegation, the Secretary of State 44 (Department of State Publication 2349, Conference Series 71, 1945).

vention. Instead of merely representing the negative corollary of the affirmative powers of the Organization, the rule of non-intervention is here given a positive role in counter-acting what seems to be regarded as a right which the Organization would otherwise have to intervene in the affairs of states. If it had been true, as indicated in the penultimate sentence of the above-quoted passage, that Article 2(7) was essential to prevent the Economic and Social Council from interfering directly in the economic, social, and cultural affairs of states, it must have been known, during the Conference itself, that there was something wrong with the drafting of the substantive provisions concerning economic and social matters. If this were so, one might wonder why these provisions were not corrected so as to confer upon the Organization the exact powers which the delegates desired that it should have.

There were, in fact, no such defects with respect to the substantive provisions in question. As Preuss states:

> There is no provision of the Charter which empowers any organ of the United Nations to penetrate directly into the domestic life of member states in order to regulate their economic and social affairs . . . If Article 2(7) has the meaning attached to it by the foregoing statements it clearly becomes superfluous, for it would prohibit action which no organ of the United Nations is in any event authorized to take.[57]

The framers of the Charter were no doubt reasonably satisfied, with respect to the articles on economic and social matters as with respect to other parts of the Charter, that these provisions reflected their intentions. Article 2(7) was inserted as reinsurance that the United Nations would not undertake to intervene in domestic affairs. However, this clause had the effect of introducing rather independent concepts, difficult to define in themselves, and which, by affording new and diverse bases of argument on controversial issues, made the bases of decision more diffuse and less explicit.

Under Article 15(8) of the League of Nations Covenant, corresponding to Article 2(7) of the Charter, intervention was prohibited as to matters which, by international law, were solely within the domestic jurisdiction of states. Had this "international law" criterion been maintained in the United Nations Charter, a

---

[57] Preuss, "Article 2, Paragraph 7 of the Charter of the United Nations and Matters of Domestic Jurisdiction," 74 Academie de droit international, Recueil des Cours 547, 578 (1949-I); citing I Oppenheim, *International Law* 379, note 1 (7th ed. Lauterpacht 1948).

standard would have been established ascertainable, at least, by a competent tribunal. Even under the legal criterion, however, the general, over-all scope of domestic jurisdiction, or of the "reserved domain" of states, is inherently flexible and uncertain since it consists of just those matters which are not covered by international law, and since international law is subject to evolution and change.[58]

The Dumbarton Oaks Proposals contained a non-intervention clause based on the "international law" criterion of the League of Nations Covenant; however, at San Francisco, this was changed and the rule made to apply, instead, to "matters which are essentially within the domestic jurisdiction of any state." The intent of the changed formula seems to have been to narrow the scope of competence of the Organization, and correspondingly to broaden that of states by including within the domain reserved to states not only those matters which were, by law, "solely" within the domestic jurisdiction but also those matters which were, by a looser "political" criterion, "essentially" within that jurisdiction. However, the result in practice was the opposite of that intended.[59] For example, by the legal criterion, there would have been, at the least, serious doubt that such cases as the Indonesian and Algerian independence movements could have been regarded as subject to United Nations intervention. However, the majority of the member states quickly made it clear that such matters were regarded as "essentially international," and the United Nations proceeded to treat most matters in this light. The change in wording of Article 2(7) encouraged this trend by eliminating the legal criterion; however, there is little reason to doubt that the same course of action—e.g. the untrammeled pursuit of political objectives—would have been followed even if this change had never taken place. It is the course of action that has been generally followed with regard to all points of Charter law.[60]

Even if we approach the matter from the standpoint of theory,

---

[58] *Case of the Nationality Decrees,* P.C.I.J., Ser. B No. 4 (1923); "Definitive Report of Rapporteur," 44 *Annuaire de l'Institut de Droit International* 137, 157 (1952-I); resolution of the Institut de Droit International entitled "The Determination of the 'reserved domain' and its effects," 45 *id.* at 299 (1954-II).

[59] Preuss, *supra* note 57, at 649; Hackworth in 45 *Annuaire de l'Institut de Droit International* 156 (1954-II).

[60] Korowicz, "Some Present Aspects of Sovereignty in International Law," 102 Academie de droit international, Recueil des Cours 1, 71-73 (1961-I).

however, the change in the formula of the "domestic jurisdiction" clause, as it applies to the United Nations, is believed to have been a desirable development. There are, as has been remarked above in Chapter 1, two main kinds of legal development. One involves the interpretation and application of existing rules of law; this is normally thought of as the judicial function. The other is the outright creation or change of law by legislative or quasi-legislative process. In the United Nations period, there has been much evolution which, if it can be described in legal terms at all, can only be regarded as within this latter category. Since the prohibition of intervention in domestic affairs is simply the obverse aspect of what the Organization is affirmatively empowered to do—the "opposite side of the coin" so to speak—the notion of what is "domestic" should evolve automatically, in step with the evolution of affirmative powers. It is therefore ventured to disagree with the authorities who would have questions concerning the application of Article 2(7) determined by the World Court.[61] The Court is limited by its nature to deciding upon the basis of existing law. While existing law was the criterion specifically laid down in the League of Nations Covenant with respect to the rule of non-intervention, this is no longer the case with respect to the United Nations.[62] It is believed appropriate, and in accordance with the rapidly evolving nature of international law in the present day, to regard the change of formula in question as having been intended to eliminate the criterion of existing law. While this course of action may be said, even from a theoretical point of view, to throw the basis of decision largely into the realm of politics, it must be realized that the evolution of an effective system must lie, to a large extent, within this realm. It is the thesis of the present discussion that, for the achievement of this goal, it is necessary that political evolution should take place on the basis of principle, that is to say, within a constitutional framework.

The rule of non-intervention in domestic affairs may then be considered in relation to the two main kinds of power possessed by the United Nations for dealing with disputes and situations: (a) the peaceful settlement function, as to which the basic power is that of recommendation, and (b) collective measures.

---

[61] E.g., Institut de Droit International in resolution cited note 58, *supra*.

[62] Indeed the San Francisco Conference rejected a proposal specifically providing that such questions concerning the "domestic jurisdiction" clause should be referred to the Court. *Cf.* ch. 2, note 6 *supra*.

The second of these powers, that of collective measures, is like every other power of the United Nations in being limited to purposes which are essentially international in character. The Charter is, moreover, explicit, in Article 1(1), in providing that this power is to be employed in fulfillment of the main United Nations "Purpose" of maintaining *international* peace and security. The point is again made explicit in Article 39 (which introduces Chapter VII), authorizing the Security Council to decide "what measures shall be taken to maintain or restore international peace and security."

Turning to the substantive power of "recommendation" as part of the "peaceful settlement" function, we may observe, first of all, that in the view of the framers, the fact that this power is non-binding does not mean that it can never amount to "intervention."[63] This view, it is believed, is consistent with the fact that the United Nations is essentially an international organization, concerned only with international matters. Since the Charter was concluded, there has been a trend in the direction of adopting United Nations recommendations as to matters theretofore regarded as essentially domestic, particularly with regard to human rights. The tendency has been to consider this matter in terms of the question of intervention in essentially domestic affairs. It is believed more readily understood by considering it from the standpoint of affirmative Charter powers, in which light the question seems rather plainly, to be: Is the subject-matter, in a given case, sufficiently international in character to justify the United Nations dealing with it?

We move a step nearer the source of confusion involved in

---

[63] This view emerged from the discussion of the last clause of Article 2(7), providing that the rule of non-intervention in domestic matters "shall not prejudice the application of enforcement measures under Chapter VII." In the original draft, as proposed by the Sponsoring Powers at San Francisco, the words "enforcement measures under" were absent. (*The United Nations Conference on International Organization: Selected Documents* 101 (1946)). They were added with the specific purpose of making clear that the Organization would *not* be able to intervene by way of "recommendation" in situations essentially domestic. See the Australian argument in support of the amendment in Doc. No. 969, I/1/39, 6 U.N. Conf. Int'l Org. Docs. 436 (1945). See Preuss, *supra* note 57, at 588-94; Lauterpacht, *supra* Ch. 5, note 1, at 21 (1947-I). That recommendations may constitute intervention is also indicated in the Report of the United States Delegation to the Conference: *Charter of the United Nations: Report to the President . . . op. cit. supra* note 56, at 44.

Article 2(7) when we consider that it purports to set up only a single standard, or criterion, as to the extent of United Nations powers under the Charter, namely, the prohibition of intervention in "matters which are essentially within the domestic jurisdiction of any state," whereas in its affirmative dispositions, the Charter differentiates several categories of situations, as to which differing kinds of action are authorized.

The most serious category of disputes and situations are those dealt with mainly in Chapter VII of the Charter, constituting aggressions, breaches of peace or threats to peace. As to such disputes and situations the Security Council may apply force or other pressures, may call upon the parties to apply "provisional measures" under Article 40, or may recommend procedures of peaceful settlement or actual terms of settlement.

The next category is that described in Chapter VI as consisting of disputes the continuance of which is likely to endanger the maintenance of international peace and security. The Council may, in such situations, recommend procedures of settlement or actual terms of settlement.

The Assembly may be said to have a broader scope of recommendatory powers in such matters than does the Security Council, since it may make recommendations on "any questions relating to the maintenance of international peace and security" (Article 11(2)), or "any questions or any matters within the scope of the present Charter" (Article 10), or may recommend "measures for the peaceful adjustment of any situation, regardless of origin, which it deems likely to impair the general welfare or friendly relations among nations" (Article 14).

Article 2(7) is rather crude, by comparison, in simply prohibiting intervention in matters essentially within the domestic jurisdiction of states.[64] It is readily apparent that emphasis upon this rule would have a natural tendency to obscure finer distinc-

---

[64] The distinction between "collective measures" and the "peaceful settlement" function can hardly be said to be ignored by Article 2(7) in view of its final clause, referred to in the preceding footnote. However, this clause has not proved to be a factor in the development of the Charter, perhaps because it does not seem calculated to add anything of a practical nature to pleas of non-intervention that might be raised, under the main body of the Article, to proposed recommendations. Further, the utility of the clause is weak if, as is believed to be the case, it does not formulate a valid distinction. True, the United Nations is forbidden to intervene by means of recommendation in essentially domestic affairs. It is equally for-

tions of Charter law, such as those just referred to. This tendency has exhibited itself throughout the history of the Organization, impeding the development of Charter law and having, it is believed, its most damaging consequences in the tendency to obscure the major distinction between the "peaceful settlement" and "collective measures" functions of the United Nations.[65]

The first case in which this tendency manifested itself was that concerning the Franco regime of Spain. As was observed in the preceding section, the Subcommittee of the Security Council, in that case, found that the situation in Spain was not a threat to peace such as would justify collective measures. However, it did say that the situation was not essentially domestic and that, if continued, it would be likely to endanger the maintenance of peace and security.[66] It thus invoked the formula, found in Chapter VI of the Charter, defining types of cases as to which the Security Council's "peaceful settlement" function is applicable. The Subcommittee proceeded to suggest that the Assembly recommend that member states break their diplomatic relations with Spain.[67]

---

bidden to do so by means of applying tangible pressures. While the clause in question may appear to be implying that, if it did not exist, enforcement measures could constitute wrongful intervention in domestic affairs, in reality this is quite impossible since such measures must, by definition, be directed to international situations. The Australian Delegation itself, which proposed the insertion of the reference to "enforcement measures" in the clause in question, candidly admitted that "to take enforcement action for the restraint of aggression is not intervening in any way at all in a matter of domestic jurisdiction." Doc. 969, *supra* note 63, at 440. While it is possible to give meaning to the clause as serving to remove any doubt that "enforcement measures" are not to be hindered or obstructed by the rule forbidding intervention in domestic affairs, it is still confusing in so far as it implies (with deliberate intent of the framers) that there is a distinction in this respect as between "collective measures" on one hand, and recommendations or other valid acts of the United Nations on the other.

[65] The tendency toward emphasizing the rule may have been furthered by the inclusion of "non-intervention" in a study initiated by the General Assembly, in 1963, of certain principles of law concerning the friendly relations of states, with a view to the progressive development, codification and improved application of these principles. Although "non-intervention" in this context had to do primarily with the relations of states, Article 2(7) has received considerable attention in the discussions. See Report of the Special Committee on Principles of International Law concerning Friendly Relations and Co-operation among States, U.N. Doc. A/5746 (1964).

[66] *Cf.* pp. 174-75 *supra.*

[67] *Cf.* text accompanying note 22 *supra.*

When this latter proposal was brought up in the Assembly, it gave rise to a considerable mixture of arguments, many of which centered around the question whether such action would constitute wrongful intervention in the affairs of Spain. The Venezuelan Delegation, which supported the proposed measure, referred to the argument that the Spanish question was essentially domestic and said that it was flatly contradicted by the report of the Subcommittee.[68] It was apparently referring to the Subcommittee's denial that the case was "essentially domestic" and its designation of the situation as one continuance of which would be likely to endanger peace. The Venezuelan Delegation may have deduced from these parts of the report that the proposed measure would not constitute intervention. However, the proposed measure consisted of "diplomatic sanctions," a type of measure defined in Chapter VII as falling within the category of "collective measures" and, as such, to be applied only in the event of aggression or other breach of peace, or a threat to peace. The Subcommittee specifically found that such a threat did not exist in the Spanish case. What was being done by means of the Venezuelan argument was to focus attention upon the "domestic jurisdiction" concept of Article 2(7) and to argue that if a situation is not "essentially domestic" with respect to the application of the "peaceful settlement" function, it is removed from the "essentially domestic" category for all purposes. Stated otherwise, the proposition would be that if the application of the "peaceful settlement" function would not constitute wrongful intervention, neither would the application of collective measures. Thus we find a clear use of Article 2(7) for the purpose of breaking down the distinction between the two basic United Nations functions of "peaceful settlement" and "collective measures."

It would be beyond the scope of the present study to attempt to identify and analyze all the cases in which the argument based on "non-intervention," including the argument based on "permission," have been mixed with other arguments in favor of United Nations competence to recommend or take some other form of measure in particular cases. Seldom, if ever, has this asserted basis of authority stood forth as the sole or principal ground for a particular course of action.

Two other cases which may be mentioned in this connection are the United Nations military operations in the Suez and Con-

---

[68] U.N. Gen. Ass. Off. Rec. 1st Sess., 2d part, 1st Comm. 229 (1946).

golese cases, which were outlined in Chapter 4, above. In both cases there emerged, by implication, the idea that the operations were legally justified on grounds of "permissiveness;" e.g. as having been deployed with the consent, or (in the Congolese case) upon the request, of the state where the force was to operate. In both these cases, the notion of "permissiveness" seems to have been a derivative of the original official policy of trying to place all "UNEF-type" forces within the "peaceful settlement" category of United Nations activity.[69] In the case of UNEF, as has been observed, this relationship was made manifest, and the notion of "recommendation" was also cited as a basis for the Force, in the Advisory Opinion in the "Expenses" case. In the case of ONUC, due to its authorization to use affirmative force for several purposes, and its actual engagement in combat operations, it was doubtless difficult to classify it as either an exercise of the "peaceful settlement" function or as a "recommendation." Perhaps for these reasons, the concepts in question were not overtly invoked. The notion of "permissiveness" was available, however, and was used. Since its connection with the broader "peaceful settlement" category did not clearly appear, its use in the case tended to convey the impression that "permissiveness" stands by itself as a legal basis for the application of United Nations measures. This exact idea was advanced by the Secretary-General, in a televised interview of August 2, 1962, when, in connection with the Katanga case, he indicated that the United Nations was entitled to come to the aid of a state in suppressing a secessionist movement, simply upon the basis of a request that it do so.[70]

The statement is interesting, among other reasons, because the notion of "permissiveness" there appeared, momentarily, as *the* basis for possible United Nations measures (including the use of force) such as were later actually taken in the Congolese case and which gave the appearance of being intended to enforce a decree of the United Nations as to the outcome of a secessionist rebellion within a state. It is true, however, that other ideas as to the legal nature of ONUC were advanced at different times so that, in the end, like the measure in the Spanish case, its legal basis appears as mixed and uncertain.

It seems certain, however, that if "permissiveness" had been invoked as a reason for United Nations intervention to put down

---

[69] *Cf.* text accompanying ch. 4, note 13 *supra.*

[70] *Cf.* p. 116 *supra.*

the Indonesian rebellion of 1948, or that of Algeria a decade later, those secessionist regimes—now governments of independent states—would have complained on grounds of wrongful intervention, or on grounds that the Organization lacked the affirmative power to make or enforce such a decision.

Closing the Gap

The discussion in the preceding sections concerns several devices resorted to when it is desired that the United Nations Organization apply tangible pressures in the handling of disputes and situations and it is desired, at the same time, to avoid the designation of the measures in question as "collective measures." The view of the present discussion has been indicated that this latter concept embraces the only valid Charter authorization for the employment of such pressures by the United Nations for the purpose indicated. The devices under discussion are believed to be unsound for this basic reason and for others which have been indicated.

It is also apparent that, when taken together, they leave a substantial range of possible situations uncovered. First, the area which they *do* cover may be summarized. This would include situations in which it appears as appropriate for the desired measures to be applied by states, and not by the United Nations itself. In such cases, the Organization sometimes recommends that the states take the action. Also covered are situations in which it is necessary that the Organization, itself, take the action and as to which the consent of the state or other party concerned is obtainable. In such cases, the notions of "recommendation" (in the sense of a recommendation by the United Nations to itself) or of "permissiveness" may furnish the ostensible juridical basis.

The area of the "gap" consists, then, of situations in which, first of all, it is desired, for some reason, not to designate the measures in question as "collective measures;" in which, secondly, it is necessary that the United Nations itself appear to be taking the action; and in which, in the third place, the consent of the states or parties affected is not forthcoming.

ONUC is believed to have fallen within the gap. It may be argued that this was not the case since the Force operated with the permission of the Congolese Government. The problem arises, however, from the fact that it had to engage in combat with a secessionist faction. The dilemma in this case was, no doubt, somewhat alleviated, in the eyes of public opinion, by the fact that the operation was initiated by the Security Council, which is recognized, generally, as having authority to apply force. It was further, perhaps, and to a lesser extent, alleviated by the fact that Chapter VII was originally cited as a juridical basis for the operation.

Such alleviating factors are not present for the General Assembly, so long as the opinion continues to prevail that it is without power to apply tangible pressures on behalf of the United Nations. It is also readily foreseeable that cases might arise in which either the Assembly must act in situations in which the consent of the affected states is not forthcoming, or in which, alternatively, the United Nations must remain paralyzed when action is deemed to be required. Such a case might be one in which responsibility devolved upon the Assembly as in the case of UNEF, after which complications should arise requiring the use of force against a state or faction, without its consent, as in the case of ONUC.[71]

A possible move to close the gap by use of the notion of "recommendation" may be contained in the following statement by the Deputy Legal Adviser of the United States Department of State, in connection with the "quarantine" measure applied pursuant to a recommendation of the Organization of American States in the Cuban missile crisis of 1962:

> Council actions under Articles 40, 41, and 42 are to be distinguished from recommendations made by the Council under Article 39 or by the General Assembly in the discharge of its responsibilities as set forth in Chapter IV of the Charter. This distinction between a Security Council measure which is obligatory and constitutes "action," on the one hand, and a measure which is recommended either by the Council or by the General Assembly, on the other, has been supported by the Advisory Opinion of the International Court of Justice on Certain Expenses of the United Nations (July 20, 1962). The Court held that the measures taken by the General Assembly and the Security Council in Suez and the Congo were not enforcement action, in part, because they were only recommendatory as to participating states.
>
> Thus, in the context of United Nations bodies, it may be persuasively argued that "enforcement action" does not include action by a United Nations body which is not obligatory on all the Members. As used in Article 53(1), "enforcement action" refers to action by a regional organization rather than to action by an organ of the United Nations, but the words are properly given the same meaning

---

[71] An incipient case of the kind, in connection with ONUC, is referred to at p. 152 *supra*.

in this context. As understood by the United States, "enforcement action" means obligatory action involving the use of armed force. Thus, "enforcement action," as the phrase appears in Article 53(1), should not be taken to comprehend action of a regional organization which is only recommendatory to the members of the organization.[72]

The immediate purpose of this resort to the "recommendatory" device was to take the action out of the category of "collective" or "enforcement" action in view of the requirement of Article 53 of the Charter that "no enforcement action shall be taken under regional arrangements or by regional agencies without the authorization of the Security Council."[73]

As to the reference to the World Court's Advisory Opinion in the "Expenses" case, found in the above-quoted passage, it is no doubt true that the Opinion contains language which can be interpreted as supporting the distinction between measures taken by recommendation, on one hand, and "action" in the sense of "collective measures" by the Security Council, on the other. While it is thus possible to argue that the Opinion supports the proposition that *some* measures taken by recommendation are not collective measures, it is not believed possible to use it to sustain the proposition that *no* measures taken by recommendation can be of that category, or the corollary proposition that any measure is removed from the limitations and restrictions of the "collective measures" category so long as it is in the nature of a "recommendation." The Advisory Opinion appears, in fact, explicitly to maintain the basic distinction between "recommendation" and "action" found in Article 11(2)[74] of the Charter, stating on this point:

> The Court considers that the kind of action referred to in Article 11, paragraph 2, is coercive or enforcement action. This paragraph . . . in its first sentence empowers the General Assembly, by means of recommendations to States or to the Security Council, or to both, to organize peace-keeping operations, at the request, or with the consent, of the States concerned.[75]

This passage has reference to UNEF, and in stating that such forces must have the consent of the states concerned, it maintains the "gap" here under consideration.

---

[72] Meeker, "Defensive Quarantine and the Law," 57 Am. J. Int'l L. 515, 521 (1963).

[73] Cf. pp. 53-55 *supra*.

[74] The pertinent portion is quoted on p. 111 *supra*.

[75] Certain Expenses of the United Nations . . . [1962] I.C.J. Rep. 164.

Whether it was within the intent of the Deputy Legal Adviser, in the statement above quoted, to move in the direction of closing the "gap," is not known. The statement has, however, some important tendencies in this direction which are worth noting. These tendencies are principally to be observed in the fact that the argument in question, while applied to a measure of the Organization of American States, is really based upon the Charter of the United Nations, and upon some aspects of it which are not found in corresponding instruments of the OAS. In the first place, the argument no doubt finds some of its basis in the traditional view that United Nations collective measures may only be instituted by means of binding orders of the Council on member states. In the case of the OAS, on the other hand, there was never any comparable expectation and, so far as concerns measures of force, this mode of instituting measures was placed out of the question by Article 20 of the Inter-American Treaty of Reciprocal Assistance (Rio Pact), which provides:

> Decisions which require the application of the measures specified in Article 8 shall be binding upon all the Signatory States which have ratified this Treaty, with the sole exception that no State shall be required to use armed force without its consent.[76]

In the second place, the corresponding instruments of the Organization of American States do not provide the same opportunity, or excuse, as does the United Nations Charter for seizing upon the word "recommendation" as the basis for "action." The Charter of the OAS[77] merely sketches out the "collective measures" and "peaceful settlement" functions without use of the word "recommendation" and refers to other treaties for more detailed descriptions of the functions. Of these the one on "peaceful settlement" is not widely in force. The treaty mainly applicable in the missile crisis was the Rio Pact, in which the relevant provisions provide that the Organ of Consultation shall meet, in the event of aggressions or threats to peace, for the purpose of agreeing on measures of a collective character. The notion of "recommendation" appears only in Article 20, just quoted. Although, as a result of this provision, OAS measures involving the use of force take on the character of recommendations, there is no suggestion that

---

[76] OAS Treaty Series 8; 62 Stat. 1681 (1948), T.I.A.S. No. 1838, 21 U.N.T.S. 77.

[77] OAS Treaty Series 1, 2 U.S.T. & O.I.A. 2394, T.I.A.S. No. 2361, 119 U.N.T.S. 3.

resulting measures are taken by the member states outside the Organization. On the contrary the language of the Rio Pact seems to contemplate that all measures shall be measures of the Organization.

Consequently, in taking a concept of "recommendation" which is based, at least in good part, in a tradition and upon words which are peculiar to the United Nations Charter, and in undertaking to apply it to the OAS in whose constitutional history and documents no comparable bases for it are to be found, the Deputy Legal Adviser seems to be moving in the direction of giving the notion of "recommendation," as a basis for "action," an independent life of its own, unrelated to particular Charter provisions.

It seems that the theory advanced by the Deputy Legal Adviser was broader than it needed to be in order to fulfil the purpose of taking the "quarantine" measure out of the category of "collective measures." It would apparently have sufficed equally for this purpose if he had advanced only that part of this argument which corresponds to the original theory of the Korean case—e.g. that the particular measure in question was not an "enforcement action" because it was carried out by the member states on their own responsibility and outside the Organization. While, in the view of the present discussion, this theory is of questionable utility, the argument does not seem to be improved by asserting that all measures initiated by "recommendation" are thereby taken outside the category of "collective measures." Also, it is worth noting that the Legal Adviser of the Department of State had, only a few months earlier than this statement by his Deputy, advanced a different interpretation designed to avoid the "authorization" requirement of Article 53 of the Charter.[78]

The possibility thus suggests itself that the Department of State modified its position as to the constitutional nature of the "quarantine" measure in order to deal with the problem of the "gap" here under discussion, and that the notion of "recommendation" was put forward with such sweeping effect by the Deputy Legal Adviser in order not only to take the particular measure out of the "collective measures" category, but also to build up the idea that a "recommendation" may be adopted with respect to any measure with the effect of removing it from that category.

---

[78] *Cf.* pp. 53-54 *supra.* See further on these arguments, Halderman, "Regional Enforcement Measures and the United Nations," 52 Geo. L. J. 89, 97-105, 107-108 (1963).

"Peace-keeping" Concept Inimical to Charter Development

As part of the trends under discussion in the two preceding sections, as well as in preceding chapters, it is now customary to make a major constitutional distinction as between "enforcement action," which is narrowly defined to include only military operations against states (and possible other political entities) and "peace-keeping operations," which include diverse measures carried out by groups or, perhaps, by individual persons. A landmark in the development of this theory of Charter interpretation was an address by the Secretary-General, U Thant, on June 13, 1963,[79] in which he said:

> There has been a tacit transition from the concept of collective security, as set out in Chapter VII of the United Nations Charter, to a more realistic idea of peace-keeping. The idea that conventional military methods—or, to put it bluntly, war—can be used by or on behalf of the United Nations to counter aggression and secure the peace, seems now to be rather impractical.

He went on to say that the Korean operation was the only "collective action" to have been taken by the United Nations, and he placed in the "peace-keeping" category UNEF; ONUC; the West Irian Force; and observer groups deployed in the Greek, Kashmir, Palestine, Lebanese and Yemini cases. All these operations, he pointed out, required the permission of the parties directly concerned.

In connection with the crisis over the financing of UNEF and ONUC, the General Assembly, in early 1965, invited the Secretary-General and the President of the General Assembly to undertake appropriate consultations on the question of "peace-keeping operations in all their aspects," and authorized the President of the General Assembly to appoint a special committee to undertake a comprehensive review of the subject.[80] In resulting proceedings and reports, the line of thought represented by the Secretary-General's statement just referred to was strongly evident. Other views were also brought forward, however, and the results of the inquiry, as reported prior to the opening of the twentieth session of the Assembly in September, 1965, were inconclusive as to the true nature of "peace-keeping operations" under the Charter.[81]

---

[79] Op. cit. supra ch. 6, note 36.

[80] Res. 2006 (XIX), U.N. Gen. Ass. Off. Rec. 19th Sess., Supp. No. 15, at 7 (A/5815) (1965).

[81] See "Report of the Special Committee on Peace-Keeping Operations," Doc. A/5915/Add. 1, 12 Aug. 1965. For a summary of the work done

The notion of the "peace-keeping operation" no doubt derives from the history of UNEF and ONUC, relevant aspects of which have been touched upon in Chapter 4, above, and particularly from the desire to exclude ONUC from the "collective measures" category. The principal substantive reason advanced for that policy at the time appears to have been concern as to the willingness of states to contribute troops for the Force. Subsequently, arguments in favor of the notion of the "peace-keeping operation" appear to have rested upon the more general view which conceives the Charter concept of "collective measures" as being limited to "enforcement action" involving the use of force to put down aggression or other breaches of peace. Reasons for considering this prevailing view to be detrimental to Charter development have been suggested above, principally in Chapter 4.

Regarding the problem from the standpoint of the "peace-keeping" concept *per se,* the development of this idea appears to form part of the trend toward enabling the United Nations (and sometimes regional organizations) to apply measures of tangible pressures freed from the restrictions surrounding the Charter concept of "collective measures."[82] The devices of "recommendation," "permissiveness," etc., discussed in the present chapter as forming part of this trend, have played important roles in the development of the "peace-keeping operation."

on this subject in 1965, pursuant to Assembly Res. 2006 (XIX), see *Annual Report of the Secretary-General on the Work of the Organization 16 June 1964-15 June 1965,* U.N. Gen. Ass. Off. Rec. 20th Sess., Supp. No. 1, at 53-57 (A/6001) (1965).

[82] *Cf.* ch. 4-5 *supra.* While the concept of "peace-keeping operations" is thus used by the United Nations as a means of avoiding certain limitations on its Charter powers, it is also seized upon by communist and some other governments for the opposite purpose of restricting the role of the Organization. This is done through the contention that all "peace-keeping operations" are within the exclusive province of the Security Council. *Cf.* p. 156 *supra.* The prevalence of the concept would also seem likely to facilitate such a claim as that made by the Soviet Representative in the Security Council, in connection with the Yemeni case of 1963, that only the Council could legally deploy an observer corps since that organ alone was competent to take decisions relating to United Nations action for the maintenance of peace and security. U.N. Security Council Off. Rec. 18th year, 1038th meeting 4 (S/PV. 1038) (1963). Such an assertion *vis-à-vis* an observer corps goes far beyond the Soviet position, taken up in connection with the Uniting for Peace resolution, that the Council has exclusive competence of "action" in the sense of "collective" or "enforcement" measures. *Cf.* p. 182 *supra.*

It is to be observed that, as part of the theory under discussion, "enforcement action" is considered to be limited to military operations. If, instead, "enforcement action" were to be regarded as comprising *all* applications of tangible pressures, the effect would have been to include in this concept diplomatic and economic measures such as were initiated, for example, in the Portuguese and South African cases. Such a definition would, however, be contrary to the trend which seeks to narrow the "collective measures" category. It will be recalled, for example, that a deliberate effort was made, in the cases just referred to, to differentiate those measures from the category in question. On the other hand, since measures short of force do not have the consent of the states against whom they are directed, they seem to be automatically excluded from the category of "peace-keeping operations." The proper constitutional nature of this important class of measures appears to be a question left unanswered by the theory of Charter law under discussion.

The theory that "enforcement action" and "peace-keeping operations," as defined above, comprise the main categories of United Nations activity in the handling of disputes and situations, cuts across the major concepts laid down in Article 1(1) of the Charter as relevant to this area of activity. If, as is believed to be the case, these latter concepts—"peaceful settlement" and "collective measures"—continue to reflect the true nature of the powers that governments and peoples agree that the Organization may exercise on a basis of mutual reciprocity, then a question naturally arises as to the real constitutional validity of the new categorizations under discussion.

A certain deference to the original Charter concepts is indicated by the Secretary-General in the address above referred to, when he says of UNEF, ONUC and the West Irian Force that "all three were designed solely for the maintenance of peace and not for fighting in the military sense; . . . all three operated with the express consent and co-operation of the States or territories where they were stationed, as well as of any other parties directly concerned in the situation." These criteria applied to ONUC, perhaps, when it was first deployed. In the end, however, it proved to be a force designed to fight in a military sense, it did engage in combat and it did not operate with either the express or implied consent of the Katangese secessionist regime, which was a party directly concerned in the case.

The deference to original Charter concepts just referred to may, perhaps, have been based on more than theoretical regard for them. When the United Nations denied any ONUC initiative in the hostilities that broke out in Elisabethville on September 13, 1961,[83] two of the reasons influencing the Secretary-General in this decision are said to have been "(1) his belief that whatever his subordinates might think, nothing in the Charter or the resolutions justified a United Nations attempt to end Katanga secession by force; (2) his realization of both the immediate and long-term consequences for the Organization of an admission that this was what had been attempted."[84] The immediate consequences thus apprehended may have concerned the strong political protests being made at the time against any ONUC action against the secessionist regime; the long-term consequences may have had reference to world public opinion, as it pertains to the United Nations. The case may thus illustrate the possibility that constitutional concepts may sometimes escape from confinement and enter directly into public consciousness through the medium of political controversy.

Although ONUC later gave the impression of suppressing the secessionist regime by force, and denials that it did so have not been consistent, denials do persist as indicated by the Secretary-General's statement under discussion. A policy issue in this connection may have involved the alternative courses of attempting to persuade the governments and peoples of the world to accept the right of the United Nations to enforce decisions as to the internal and/or external relations of states, or of convincing them that ONUC did not engage in hostilities against the Katanga regime. The latter project may have been considered more likely of success than the former.

The Katanga case may thus have illustrated the unreadiness of the peoples of the world to recognize a quasi-legislative role in the United Nations. At the same time, however, to the extent that ONUC gave the impression of enforcing a substantive decision—and also, perhaps, by reason of the confusion surrounding the constitutional question of what the Force was doing—the case may have encouraged majorities of members to cause the United Nations to pursue the quasi-legislative endeavors undertaken by

---

[83] Cf. p. 115 supra.

[84] Hoskyns, The Congo Since Independence: January 1960–December 1961, at 421-22 (1965).

that Organization, at about the same time, in the Portuguese and South African cases.

Like other devices discussed in this chapter, the notion of the "peace-keeping" operation thus seems designed to break down the Charter distinction between the basic "peaceful settlement" and "collective measures" concepts of the Charter. These devices seem to have, by the same token, the unintended and inadvertent further effect of raising severe obstacles to the development of the Charter as the basis of a rule of law in international relations.

This discussion should not be concluded without taking note of the force of the current which is sweeping away constitutional limitations upon what the United Nations may do. Not only do a number of states now unhesitatingly demand that the United Nations make and enforce decisions as to substantive issues in dispute, but arguments are heard that the prestige of the Organization calls for such measures.[85] There is a great deal of impatience with the substantive power of "recommendation," on the ground that it has been ineffective in such cases as those of the Portuguese overseas territories and the policy of *apartheid* in the Republic of South Africa. Such attitudes form part of the current trend of development; this trend, in turn, encourages and accentuates these demands. So far as concerns the role of the Charter, the trend might be compared with the employment of a currency to produce a demand for goods in excess of what the given economic system can produce. The result is, in other words, inflationary.

In devaluing the Charter governments are, at the same time, damaging the most promising potential basis for a system which might, in time, be able to exert effective pressures in the interests of achieving just demands. This objective cannot, it is believed, be achieved by causing the United Nations to try to do things which its members are not agreed, in principle, that it has power to do. If, on the other hand, the Organization stays within its generally agreed powers, there is then the possibility of gradually developing these powers with the consent of all concerned.

Involved in this problem of development are various factors, some of which have been discussed above. The matter of particular concern in this Chapter is the evidence of a powerful trend on the part of some governments and peoples to dismantle Charter limitations surrounding the "peaceful settlement" and "collective meas-

---

[85] E.g., U.N. Gen. Ass. Off. Rec. 17th Sess., Spec. Pol. Comm. 7 (A/SPC/SR. 327) (1962) (Ghana); *id.* 15 (A/SPC/SR. 329) (Liberia).

ures" functions of the Organization to the end that the United Nations may take such decisions, and initiate such measures, as may be determined by majority votes. The trends under discussion thus result in emphasis being placed on voting victories, rather than in developing international principles. This trend is, in turn, part and parcel of the larger and prevalent tendency on the part of member states to use the Organization primarily as an instrument for the advancement of immediate, or apparent, policy interests.

Chapter VIII

Legal Versus Political Approach

Realism and Idealism

By pursuing a legal approach to international relations, this discussion invites the charge of being wrongly based on abstract idealism rather than on the political and power basis that "realists" regard as the only true criterion of international conduct. The present writer agrees, however, with a leader of the realist school when he says:

> The realist parts company with other schools of thought before the all-important question of how the contemporary world is to be transformed. The realist is persuaded that this transformation can be achieved only through the workmanlike manipulation of the perennial forces that have shaped the past as they will the future. The realist cannot be persuaded that we can bring about that transformation by confronting a political reality that has its own laws with an abstract ideal that refuses to take those laws into account.[1]

Professor Morgenthau goes on to give this summary of the correct basis for the conduct of international relations:

> [I]f we look at all nations, our own included, as political entities pursuing their respective interests defined in terms of power, we are able to do justice to all of them. And we are able to do justice to all of them in a dual sense: We are able to judge other nations as we judge our own and, having judged them in this fashion, we are then capable of pursuing policies that respect the interests of other nations, while protecting and promoting those of our own. Moderation in policy cannot fail to reflect the moderation of moral judgment.[2]

This last paragraph is, in the view of the present writer, only a step or two away from postulating law as the basis for the successful conduct of international relations. If citizens of a state are to judge other nations on the basis of their ordinary notions of justice,

[1] Morgenthau, *Politics Among Nations* 10 (3d ed. 1961).
[2] *Id.* at 11.

international clash and conflict will be the inevitable result as it has been in the past. It is the purpose of law to provide standards of judgment which are mutually acceptable. It is the potential role of the United Nations to provide such standards of a loose and flexible kind, together with the means of applying them, when necessary, in a way that will at least prevent outright conflict. To this end, a "transformation" of the contemporary world is necessary to the extent that the minimal elements of an effective rule of law must come to life in world public opinion. It is the purpose of this study to demonstrate that some progress toward this goal can be made through uses of the United Nations which are politically possible. It is not a question of confronting political realities with an abstract ideal, but rather of bringing into the calculation the long-range "interests defined in terms of power" which states have in avoiding destructive war.

Political realities derive, in the end, from people; and that there is a dynamism in the thinking of people, which brings developments of the kind under discussion within the realm of practical possibilities, appears beyond question. The complex and efficient self-governing systems that are to be found in various parts of the world today all evolved from the most primitive beginnings. They all involved the development of community thinking and the "rule of law." That most of the peoples of the world desire such development on a worldwide basis, to the extent necessary to assure the preservation of peace, seems to have been demonstrated, in principle, by the adoption of the League of Nations Covenant and of the United Nations Charter. That it is possible, through intelligent and persistent efforts of various kinds, to make *some* progress toward effective realization of this goal seems to be beyond question. If this is so, how can it be said with certainty that such efforts must necessarily fall short of fulfillment?

Again, Professor Morgenthau states:

> Realism maintains that universal moral principles cannot be applied to the actions of states in their abstract universal formulation, but that they must be filtered through the concrete circumstances of time and place.[3]

The present discussion, it may be observed, does not involve an attempt at deduction from an idealistic general principle. Instead it is based, mainly, on several concrete powers which the

---

[3] *Id.* at 10.

"peoples of the world" conferred upon the United Nations. It is true that the particular form of a legal order envisioned at San Francisco proved unworkable in the conditions that developed; however, the principles themselves are more important than any question of form. They are flexible, capable of being adapted to use in varying situations and thus of playing their essential role, in terms of political realities, in the development of a dynamic system capable of maintaining peace and security in an evolving world. However, the potential inherent in those principles has not been realized for the reason, at least in part, that little leadership has been forthcoming tending to promote such realization. Statesmen have been glad to avail themselves of basic United Nations principles when these have been seen as contributing to immediate policy objectives; with equal eagerness they have overridden, twisted and ignored these principles when they have seemed to stand in the way of such objectives.

Scope of Constitutional System

If a constitutional system is to be successful in regulating a society of free and equal members, it must be able to handle all important political issues. If it is not able to do so—if, in other words, some such matters fall outside the scope of the constitution —the constitution is incomplete and the situation anarchic as respects such matters.

In states having successful constitutional systems, it is the general practice to designate as "political" those governmental issues and procedures as to which political forces are determinative. The forces must, of course, be peaceful and in accordance with the constitution. They generally fall into categories designated as legislative, executive and administrative. They are outside the judicial function, since this function is supposed to exclude political factors. The United States federal courts designate as "political" those matters which fall outside their competence. Particularly noteworthy has been the practice of these courts, at least until recently,[4] of holding as "political," and outside their jurisdiction, issues concerning the delimitation of electoral districts pertaining to the governments of the constituent states. These matters were certainly within the constitutional system as a whole, since they were regulated by the states. Nor does the designation

[4] Baker v. Carr, 369 U.S. 186 (1962).

of such matters as "political" infer that they are not subject to adjudication, in the state courts, in appropriate cases.

Within effective constitutional systems, then, the designation of issues as "political" does not mean that such issues are outside the system.

People naturally tend to carry over into their thinking on international affairs the same distinction between what is "legal" or "justiciable" on one hand, and what is "political" on the other. However, due to the absence of any effective system of regulation of international political affairs, there is, in this realm, generally lacking any tendency, corresponding to that found with respect to domestic societies, to regard "political" matters as falling within a broad constitutional framework. Except for the elementary requirement of obtaining requisite majorities for United Nations decisions, international "political" affairs are generally regarded as being subject to no restriction upon the free play of political forces. Nevertheless, the commonplace definition of international "political" matters as those which are not "justiciable" can be said to have a juridical basis.

Approaching this problem from such a juridical, or constitutional, point of view, it is possible to regard the lack of effective constitutional norms regulating "political" matters as a defect of international relations which can and must be remedied by work, effort and sacrifice. However, the more customary attitude has been that "political" matters not only cannot be, but *must not be,* subject to any international rules or restriction and that, moreover, the concept of what is "political" is readily expandable to cover any situation to which parties do not desire to see law or principle applied. The word is flexible enough, for example, to be used to cover any situations which are deemed to affect important national interests or national prestige.

The word "political," then, in international relations, is used to describe situations and disputes which are deemed to be outside legal regulation; it is therefore an appropriate means of describing the general mode of conduct of international relations—the "political approach," "power politics," etc. Also it is a word that can be and is used as a means for perpetuating this political approach. This approach is, indeed, perpetuated and continues to prevail out of the supposed self-interest of states, notwithstanding that it has been used since the beginning of history and has never succeeded in establishing peaceful relations on a secure basis.

It is herein believed erroneous to regard any important disputes and situations to be inherently beyond the reach of constitutional principles;[5] on the contrary, it is considered essential to the achievement of a secure peace that a set of principles and procedures be evolved which is capable of handling any such situations as might, in the language of Article 1(1) of the Charter, lead to a breach of the peace. The problem of evolving such Charter principles has been the subject of concern in previous chapters; in this chapter we may consider it in terms of achieving a "constitutional approach" to disputes and situations of a kind now generally regarded as political.

An approach along this line was attempted by the British Delegation to the General Assembly in 1951. Referring to the aim of the United Nations expressed in the preamble of the Charter "to establish conditions under which justice and respect for the obligations arising from treaties and other sources of international law can be maintained," that Delegation suggested that the objective could not be achieved unless the Assembly adopted regular and satisfactory methods and procedures for dealing with legal matters.[6] Among several proposals advanced having this objective, the one most relevant to the present discussion was to assure that, whenever the legal elements of an item on the Assembly's agenda appeared to be of equal importance with the non-legal, the item should, if not referred to the Legal Committee in its entirety, be referred in its legal aspects to that Committee. Other aspects would then be referred to the appropriate political, economic or other committee. Also, under the proposal, the legal elements of predominantly non-legal items should also, if they affected the ultimate decision, be referred either to the Legal Committee or to an *ad hoc* legal subcommittee established for the purpose. The British proposal went on to suggest a study of methods for securing the objective determination of the legal or non-legal character of any agenda item, and the nature and degree of its legal content.

The resulting resolution of the Assembly, adopted in the following session, did no more than recommend

> That, when a Committee considers the legal aspects of a question important, the Committee should refer it for legal advice to the

---

[5] See Ch. 1, note 9 *supra*.

[6] U.N. Gen. Ass. Off. Rec. 6th Sess., Annexes, Agenda Item No. 63, at 2 (A/C. 6/L. 175) (1951).

Sixth Committee [e.g., the Legal Committee] or propose that the question should be considered by a joint Committee of itself and the Sixth Committee.[7]

Although it attempted to do more than was possible in the circumstances, the British proposal appears as inherently inadequate to deal satisfactorily with the problem herein under discussion since it recognized a distinction in kind as between the legal and non-legal aspects of disputes and situations. The British spokesman, in introducing the proposal, said that "the United Nations was a political institution in which political considerations must predominate."[8] While this opinion that a basic distinction exists between what is "political" and what is "legal" received widespread endorsement in the ensuing debate, little effort was made to describe what was meant by either term. The task of defining this distinction in terms of the handling of disputes by the Assembly and Security Council is indeed difficult for the reason, it is believed, that the distinction itself is not soundly based.

The serious issues involved in important and sensitive disputes and situations are seldom, if ever, regarded as anything but "political." This view would be reasonable enough were it not for the fact that, in international relations, what is "political" is regarded as being outside the bounds of constitutional limitations. The Assembly has, also, some agenda items which appear more "legal," relatively speaking, than "political." These include such matters as those pertaining to international law, or the judiciary, or which involve the drafting of instruments or the formulation of definitions intended to have legally operative effect. It was this notion of legality which was apparently in mind in the debate on the British proposal referred to above, and which has generally been followed by the Assembly in deciding whether or not particular items should be referred to the Legal Committee. In the Assembly session in which the British proposal was initiated (sixth session), the following items[9] were referred to the Legal Committee:

Draft Declaration on Rights and Duties of States . . .

Report of the International Law Commission . . . including:

    (a) Reservations to multilateral conventions;

    (b) Question of defining aggression;

[7] Res. 684 (VII), *id.* 7th Sess., Supp. No. 20, at 61 (A/2361) (1952).
[8] *Id.* 6th Sess., 6th Comm. 27 (A/C. 6/SR. 256) (1951).
[9] Taken from *Yearbook of the United Nations 1951* at 18-22.

(c) Review of the Statute of the International Law Commission with the object of recommending revisions thereof to the General Assembly;

Reservations to the Convention on the Prevention and Punishment of the Crime of Genocide: advisory opinion of the International Court of Justice

Designation of non-member states to which a certified copy of the Revised General Act for the Pacific Settlement of International Disputes shall be communicated . . . for the purpose of accession . . .

Regulations to give effect to Article III, section 8, of the Headquarters Agreement . . .

Ways and means for making the evidence of customary international law more readily available . . .

Request of the Government of China for revision of the Chinese text of the Convention on the Prevention and Punishment of Genocide

Application of the Headquarters Agreement to representatives of non-governmental organizations

Consideration of the Assembly's methods and procedures for dealing with legal and drafting questions.

The political committees received the important disputes and situations on the agenda, but they also were given the following items which seem little different, in principle, from some of those assigned to the Legal Committee except in being, perhaps, more politically sensitive:

International control of atomic energy: report of the Committee of Twelve . . .

Methods which might be used to maintain and strengthen international peace and security in accordance with the Purposes and Principles of the Charter: Report of the Collective Measures Committee.

The foregoing allocations of agenda items are fairly representative of what has been done in this respect throughout the history of the United Nations. Matters referred to the Legal Committee may generally give the appearance of being more "legal" than items referred to other committees; in fact it is difficult to define the sense in which this is so. Certainly, from the point of view of the present discussion, actual international disputes and situations, which are generally assigned to the "political" committees, have a far greater potential for the development or non-development of law as the basis of international relations than do most of the items assigned to Committee VI.

The designation of one of the main Assembly committees as the "legal" committee may have an unfortunate effect in respect to the problem of advancing the rule of law. As was just observed, the General Assembly is commonly regarded as being essentially a "political" body. The practice, then, of separating out certain agenda items having a "legal" appearance, and which are generally concerned more with words than deeds, and assigning them to the Assembly's "legal" committee, would seem to carry the implication that all else is doubly political.

It seems certain that the key to the major problem here under discussion, namely that of promoting the rule of law through the handling of international disputes and situations in the United Nations, is not to be found in the Legal Committee of the General Assembly. As was frequently stressed by its members during the discussion of the British item mentioned above, delegates assigned to this Committee are exactly like those assigned to the political, economic, social, trusteeship and finance committees in that they are all subject to the instructions of their governments. The solution of the problem is to be sought, primarily, in the places where national policies are formulated including, to varying degrees with respect to different countries, their respective bodies of public opinion.

Defining Constitutional Issues

When we turn to consider what might be done, in the practical handling of disputes and situations, to substitute a "constitutional" approach for the "political" approach usually followed in such matters, it would seem to the present writer that efforts might be most productive which sought to assure that when disputes and situations are brought before the Assembly or Security Council, the correct issues, from a "legal" or "constitutional" point of view, are debated and otherwise elucidated and, finally, voted upon.[10]

---

[10] A prior question, logically, is whether some cases ought to be brought into the United Nations at all. It is, in one sense, a part of the question of "legal versus political approach" here under discussion. The German case is an example of a dispute which neither side apparently wishes to bring before the United Nations. The Soviet attitude on this point is readily understandable. As to the western powers involved in the dispute, they might presumably have brought the case into the United Nations and have

Cases in which United Nations debates have inextricably confused such issues, and as to which clarification would have been necessary to a successful constitutional approach, were the Suez "troops" and "ships" cases discussed in Chapter 1, above.

A recent case of the kind was the West Irian dispute between the Netherlands and Indonesia. Indonesia claimed sovereignty over the territory in question, asserting that the Netherlands had relinquished it to Indonesia as part of the agreement recognizing Indonesian independence.[11] The Netherlands, which had been in control of West Irian for several centuries, in effect denied that that territory had been included in the agreement and proposed that the future of the area be determined in accordance with the wishes of its people.[12] Indonesia rejected recourse to the International Court of Justice for the solution of the dispute as to the location of sovereignty on the ground that, in a dispute of this kind before the Court, the former colonial power would always have an advantage.[13]

As has been mentioned in Chapter 1, above, when, as frequently happens in present world conditions, states refuse to submit proper cases for adjudication the only remaining alternative from a constitutional point of view is for the parties to a given case to conclude a new agreement, based on principle, governing the situation in question, or at least to attempt to do so. Various other recourses exist, but of a "political" and "non-constitutional" character: e.g., a state may seek to aid its cause by gaining a favorable vote in the

gained a considerable success in the eyes of world public opinion by focusing attention on the right to self-determination of the East German people. Debate of this issue might, in particular, have impressed Asian and African governments, which have been notably ill-informed and indifferent to this question. The states having this opportunity may have refrained from pursuing it, and acquiesced in keeping the case out of the United Nations, in part because it was feared that to have pursued the issue in that forum would have heightened east-west tensions, and reduced the chances of reaching an agreed solution. It remains true that such an important issue lying outside the realm of a constitutional system is a subject of anarchy. That the situation exists in fact is, at the same time, symptomatic of the state of present-day international relations.

[11] See e.g. U.N. Gen. Ass. Off. Rec. 16th Sess., Plenary 617-18 (A/PV. 1050) (1961).

[12] Id. at 587-89 (A/PV. 1049); id. Annexes, Agenda Items 88 and 22 (a), at 24 (A/L. 354) (1961).

[13] For the Netherlands proposal of adjudication see id. Plenary 589; for Indonesia's rejection of the proposal see id. at 848 (A/PV. 1065).

United Nations by political means, or by threatening force, or by other methods. In the case under discussion the principle apparently most applicable to the situation was that of self-determination. It was, however, flatly rejected by Indonesia on the ground that Indonesia was sovereign of the territory, and that the principle in question therefore did not apply.[14] The question of sovereignty was, however, as has just been pointed out, inescapably controversial by virtue of the circumstances of the case. Indonesia also sought to gain support in the United Nations on the plea that it was maintaining an anti-colonial position, and candidly threatened the use of force to gain its ends.[15] When a settlement was finally agreed to,[16] transferring administration of the territory to Indonesia in 1963, and providing that an act of self-determination by the people of West Irian need be carried out only at a later date, some time before 1970, the Netherlands Delegation to the General Assembly claimed that the settlement represented a yielding to the Indonesian threat of force.[17] This contention does not seem to have been denied by Indonesia.

The desire for a purely "political" solution untrammeled by consideration of principle was implied by the Indonesian Delegation in asserting that the Assembly should not impose a solution which was not acceptable to either or both countries.[18] To similar effect was the following statement by the Indian Delegation:

> My delegation believes that the only line the United Nations can take is to get negotiations going between the parties and to assist them in this process. When two Member States are deadlocked in a long-standing dispute of this character, there is no substitute for negotiations. Any dictation by the United Nations would be pointless, unwise and contrary to the spirit of the Charter.[19]

Both these delegations knew that the General Assembly is not empowered to impose or dictate settlements of substantive issues of international disputes. On the other hand, the Assembly could

---

[14] *Id.* at 848. On this page, Indonesian statements rejecting self-determination and adjudication, respectively, are juxtaposed in paragraphs 157 and 158.

[15] *Id.* at 848-49.

[16] 437 U.N.T.S. 273; U.N. Gen. Ass. Off. Rec. 17th Sess., Annexes, Agenda Item No. 89, at 2 (A/5170) (1962). The General Assembly expressed appreciation of the agreement by its resolution 1752 (XVII), *id.* Supp. No. 17 at 70 (A/5217) (1962).

[17] *Id.* Plenary 51 (A/PV. 1127) (1962).

[18] *Id.* 16th Sess., Plenary 850 (A/PV. 1065) (1961).

[19] *Id.* at 845.

make recommendations based on principle. The desire of one side of a dispute to get a case out of the Assembly, and returned to direct negotiations between the parties, may represent an admission that that side's position could not stand scrutiny from the standpoint of principle.[20] The invocation of the "spirit of the Charter" has somewhat similar connotations.

The "constitutional approach" to this case was upheld by several delegations, including that of Australia which said:

> What we oppose is any suggestion that the parties should be pressed to negotiate on a basis which excludes self-determination and which is, therefore, inconsistent with Charter principles.[21]

---

[20] Article 33 of the Charter, providing that parties to disputes should first of all seek a solution by negotiation or other peaceful means of their own choice, may encourage the United Nations to recommend voluntary negotiations when such procedure can no longer contribute to a solution of a given dispute. Thus, in the Security Council's first case, which was an Iranian complaint concerning the presence of Soviet troops in Azerbaijan Province, the U.S.S.R. attempted to persuade the Council to leave the dispute to negotiations between the parties and not even to include the case on its agenda. The purpose was evidently to keep the United Nations out of the case while the Soviet Union used its position in Azerbaijan Province, gained during World War II, to strengthen its influence there, and in the whole of Iran. Less extreme uses of the "negotiation" procedure may still be inimical to the development of the rule of law. By obtaining a United Nations recommendation of negotiations between the parties, one side may be able to have an agreed settlement reopened, and to place itself immediately on an equal footing with the other, notwithstanding the contention of the latter that it has fully carried out the agreement. Also "negotiations" may be a device for excluding the application of law and principle and, at the same time, for keeping a dispute open and unsettled while a party endeavors to obtain a solution by "political" means, including, possibly, the obtaining of the requisite majority for a favorable United Nations recommendation.

Secretary-General Hammarskjöld is believed to have been correct in saying:

> "[T]he obligation of States to settle their disputes by peaceful methods does not mean that principles of justice and international law may be disregarded. The Charter reconciles the obligation of peaceful settlement with the objective of justice and equity through its emphasis on peaceful negotiation in which the full weight of the world community, as organized in the United Nations under the Principles of the Charter, is brought to bear on the issue at stake."

Introduction to the Annual Report of the Secretary-General on the Work of the Organization 16 June 1955-15 June 1956, id. 11th Sess., Supp. No. 1A, at 2 (A/3137/Add. 1) (1956).

[21] U.N. Gen. Ass. Off. Rec. 16th Sess., Plenary 851 (A/PV. 1065) (1961).

While it may, therefore, be said that the issues were at least identified in the debate, this was not done in such a way as to pose them in consistent and clear-cut fashion before the delegations or the public. It would seem logical, in this connection, to suppose that attention would be focused, to some extent, upon the resolutions brought before the Assembly. The resolution proposed by the Netherlands in this case[22] would have provided a procedure designed to bring about an ultimate solution of the dispute on the basis of self-determination. This proposal, however, was not brought to a vote. As indicative of what happened, the United States Delegation expressed sympathy for the Netherlands proposal, but doubted that it could form the basis of a settlement since it did not take adequately into account the intense Indonesian interest in the territory.[23] Another proposed resolution[24] would have called for negotiations and, if these failed, the appointment of a commission to investigate the possibilities of an interim administration for the territory. A statement in the preamble that any solution affecting the final destiny of a Non-Self-Governing Territory must be based on the principle of self-determination of peoples was voted upon separately; while receiving a simple majority of the Assembly, it failed for lack of the necessary two-thirds,[25] as did the resolution as a whole when voted upon.[26]

The possibility that, in present world conditions, the United Nations might adopt procedures designed to assure the debate and elucidation of proper constitutional issues of all disputes brought before it would seem to be remote. The possible nature of such procedures are, nevertheless, believed to be worth a moment's consideration, since to the extent that they could be obtained, or their effects secured on a case-by-case basis, the role of law in international relations would be measurably advanced.

A system based on the "rapporteur" system of the League of Nations Council might serve to secure the ends here in mind.[27]

[22] *Id.* Annexes, Agenda Items 88 and 22(a), at 24 (A/L. 354) (1961).

[23] *Id.* Plenary 774 (A/PV. 1061) (1961).

[24] *Id.* Annexes, Agenda Items 88 and 22(a), at 26 (A/L. 368) (1961).

[25] *Id.* Plenary 873 (A/PV. 1066) (1961).

[26] *Id.* at 875.

[27] Interesting suggestions along this line were made by Benjamin V. Cohen in *Hearings Before the Committee on Foreign Relations,* U.S. Senate, 89th Cong., 1st Sess. on S. Con. Res. 32 *(For Planning for Peace)* at 37, 44-46 (1965). *Cf.* Gardner, *In Pursuit of World Order* 95-96 (1964); Wilcox and Marcy, *Proposals for Changes in the United Nations* 124-25 (1955).

This system involved the appointment of a "rapporteur" for individual cases brought before the Council. This function has been described as follows:

> The task of the Rapporteur was to elucidate the issue involved in the dispute and to make proposals for its solution. To this end it was his duty to study the documents relating to the dispute, to engage in private conversations with the disputants and to guide discussion in the Council. In several instances, he was authorized to call upon outside experts for advice and assistance. . . . In his report the Rapporteur would submit to the Council proposals for the solution of the dispute. . . .[28]

The function, as herein envisioned, would be somewhat different, consistent with the thesis of the present discussion in being designed less consciously toward finding solutions of particular disputes, and more toward the application of the correct constitutional principles to these disputes.[29] Juridical talent would thus be called

---

[28] "Interim Committee of the General Assembly . . . Measures and Procedures of Pacific Settlement Employed by the League of Nations" (Memorandum prepared by the Secretariat) 8 (A/AC. 18/68) (June 29, 1948).

[29] The ultimate object would, of course, be to find a more effective means of achieving actual settlements. The distinction indicated in the principal text—the same, in essence, as has been noted above in various contexts as between the "political" and "legal" approaches—might also be described in terms of a "quantum" versus a "continuous flow" theory of international relations. The former would represent the traditional theory in which individual disputes—"quanta"—are essential elements of the problem of peace, and under which the task is to find peaceful settlement, regardless of means, of all disputes which, if left unsettled, might lead to war. See in this connection the discussion in Chapter 1, above, of the prevalent theory of the role of the World Court—that it is to decide, in their entirety, any disputes brought before it—as this evolved from the notion of arbitration. (Cf. pp. 19-20 supra) It is believed that this "quantum" theory has proved inadequate and that what is required is something more in the nature of a "continuous flow" theory which would seek to apply applicable law and principle to all disputes in a dispassionate manner. Granted that this approach cannot solve all disputes, at least in the beginning, it would also have the objective of establishing a basis in law which would, in time, prove more conducive to settlement than is the present essentially political basis upon which the peaceful settlement function is attempted to be applied. This approach would seem to correspond with the theory enunciated in Article 1(1) of the Charter where it is declared to be a major "Purpose" of the Organization

> "to bring about by peaceful means, and *in conformity with the principles of justice and international law,* adjustment or settlement of international disputes or situations which might lead to a breach of the peace." [Italics added.]

for in the position of rapporteur, and the reporting function, which is the normal task of this official, would be central to the system. In Assembly cases, then, the rapporteurs might be given the task of drawing up the reports of the committees to the plenary session. In the Security Council, these officials might be charged with preparing the report on the particular cases to which they are assigned, to be incorporated in the annual report of the Security Council to the General Assembly. As a first step in the fulfillment of his task, the rapporteur might study the documents, consult with representatives of the parties and otherwise familiarize himself with the case. He might then submit to the Assembly committee or to the Security Council (as the case might be) a proposal, with supporting documentation, as to the issue to be first discussed.[30] It might, for instance, be explained that the dispute, or a basic part of it, involved an existing rule of law, and that the parties were unable to agree to submit it for adjudication; the rapporteur might, then, propose that the Assembly or Security Council recommend to the parties that they so submit the dispute. He might suggest, as another example, that progress had been made since the case came before the United Nations, and that the case might well be returned to the parties for further negotiation. Or he might propose that certain subsidiary issues of the dispute be taken up and debated in a certain order, with a view to a final recommendation by the competent organ as to procedures that should be followed by the parties in seeking a settlement, or as to actual terms of settlement. As each phase of the Assembly committee's or Security Council's consideration of the case was completed, the rapporteur should propose the next sub-agenda item to be taken up in debate. The organ in question would, of course, have the decision as to whether to follow such recommendation.

Thus, in the West Irian case, the first item for discussion might have been the dispute as to sovereignty of the area in question. When Indonesia made clear its refusal to consider adjudication of this question, the next step, on the basis of a constitutional ap-

---

[30] Hasluck contributes valuable suggestions (with particular reference to the Security Council, but also applicable to the Assembly) as to uses of rapporteurs in stages leading up to, as well as including, the general debate. He considers it a mistake that the admission of an item on the agenda should be regarded as a decision to debate it substantively and considers, on the other hand, that such substantive debate should not take place until the issues are defined and it is decided that a *prima facie* case exists. Hasluck, *Workshop of Security* 86-101, 109-11 (1948).

proach, might have been to seek a new agreement between the parties for the regulation of the subject-matter of dispute. The first issue to be taken up in this connection could then, logically, have been the question of the applicability of the Charter principle of self-determination. If Indonesia then denied the applicability of this principle on the ground that it was sovereign of the territory in question, this denial would have been clearly juxtaposed against the fact that sovereignty was in dispute, and that Indonesia had rejected the only means of determining such a disputed interpretation of a legal situation.

If a logical exposition of a dispute could thus be carried out on the basis of the sub-agenda items proposed by the rapporteur, these items could then serve as the headings for sections of his final report on the case. The report should have the function of informing not only the Assembly, but also the world public, as to the handling of the case in the light of Charter principles.

Voting

What has been said concerning the importance of defining the issues in connection with the discussion of disputes and situations in the United Nations applies equally to voting. The ultimate purpose of defining the issues is, in a sense, to assure that the proper issues are voted upon when decisions are necessary. The essential importance of voting, from the standpoint of a constitutional approach, is regarded as lying in its effect on governmental and public opinion in compelling reasoned choices.

The prevalent "political" approach to the use of the United Nations in the handling of disputes and situations has, however, led to a tendency on the part of governments to regard victories in United Nations votes as ends in themselves. In this view, defeat in a United Nations body would be evidence of failure of the policy involved. Pursuant to such a policy, governments might decide what to do, in part, by estimating the chances of winning or losing votes in the Security Council or General Assembly. It seems clear that, so far as this policy is followed, political considerations have the ascendancy over considerations of principle in the formulation of national policies.[31] Also, it is probably by

[31] The prevalent exaggerated importance given to voting no doubt played a part in connection with the crisis which paralyzed the 19th Session of the General Assembly. Certain states at that time attempted to enforce against certain others the rule of Article 19 which provides that a state shall lose its

token of this attitude that complaints are heard, in some of the larger states, that these countries do not have voting power commensurate with their size, power and international responsibilities. On the contrary, it is objected, such a country as the United States, with all its burdens and responsibilities for the maintenance of peace and security, has exactly the same vote in the General Assembly as the smallest, or least responsible, state. As part of an argument in answer to such objections, an official of the United States Department of State recently said, in an unofficial publication, that:

> Anyone who believes that United States influence in the United Nations is measured by the fact that it has less than one-hundredth of the votes in the General Assembly fails completely to understand the realities of power as they are reflected in the world organization. These realities include the fact that the U.S. is the principal contributor to the U.N.'s regular budget and by far the largest supporter of the U.N.'s peacekeeping and development programs, and that the U.S. is making by far the largest individual contribution to the defense and development of the non-Communist world. On U.N. decisions of vital importance to the United States, the voting of other countries has been considerably influenced by U.S. views.[32]

While this authority is undoubtedly correct in what he says, the "realities of power" can hardly be considered as constituting the most desirable factor in determining voting influence in the United Nations. Other countries than the United States, of course, have various kinds of power at their disposal, and if these are to constitute the predominant factor entering into United Nations decisions, the Organization must become, as a result, nothing more than an area for conflicts of power and an instrumentality which states try to use for the advancement of their interests. As Hasluck states, speaking of another aspect of the voting problem:

> If in the work of the Council the serving of national interests is the primary concern the veto will continue to be used, and, even if there were no veto, other means of obstruction would be found. If the Charter method of international co-operation on a basis of principle is followed the veto will be used less and less.[33]

---

vote in the General Assembly in certain contingencies involving arrears in financial contributions.

[32] Gardner, *op. cit. supra* note 27, at 37.

[33] Hasluck, *op. cit. supra* note 30, at 139.

"A voting victory or a voting defeat may be of short-lived significance. What is regarded as responsible world opinion as reflected in the

A case involving the question under discussion concerns the action of India, in 1961, in forcibly wiping out the Portuguese territories of Goa, Damão and Diu and incorporating them in India. The action was condemned as a wrongful use of force by several members of the Security Council; however, a proposed resolution calling for the withdrawal of Indian forces and the working out of a peaceful solution of the difficulty was defeated in that body.[34] The resolution received seven affirmative votes against four negative, which would have been enough for passage except that one of the negative votes constituted a Soviet veto. Other votes against the resolution were those of two African and one Asian state. The issue of principle represented by the resolution, namely that force as a means of settling international disputes is wrongful and not justified by the plea of "anti-colonialism," was given able expression by representatives supporting the resolution.

Following its defeat in the Security Council, the resolution was not taken into the General Assembly for the reported reason that its sponsors ascertained that most Asian and African delegations would vote against it and that, consequently, the two-thirds vote required for passage could not be obtained.[35] Regarding the matter, momentarily, solely from the point of view which looks to the long-range development of the rule of law, it would seem highly desirable that issues such as this should be brought to vote in the General Assembly. It is this organ, not the Security Council, which now appears as the key to the development of a constitutional basis for international relations. The original theory upon which the Security Council was entrusted with "primary" responsibility in these matters—namely the collaboration of the permanent members—was never realized in practice, and it seems clear that if the Organization is ever to achieve its fundamental purpose it must do so through the development of law and principle on a

---

voting and in the debates is in many respects more important than any formally registered result." *Introduction to the Annual Report of the Secretary-General on the Work of the Organization 16 June 1959-15 June 1960,* U.N. Gen. Ass. Off. Rec. 15th Sess., Supp. No. 1A, at 2 (A/4390/Add. 1) (1960).

[34] For the debate see U.N. Security Council Off. Rec. 16th year, 987th and 988th meetings (S/PV. 987; S/PV. 988) (1961). For text of the draft resolution see *id.,* 988th meeting 21-22.

[35] N.Y. Times, Dec. 20, 1961, p. 1, col. 1.

wider basis. The Assembly, as the competent organ possessing the most nearly universal representation of governments and peoples, is the obvious focal point through which such development must be attempted, in so far as concerns the handling of disputes and situations by the United Nations.

The sponsors of the above-mentioned resolution in the Goan case, in withholding it from the Assembly on the grounds indicated, evidenced their belief that the Assembly was essentially a "political" organization in that it would act in accordance with what they regarded as essentially short-range considerations— e.g., "anti-colonialist" sentiments and pro-Indian sympathies—rather than on the basis of the Charter principle prohibiting the resort to force for the solution of disputes which, in their view, represented the true long-range interests of all concerned. Whether the Asian and African states concerned would share this view of the matter or whether this view is, in fact, right or wrong, are considerations irrelevant to the present discussion. The essential point is that the sponsoring delegations conveyed the impression that they anticipated a "political" vote and, consequently, withheld the issue from the Assembly. They offered no alternative and thus tended to confirm the general impression that the Organization is, in fact, essentially "political" in the sense of being used by states only for the advancement of their immediate or apparent interests.

It is submitted that different consequences, far more encouraging to the development of the Organization toward the fulfillment of its ultimate goal, would have ensued if the resolution in question could have been carried into the Assembly, debated on its merits, and voted upon, even though it were defeated. Asian and African delegations, even though convinced that the Indian action in Goa was justified as an "anti-colonial" measure, would at least have been compelled to listen to arguments to the effect that the action violated a basic Charter principle concerning the use of force. In voting, moreover, they would have been faced with the responsibility of choosing between the alternatives placed before them. Regardless of how the states would then have actually voted, the process would have wrought *some* degree of transformation in the views of all concerned, for all time to come, both as regards the particular issue in dispute, and the general issue as between "politics" and "principle" in the use of the United Nations. If states can be said sometimes to vote wrongly in such matters by the standard of their true long-range interests, there is believed to be no better corrective of such tendencies, in the long run, than through the continued process of debate and decision. These processes affect the thinking not only of delegations but also, of course, their governments and, to greater or less extent in different countries, public opinion. These are the exact areas in which the United Nations must put down roots if it is ever to become more than a paper organization.

Another case that might be mentioned in the present connection has to do with Indonesian attacks against Malaysia in the summer of 1964 and the failure of the attempt, on September 17, 1964, to obtain a Security Council resolution deploring a specific incident, namely the dropping of Indonesian paratroopers into Malaysia on September 2 of that year.[36] The Indonesian spokesman appears to have admitted not only the specific incident referred to in the proposed resolution, but other uses of force against Malaysia as well. Such force was justified generally, as in the Goan case, on the ground that it was directed against "colonialism."[37]

The resolution received a favorable vote of 9 to 2, but since one of the negative votes was a Soviet veto, it was defeated. The resolution has not been taken into the General Assembly. As in the Goan case, the sponsors may have anticipated a defeat in that body. It is believed, nevertheless, for reasons just indicated in connection with the Goan case, that the benefits of forcing the issue in the Assembly, in terms of long-range Charter development, might well have outweighed the immediate disadvantages of a defeat in the voting.

Practice as Affecting Charter Development

As to the resolution in the Malaysian case, Mr. Thomas J. Hamilton has written:[38]

> Malaysia's appeal to the United Nations Security Council against Indonesia's "blatant and inexcusable aggression" has come to a frustrating end. A Soviet veto defeated the mild resolution intro-

---

[36] For debate see U.N. Security Council Off. Rec. 19th year, meetings 1144, 1145, 1148-1150, 1152 (1964). For text of the proposed resolution see Doc. S/5973, Sept. 15, 1964.

[37] See e.g. Indonesian statement in U.N. Security Council Off. Rec. 19th year, 1144th meeting 13-27 (S/PV. 1144) (1964).

[38] N.Y. Times, Sept. 20, 1964, §4, p. 11, col. 7. © 1964 by the New York Times Company. Reprinted by permission.

duced by Norway, which would merely have "deplored" the landing of 30 Indonesian paratroopers near Singapore. . . .

* * *

Thanks to the cold war, this nonaggression commitment [e.g., Article 2(4) of the Charter], is honored more in the breach than in the observance. From the time Malaysia submitted the complaint it was known that the Soviet Union, which unfailingly backs African and Asian neutralists against the West, would veto any resolution unacceptable to Indonesians.

In the early years of the United Nations, however, the Western powers would have complied with the Malaysian's demand for a condemnation of the aggression. Up until a few years ago the United States and its associates felt that the moral effect of such condemnation was salutary despite the veto.

* * *

Despite these and other efforts to avoid irritating Indonesia, it was touch and go until the end whether the two African members of the Council . . . would vote for the Norwegian proposal.

No Asian members of the African-Asian group are on the Council . . . and this apparently convinced Western delegates that it was absolutely essential to water down the proposal to the point where it would be acceptable to the Ivory Coast and Morocco.

As a result of these tactics, there was a vote of 9 to 2 for the Norwegian resolution, which was some consolation to Malaysia, but not much. The resolution was so non-committal that it would probably have had little effect on Dr. Sukarno if it had passed. But it was killed by the Soviet Union and Indonesia has gotten by with a clear-cut violation of the Charter without even a slap on the wrist from the Council.

He went on to say:

This is not the first time that a newly independent Asian or African state has done so. The same factors, the Soviet veto and the desire of the Western powers to go along with the Asian and African members of the Council enabled India to get by with its seizure of Goa.

Later, when Dr. Sukarno moved more than 1,000 agents and paratroopers in the Netherlands New Guinea [e.g., West Irian], the United Nations, with the support of the United States went even further. Far from criticizing this use of force, Washington pressured The Netherlands into surrendering, and the United Nations drew a cloak of legality over Indonesia's annexation of the colony.

He expresses the conclusion that:

In all these cases the newly independent African and Asian states, or most of them, seem to follow a double standard: they appear to believe that aggression is not aggression if it is committed against a colonial power or a former colony which, as in the case of Malaysia, remains allied with its former ruler.

. . . The tragedy of the situation is the failure of many African and Asian members to realize that if they do not help the United Nations to take a stand against aggression, no matter who committed it, they themselves cannot expect any protection from the Organization.

While this last statement is undoubtedly true, it is not believed that it should be taken as implying that the whole problem is to be attributed to the governments of the newly independent Asian and African states. The attempt is made, in the present discussion, to demonstrate that the problem is broader and deeper than anything that could be attributed to policies of a few states. It is, rather, a problem of developing a rule of law on a broad basis.

From this point of view, all the uses made of the United Nations since its inception have had their bearing on, for example, the few Asian cases just mentioned. It is, of course, possible to go back farther in history. Some well-known cases are to be found in the history of the League of Nations. Had more of the statesmen handling those cases shared the prophetic sense of some of them as to their potentialities for disaster, the cases might have been handled in ways that would have made the League a more effective instrument, that might have avoided World War II, and might have contributed directly to the creation of an effective system, based on law, capable of maintaining peace on a secure basis.

To take a narrower range of cases to illustrate the point under discussion, we may consider the three Asian cases just mentioned— West Irian, Goa and Malaysia-Indonesia—in juxtaposition with the question discussed above, in Chapter 2, as to whether United Nations authorization should have been sought, under Article 53 of the Charter, for the OAS diplomatic and/or economic measures against the Dominican Republic in 1960, and against Cuba in 1962 and 1964.[39]

While various questions have been raised as to whether the Charter requires authorization in such cases, it is assumed for purposes of present discussion that it does. It will be recalled that the provision was placed in the Charter because it was felt that to permit regional organizations to apply measures of force or other tangible pressures in international situations, on their own

---

[39] Cf. pp. 37-49 *supra.*

decision and volition, would be divisive, tending to break the world up into regional blocs, and incompatible with the overall responsibility of the United Nations for the maintenance of peace and security. Consequently we are considering the "authorization" requirement not as a technicality, but as one of the basic principles of the Charter.

In the 1960 Dominican case and in the 1962 Cuban case, the American states denied the applicability of the "authorization" clause for the reason, it is believed, that they feared that through it the Soviet Union could, by use of the veto, frustrate desirable regional action. Thus, the use of the "authorization" clause in the 1960 case was opposed by these states, notwithstanding that authorization could apparently have been obtained without difficulty. In the 1962 case, by contrast, an application for United Nations authorization of the OAS arms embargo against Cuba would certainly have met with a Soviet veto. Had the case then been taken into the General Assembly, a failure to obtain the necessary majority in that organ would have been a real possibility, but for reasons somewhat different from that underlying the Soviet veto in the Council. That veto would have been but an automatic move in the major east-west struggle. However, if Assembly delegations of neutralist persuasion had voted in favor of Cuba, it might have been because their governments were genuinely unable, at that time, to see the Cuban situation as constituting such a threat to peace as to justify the imposition of tangible pressures against that country.

As was pointed out above, in Chapter 2, public opinion in the Americas was undoubtedly unready to see these governments seek United Nations authorization and sustain a defeat in this effort, thereby bringing about frustration of a desired regional policy. An attempted justification on the ground of upholding an important principle of the United Nations Charter would probably not have been understood nor accepted. Thus, the course of action in question was not really open to the American policy-makers.

The 1964 Cuban case was in sharp contrast to the 1962 case in that it involved overt and provable acts of terrorism in Venezuela, as well as clandestine arms shipments into that country, by Cuban agents. The charges were proved to the satisfaction of the OAS, and far-reaching diplomatic and economic sanctions were imposed by that Organization against Cuba. United Nations authorization under Article 53 was, again, not sought. Had this "authorization" principle been invoked and had the case thereby been fully debated in the Assembly, certain immediate and practical advantages would have accrued to the American states in addition to the longer-range advantages deriving from the upholding of an important Charter principle. If the resolutions of the Punta del Este Conference of 1962 asserted, in effect, that the introduction of communism constituted a threat to the peace of the hemisphere, the 1964 case enabled the Venezuelan spokesmen to prove that this was so, citing chapter and verse in terms of terroristic outrages and clandestine arms shipments. If it was of psychological value, from the standpoint of those opposing the Cuban actions, to have the proofs brought out in the regional OAS forum, it would have been of correspondingly greater value to have had them made, fully debated and voted upon in the world forum which is the General Assembly. The psychological value would have been great, even if actual authorization for the OAS measures could not have been obtained.

The practical benefits of this course of action, including the chances of obtaining a favorable vote on the question of authorization, would both have been improved if the American states could have acted, in the earlier 1960 and 1962 cases, so as to uphold the "authorization" principle. So far as concerns the 1962 case, this is assuming the impossible, for reasons, which have just been indicated, pertaining to the unreadiness of public opinion. For the peoples of the Americas to have been willing to accept the sacrifices involved in sustaining a defeat in that 1962 case, a course of action designed to have built up public opinion to the requisite point would have had to be started much earlier. We may assume, for discussion purposes, that this had been done, that the American states sought authorization in the 1962 case, that the request was fully debated and refused by vote of the General Assembly, and that the American states accepted the verdict and refrained from applying the arms embargo in question. This course of action would seem inevitably, and substantially, to have strengthened the position of these states if they had then brought the 1964 Cuban-Venezuelan case into the General Assembly with a request either for authorization of OAS measures, or for measures by the United Nations itself.

Put somewhat differently, the hypothetical course of action referred to would have tended to strengthen the capability of the United Nations, as such, to handle the later case effectively. So would, it is believed, stronger efforts by states in the West Irian and Goan cases to persuade the members to support their positions in opposition to the use and threats of force in those cases, and in support of the principle of self-determination. Stronger efforts along these lines might well have been defeated; however, they would seem to have been bound to strengthen the fabric of the United Nations by compelling governments to consider the issues.

By the same token, if the American states could have made the effort to obtain United Nations authorization in the Cuban case of 1962, even if this had failed, the United Nations, as a whole, would have been rendered more capable of effectively handling the later Malaysian-Indonesian case of 1964.

The argument is, in effect, that efforts made to cause the United Nations to act in accordance with principle will strengthen its capability as to all future cases, and the effect of such efforts, even in highly disparate cases, will be cumulative. The argument is, perhaps, an exercise in the obvious. However it provides a perspective from which it is possible to envision that efforts of this kind, combined with efforts in other promising fields of activity, may lead to ultimate success in establishing the Charter as the basis of a system which is actually capable of maintaining peace.

It may be worth noting that, as the 1964 Cuban case was much more favorable, on its facts, to effective United Nations actions against Cuba than was the 1962 case, so, to a lesser extent, were the facts of the 1964 Malaysian-Indonesian case more favorable than were the earlier West Irian and Goan cases to an effective United Nations position opposed to the use and threat of force. The reason was that the West Irian and Goan cases—involving Asian countries against the Netherlands and Portugal, respectively —were more calculated to arouse the "anti-colonialist" sentiments of some delegations than was the Malaysian-Indonesian case which, notwithstanding Indonesian claims of British "neo-colonialism" in the creation of Malaysia, inescapably pitted one Asian country against another. Therefore if, in the handling of the earlier cases, efforts had been made which tended to strengthen the United Nations, the Organization's enhanced capability in regard to the later cases would have been supplemented, and the chances of success further improved, by the coincidental factor that these later cases were more conducive on their facts than were the earlier cases to a successful handling on the basis of United Nations principles. If these circumstances were accidental, they still serve to emphasize the point that the development of the role of the Organization must depend upon its readiness to seize opportunities for progress when they present themselves.

It must be emphasized that the Cuban case is not here being cited for the proposition that policies in accordance with the long-range interests represented by the United Nations, carried out in an early phase of a case, are likely to bring "practical" advantages to the parties concerned in later phases of the same case. It is true that, in the above hypothetical discussion, certain advantages were suggested which would have been of this character—namely, the advantage to be derived from using the world forum of the United Nations to bring the case to the attention of the world public, and the improved chances of securing United Nations authorization for OAS action. These advantages are, however, also of a long-range character since the developments in question would tend to bring into sharp juxtaposition, before the eyes of the world public, the attitudes toward law and justice of the American states versus the communist states, and the meaning of the United Nations and OAS Charters in the relevant context. This long-range benefit, which might have been derived from the upholding of the "authorization" principle of Article 53 of the Charter, is quite different from the purpose for which this principle was originally incorporated in the Charter. This was, it will be recalled, to prevent regional groups from taking actions which might lead to the breakdown of the world system represented by the United Nations. The hypothetical possibilities of the Cuban case, as discussed above, are believed of interest as being symbolic (a) of the general rule that policies tending to strengthen the Charter and the rule of law will, in the long-run, prove advantageous to those who believe in the rule of law, and (b) that proper use of a given Charter principle may tend to promote the rule of law in ways different from those anticipated when the particular principle was placed in the Charter. The effort of course is to find a way, not into a compartmentalized aspect of the rule of law, but into the broad reality which must, necessarily, be comprehensive in scope.

A factor entering into policy formulations in such cases is undoubtedly the major east-west struggle, one aspect of which is the invariable Soviet policy of support for Asian and African "anticolonialist" positions. Other countries may apprehend that, by following policies based on principle, they may come into opposition to the "anti-colonialist" countries and encourage the latter to feel that they form, or should form, a front with the communist states against the threat of "neo-colonialism." "Practical" and "long-range" considerations are inextricably mixed in the consideration of this question. Whether Soviet policy has produced substantial advantages for the communist cause is a question generally beyond the scope of this discussion; however, reference may be made in this connection to the "troika" proposal by which the Soviet Union attempted to paralyze the decision-making powers of the Secretary-General. Although the Soviet Union had strenuously attempted to inflame Asian and African sentiments against the United Nations in connection with the Congolese case, and proposed the "troika" as part of this campaign, the Asian and African states appear, in general, to have seen it in their interest to support the United Nations as a bulwark of the independence of small states.

It seems logical to anticipate that this latter consideration will gradually move nearer the focal point of attention of these counries, along with more general concern as to their independence and security; and that "anti-colonialism" will gradually recede in importance as traditional "colonialism" continues its decline. Such a possible shift in outlook on the part of Asian and African states would naturally represent a move toward increasing solidarity with any states which, meanwhile, had demonstrated a regard for principles of law and the Charter. This opinion is predicated in part on what would seem to be the logical probability that the Charter is, in the long run, bound to prove conducive to solidarity as among states which subscribe to the principles of freedom, equality and the rule of law, for the reason that the Charter is, itself, based on these principles.

The view may be emphasized, in concluding the discussion, that the effort to develop constitutional principles through their application to concrete disputes and situations is but one of several essential lines of approach to the development of the rule of law. It is believed to be a vital one, however, having the potential of crystallizing other efforts into an effective pattern of international relations. Whatever else may be done, it seems essential that principles and procedures be devised which, in the end, can prove capable of resolving disputes which might otherwise lead to war. Underlying this requirement is the prerequisite that all concerned be satisfied that these principles and procedures will be applied equally and dispassionately in a genuine effort to do justice.

If the effort to achieve permanent and secure peace is regarded as, essentially, the effort to improve communication and understanding between peoples, then, it is believed, effective United Nations principles and procedures may be regarded as media of communications established at the most critical point, namely that at which the ultimate decision on a question involving war or peace may have to be made.

To state in simplest form what is believed to be the basic requirement for practical progress, it is to give due priority to those long-range interests which are reflected in the United Nations, its purposes and principles. The writer recalls as a commonplace point of view among his colleagues of the "working level" of the San Francisco Conference that if the United Nations were to succeed, these principles and purposes would have to be given the necessary priorities in the formulations of national policies. It would appear, however, that, in practice, the Organization has been regarded most commonly as an instrumentality for the pursuit of national foreign policy objectives. As has been noted at various points of the present study, it is not unusual to see the United Nations twisted so as to serve the immediate policies of states; it is unusual to see states modifying their own policies in order to further the long-range interests represented by the United Nations.

It would follow inescapably from this analysis that sacrifices are required in the interests of establishing a secure and permanent peace. While voluntary sacrifices of what states regard as vital interests are not to be expected, it becomes all the more important, by the same token, that practical opportunities for progress be seized when they arise.

The opinion may be ventured that if states in a position to do so exert conscientious efforts, in concrete cases, to cause the United Nations to handle disputes and situations in accordance with principles which are deemed sound and just; and if states in a position to do so in particular cases endeavor to shape United Nations debates and other activities so as to promote the development of such principles among peoples and governments of the world, some progress toward a secure peace will be made. Whether, taken together with intelligent efforts in other areas of international activity, such endeavors can ultimately bring about the achievement of this goal cannot be said with any certainty; at the same time no one is in a position to say that such achievement is impossible.

Charter of United Nations

Articles quoted (in whole or part) in the text.

Index

Abuse of right, 85

Adjudication. *See* Judicial process

Aggression, 94, 151

Albania. *See* Corfu Channel dispute; Greece, dispute with Albania and Bulgaria

Algeria, 138, 140, 194, 201

"Anti-colonialist" attitudes, 10, 140-42, 221, 222, 229-33, 237-38
  self-determination, 140-42, 220 n., 222

Arbitration, 9, 20

Armaments, international control of, 11

Armed force of international organizations
  Organization of American States, deployment by. *See* Collective measures, regional; Cuba: missile crisis; Organization of American states: Dominican Republic, U.S.-OAS intervention, 1965
  United Nations, deployment by. *See* Collective measures function of United Nations; Cyprus; Korea; Recommendations, substantive, of United Nations; ONUC; United Nations Emergency Force; Rhodesia
  policy guidance for forces, 120-22

Armistice, Egyptian-Israeli
  belligerent rights, effect on, 16, 18, 84-85, 88-89
  Observer corps, 206
  United Nations Emergency Force, function regarding, 96

Barents Sea, aircraft incident over, 73 n.

Belligerent rights. *See* Armistice, Egyptian-Israeli

Bulgaria. *See* Greece, dispute with Albania and Bulgaria

Certain Expenses of the United Nations (Article 17, paragraph 2, of the Charter), 110, 111-14, 186-87, 190, 200, 202-203

Change of international legal relationships, problem of effectuating (*see also* Charter, United Nations; System capable of maintaining international peace and security), 6-22, 23, 50-52, 195

Charter, United Nations
  amendment, 23
  evolution of, 10, 23, 95, 140, 161
  interpretation, organs empowered, 26, 133-34
  modification through informal acquiescence of members, 23-25, 27-55, 56, 57, 62-63, 66-67, 154-62

China, People's Republic of, 142, 150-51

Codification of international law, 19

Collective measures function of United Nations (*see also* Armed forces of international organizations; Measures of tangible pressure; Measures short of force), 31, 37-38, 40, 52, 54, 62, 76-77, 81, 83, 91-95, 96-114, 115, 120-25, 135-37, 144-47, 149-65, 172-89, 196-97, 198-99, 201, 202-205, 206-208, 210-11
  definition, Charter, 37-38, 76-77, 93, 95, 112-13, 159
  discretionary power of United Nations, 93-94, 99-100, 106-107, 123-24
  enforcement action against states, relationship to (*see also* Enforcement action, this index), 91-95, 103, 105-106, 108, 112-13, 123, 207-208
  force, as aspect of, 40-41, 159
  General Assembly, power, question of, 92, 97-100, 135, 144, 149-62
  orders of Security Council, as sole means of initiating, 54-55, 145, 149, 162-65, 178-79, 185, 204
  recommendations. *See* Recommendations, substantive, of United Nations
  Security Council, exclusiveness of authority, question of, 136, 149-65, 182-83, 207 n.
  "situations" as objects of, 98
  states (or other political entities) as exclusive objects. *See* enforcement action against states, this heading